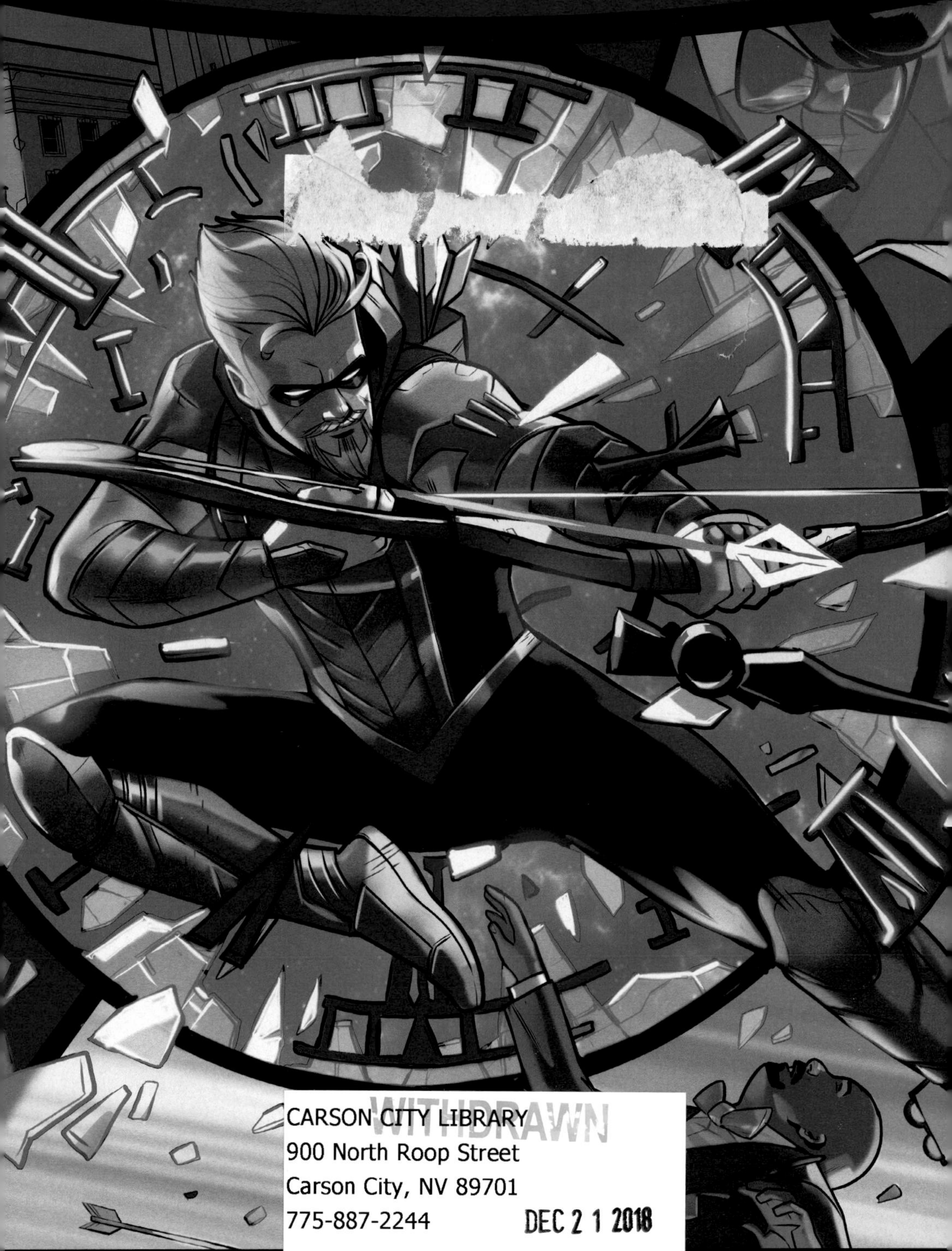

GREEN ARROW

VOL. 6 TRIAL OF TWO CITIES

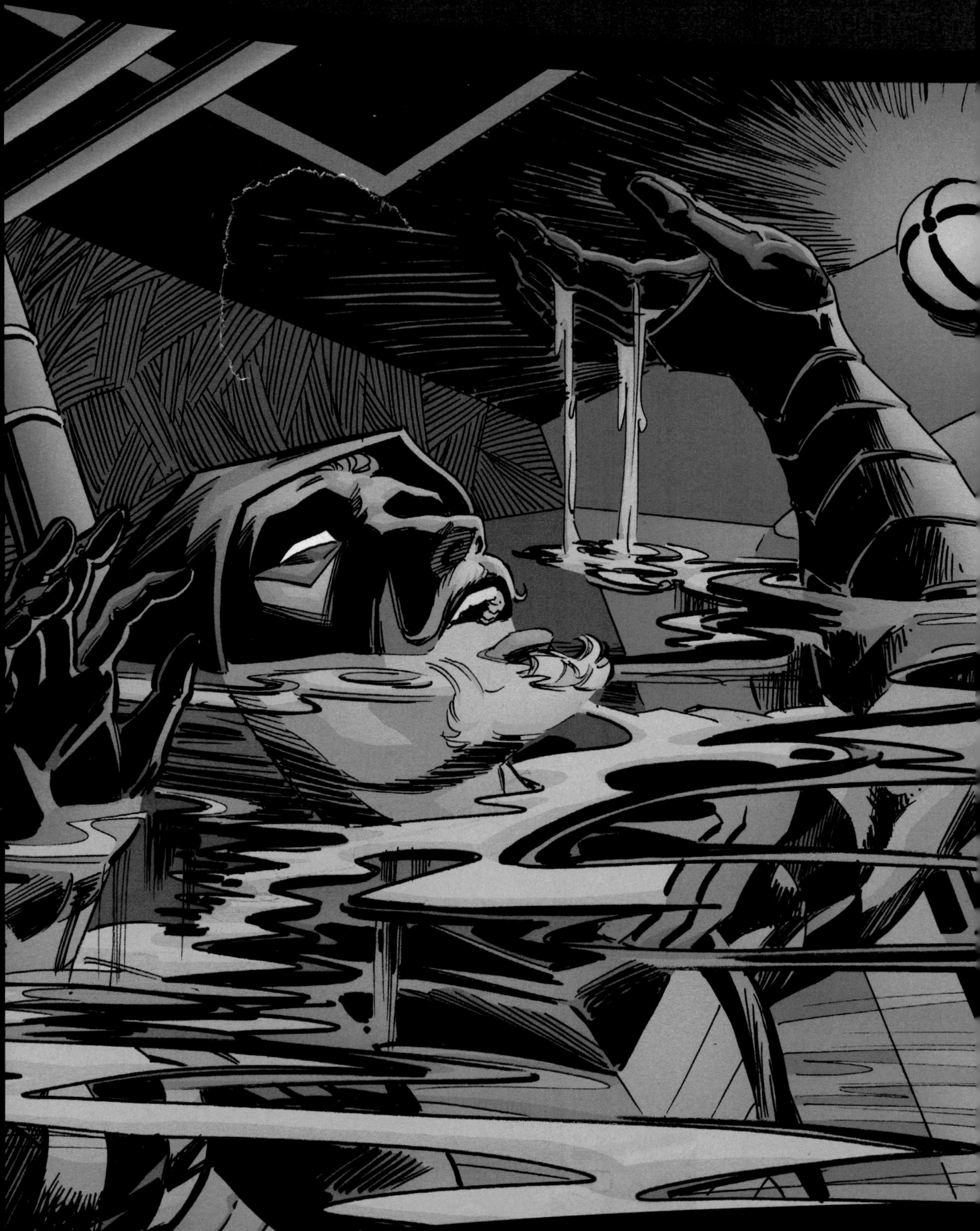

GREEN ARROW
VOL.6 TRIAL OF TWO CITIES

BENJAMIN PERCY
writer

JUAN FERREYRA
JAMAL CAMPBELL * STEPHEN BYRNE
artists

JUAN FERREYRA
JAMAL CAMPBELL * STEPHEN BYRNE
colorists

DERON BENNETT
letterer

JAMAL CAMPBELL
collection cover artist

SUPERMAN created by **JERRY SIEGEL** and **JOE SHUSTER**
By special arrangement with the Jerry Siegel family

ALEX ANTONE REBECCA TAYLOR Editors - Original Series * **DAVE WIELGOSZ** Assistant Editor - Original Series
JEB WOODARD Group Editor - Collected Editions * **ERIKA ROTHBERG** Editor - Collected Edition
STEVE COOK Design Director - Books * **MONIQUE NARBONETA** Publication Design

BOB HARRAS Senior VP - Editor-in-Chief, DC Comics
PAT McCALLUM Executive Editor, DC Comics

DAN DiDIO Publisher * **JIM LEE** Publisher & Chief Creative Officer
AMIT DESAI Executive VP - Business & Marketing Strategy, Direct to Consumer & Global Franchise Management
BOBBIE CHASE VP & Executive Editor, Young Reader & Talent Development * **MARK CHIARELLO** Senior VP - Art, Design & Collected Editions
JOHN CUNNINGHAM Senior VP - Sales & Trade Marketing * **BRIAR DARDEN** VP - Business Affairs
ANNE DePIES Senior VP - Business Strategy, Finance & Administration * **DON FALLETTI** VP - Manufacturing Operations
LAWRENCE GANEM VP - Editorial Administration & Talent Relations * **ALISON GILL** Senior VP - Manufacturing & Operations
JASON GREENBERG VP - Business Strategy & Finance * **HANK KANALZ** Senior VP - Editorial Strategy & Administration
JAY KOGAN Senior VP - Legal Affairs * **NICK J. NAPOLITANO** VP - Manufacturing Administration
LISETTE OSTERLOH VP - Digital Marketing & Events * **EDDIE SCANNELL** VP - Consumer Marketing
COURTNEY SIMMONS Senior VP - Publicity & Communications * **JIM (SKI) SOKOLOWSKI** VP - Comic Book Specialty Sales & Trade Marketing
NANCY SPEARS VP - Mass, Book, Digital Sales & Trade Marketing * **MICHELE R. WELLS** VP - Content Strategy

GREEN ARROW VOL. 6: TRIAL OF TWO CITIES

DC Comics, 2900 West Alameda Ave., Burbank, CA 91505
Printed by LSC Communications, Kendallville, IN, USA. 10/26/18. First Printing.
ISBN: 978-1-4012-8171-7

Library of Congress Cataloging-in-Publication Data is available.

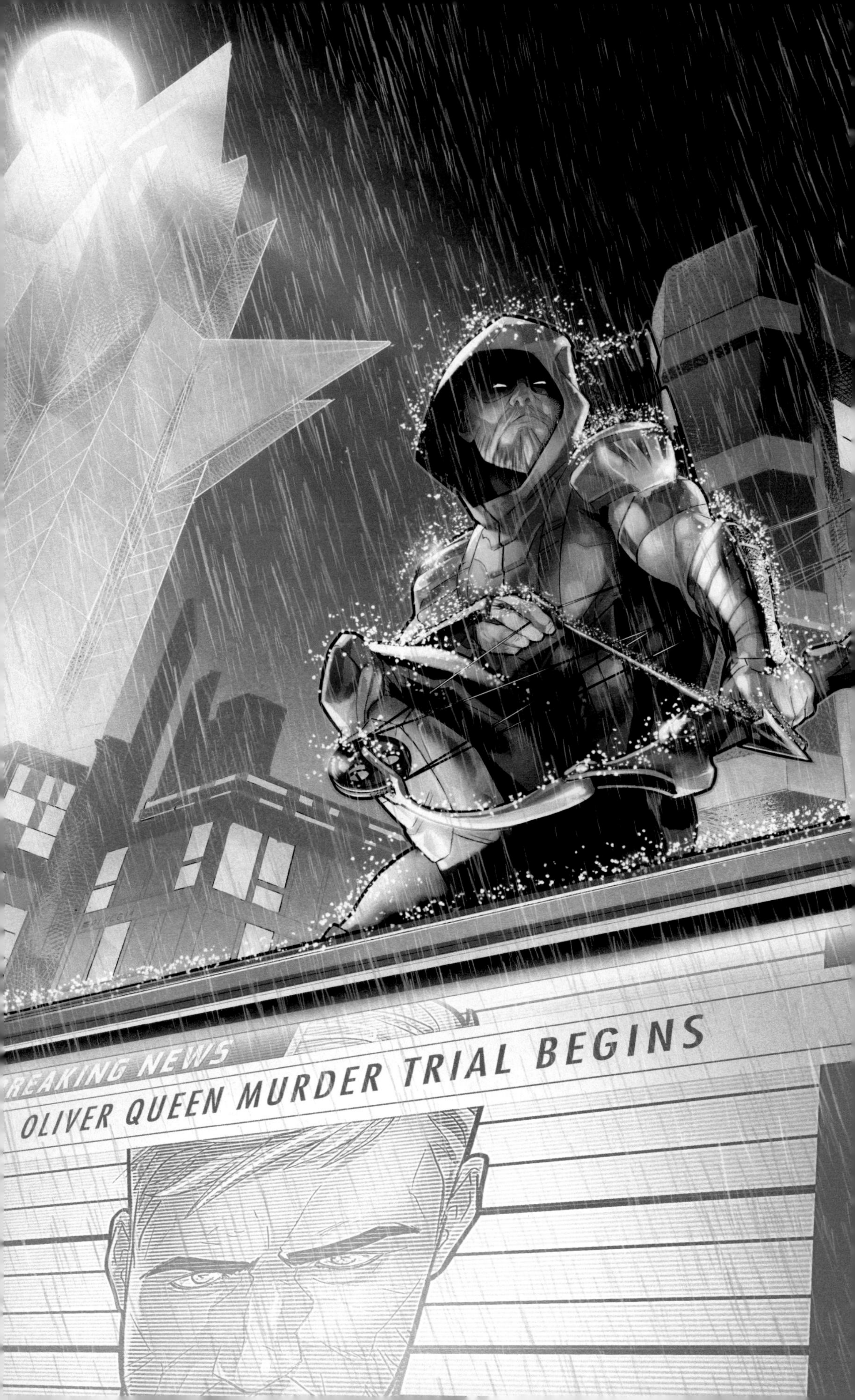
REAKING NEWS
OLIVER QUEEN MURDER TRIAL BEGINS

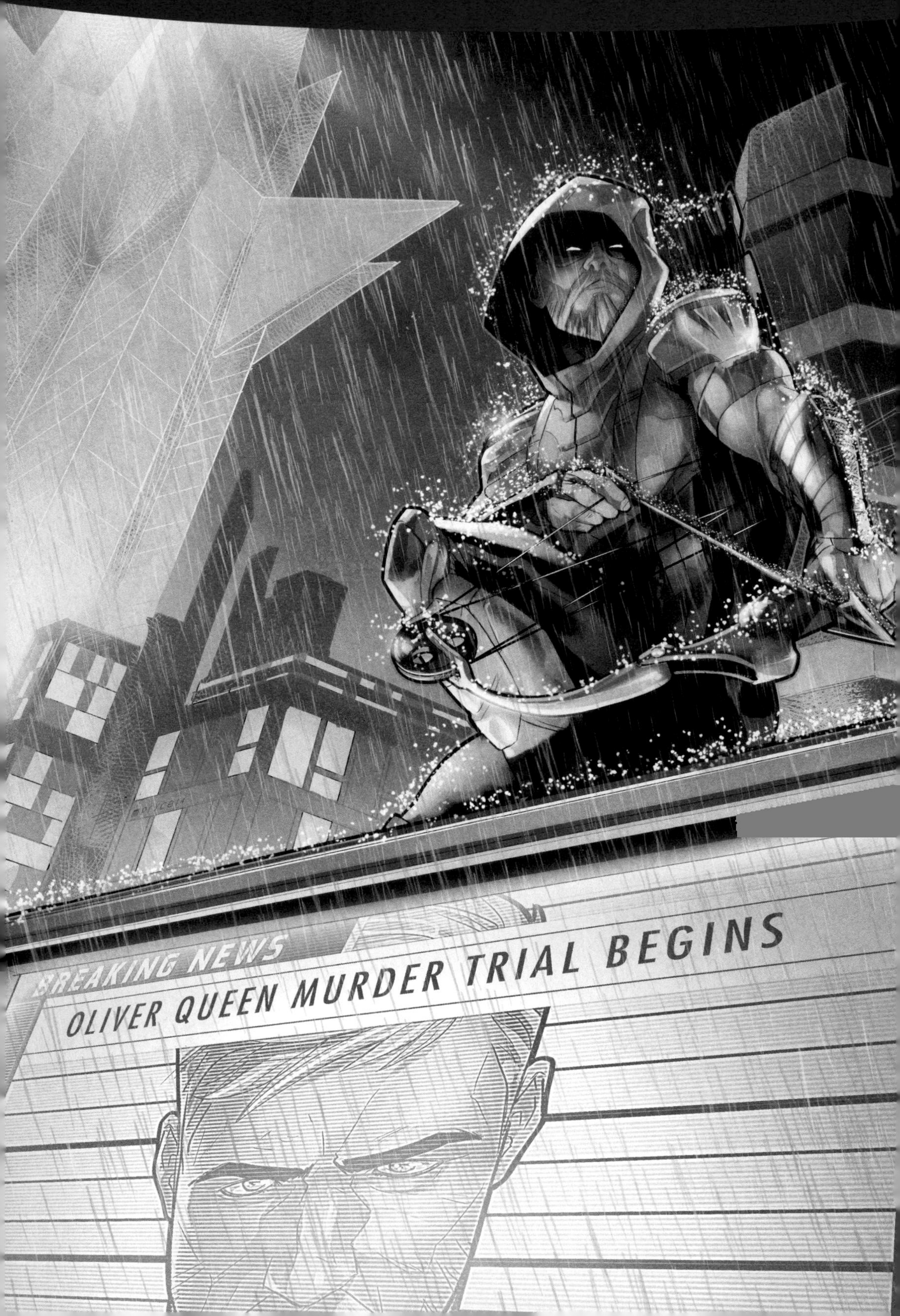
BREAKING NEWS
OLIVER QUEEN MURDER TRIAL BEGINS

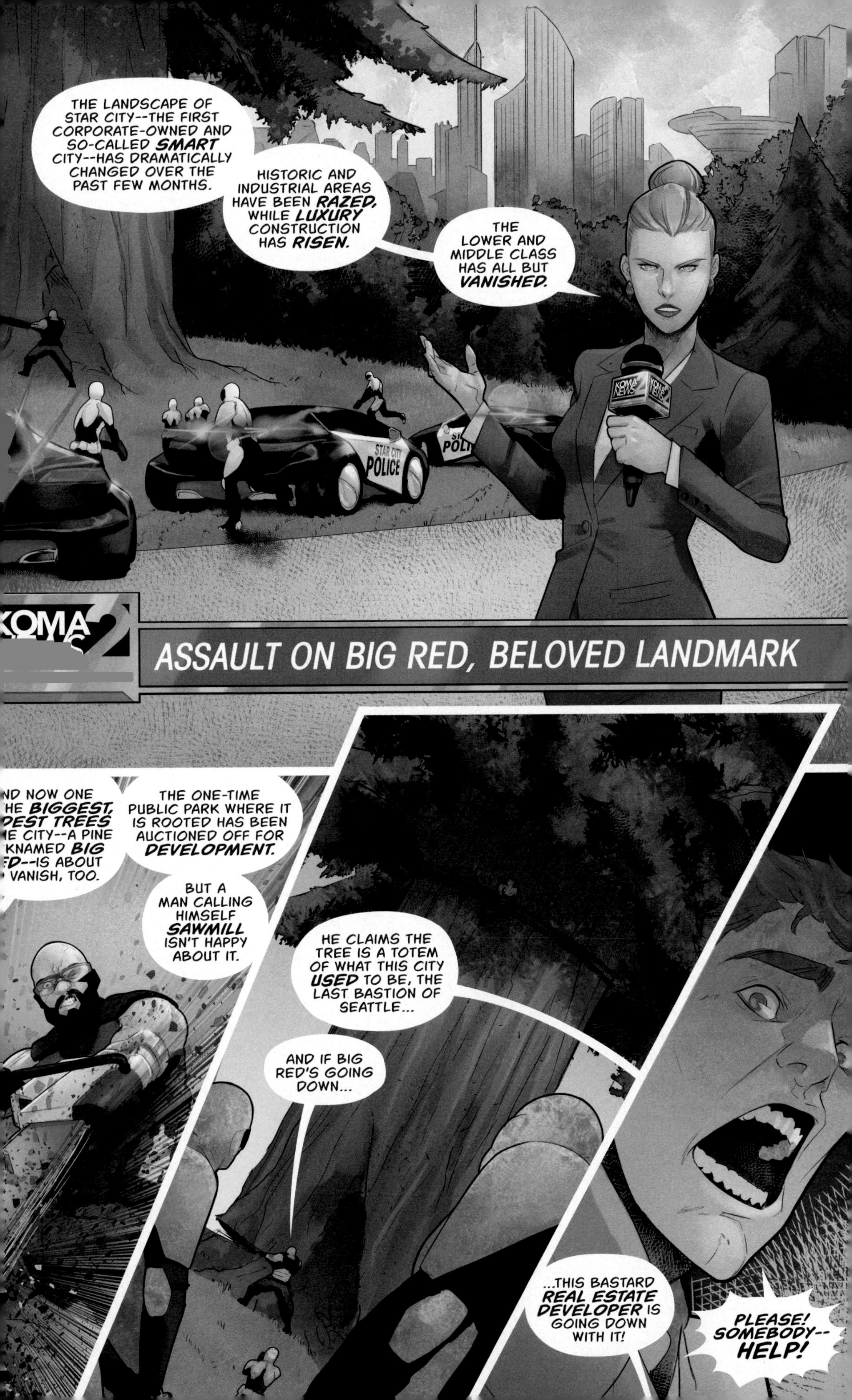
THE LANDSCAPE OF STAR CITY--THE FIRST CORPORATE-OWNED AND SO-CALLED SMART CITY--HAS DRAMATICALLY CHANGED OVER THE PAST FEW MONTHS.
HISTORIC AND INDUSTRIAL AREAS HAVE BEEN RAZED, WHILE LUXURY CONSTRUCTION HAS RISEN.
THE LOWER AND MIDDLE CLASS HAS ALL BUT VANISHED.
STAR CITY POLICE
KOMA NEWS 2
KOMA
ASSAULT ON BIG RED, BELOVED LANDMARK
ND NOW ONE HE BIGGEST, DEST TREES E CITY--A PINE KNAMED BIG D--IS ABOUT VANISH, TOO.
THE ONE-TIME PUBLIC PARK WHERE IT IS ROOTED HAS BEEN AUCTIONED OFF FOR DEVELOPMENT.
BUT A MAN CALLING HIMSELF SAWMILL ISN'T HAPPY ABOUT IT.
HE CLAIMS THE TREE IS A TOTEM OF WHAT THIS CITY USED TO BE, THE LAST BASTION OF SEATTLE...
AND IF BIG RED'S GOING DOWN...
...THIS BASTARD REAL ESTATE DEVELOPER IS GOING DOWN WITH IT!
PLEASE! SOMEBODY-- HELP!

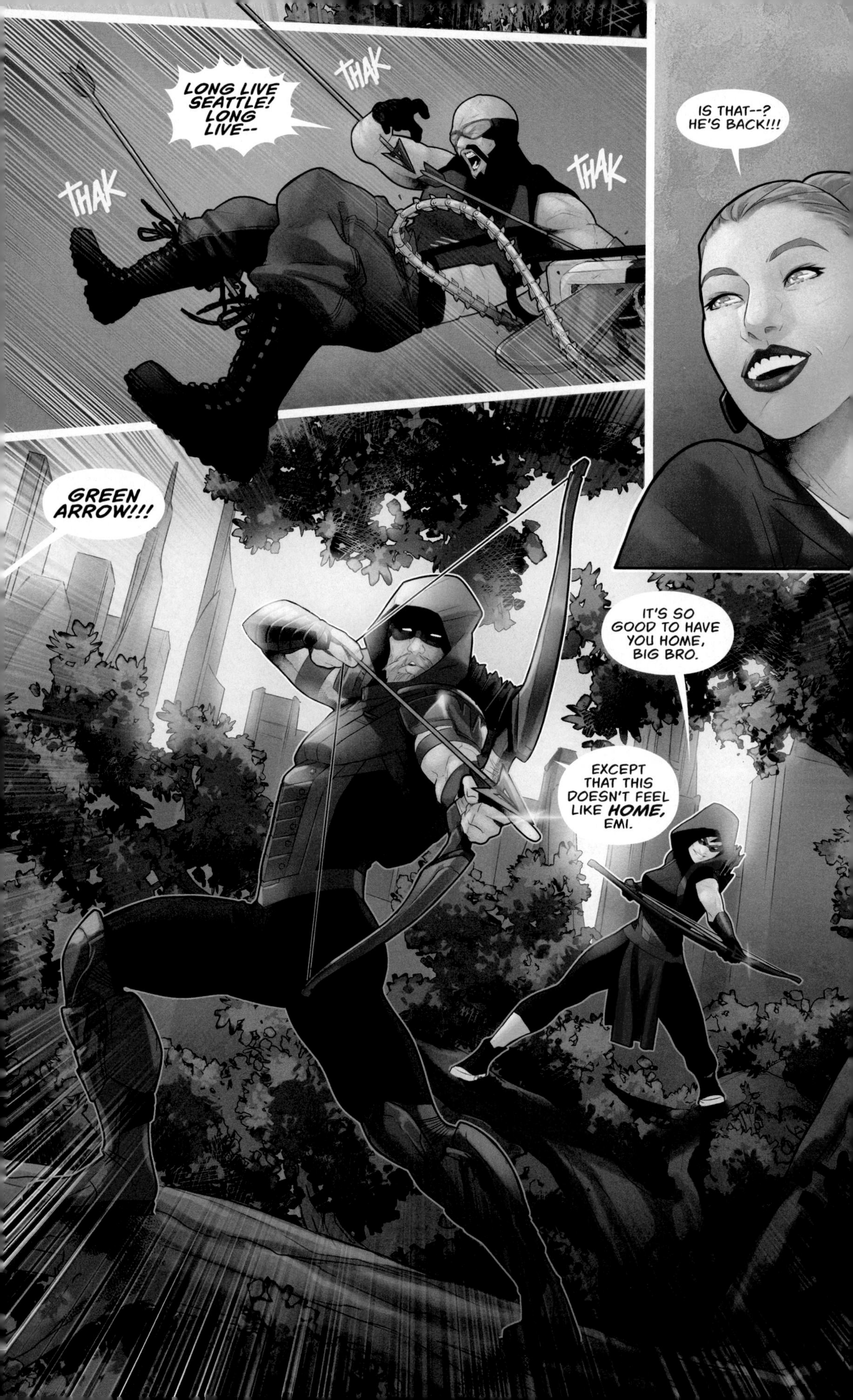
THAK
LONG LIVE SEATTLE! LONG LIVE--
THAK
THAK
IS THAT--? HE'S BACK!!!
GREEN ARROW!!!
IT'S SO GOOD TO HAVE YOU HOME, BIG BRO.
EXCEPT THAT THIS DOESN'T FEEL LIKE *HOME,* EMI.

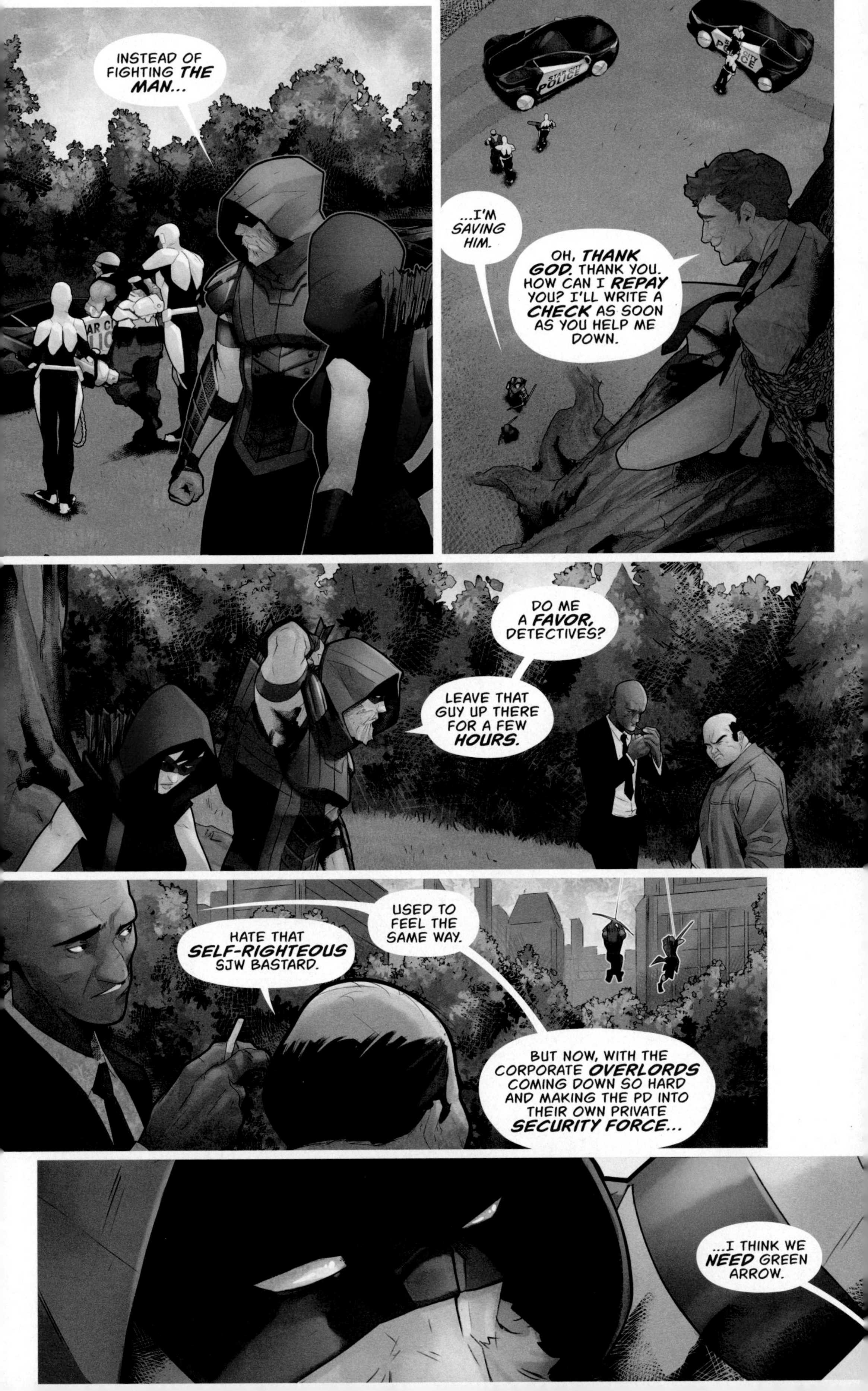
INSTEAD OF FIGHTING THE MAN...
...I'M SAVING HIM.
OH, THANK GOD. THANK YOU. HOW CAN I REPAY YOU? I'LL WRITE A CHECK AS SOON AS YOU HELP ME DOWN.
DO ME A FAVOR, DETECTIVES?
LEAVE THAT GUY UP THERE FOR A FEW HOURS.
HATE THAT SELF-RIGHTEOUS SJW BASTARD.
USED TO FEEL THE SAME WAY.
BUT NOW, WITH THE CORPORATE OVERLORDS COMING DOWN SO HARD AND MAKING THE PD INTO THEIR OWN PRIVATE SECURITY FORCE...
...I THINK WE NEED GREEN ARROW.

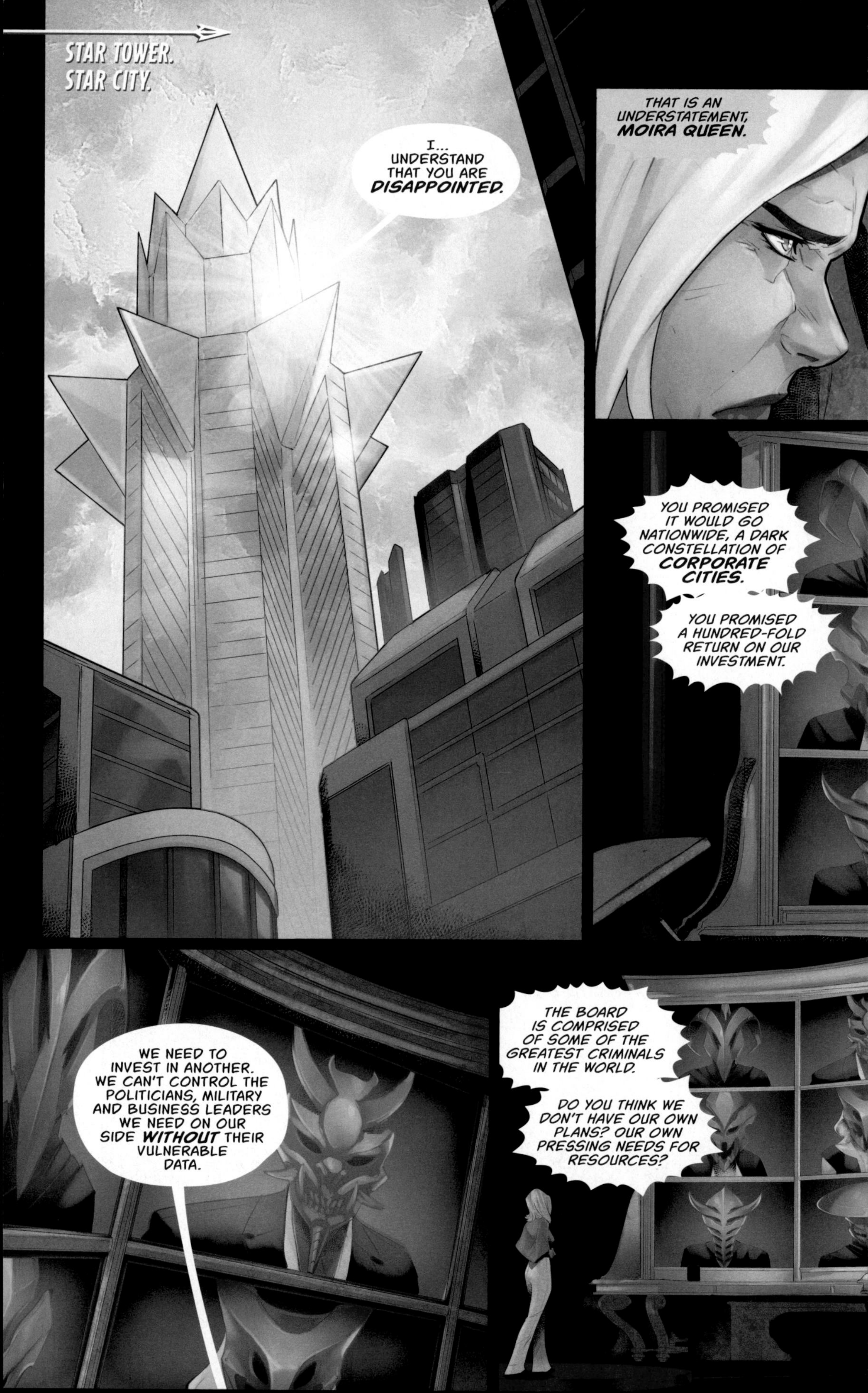
STAR TOWER. STAR CITY.
I... UNDERSTAND THAT YOU ARE DISAPPOINTED.
THAT IS AN UNDERSTATEMENT, MOIRA QUEEN.
YOU PROMISED IT WOULD GO NATIONWIDE, A DARK CONSTELLATION OF CORPORATE CITIES.
YOU PROMISED A HUNDRED-FOLD RETURN ON OUR INVESTMENT.
WE NEED TO INVEST IN ANOTHER. WE CAN'T CONTROL THE POLITICIANS, MILITARY AND BUSINESS LEADERS WE NEED ON OUR SIDE WITHOUT THEIR VULNERABLE DATA.
THE BOARD IS COMPRISED OF SOME OF THE GREATEST CRIMINALS IN THE WORLD.
DO YOU THINK WE DON'T HAVE OUR OWN PLANS? OUR OWN PRESSING NEEDS FOR RESOURCES?

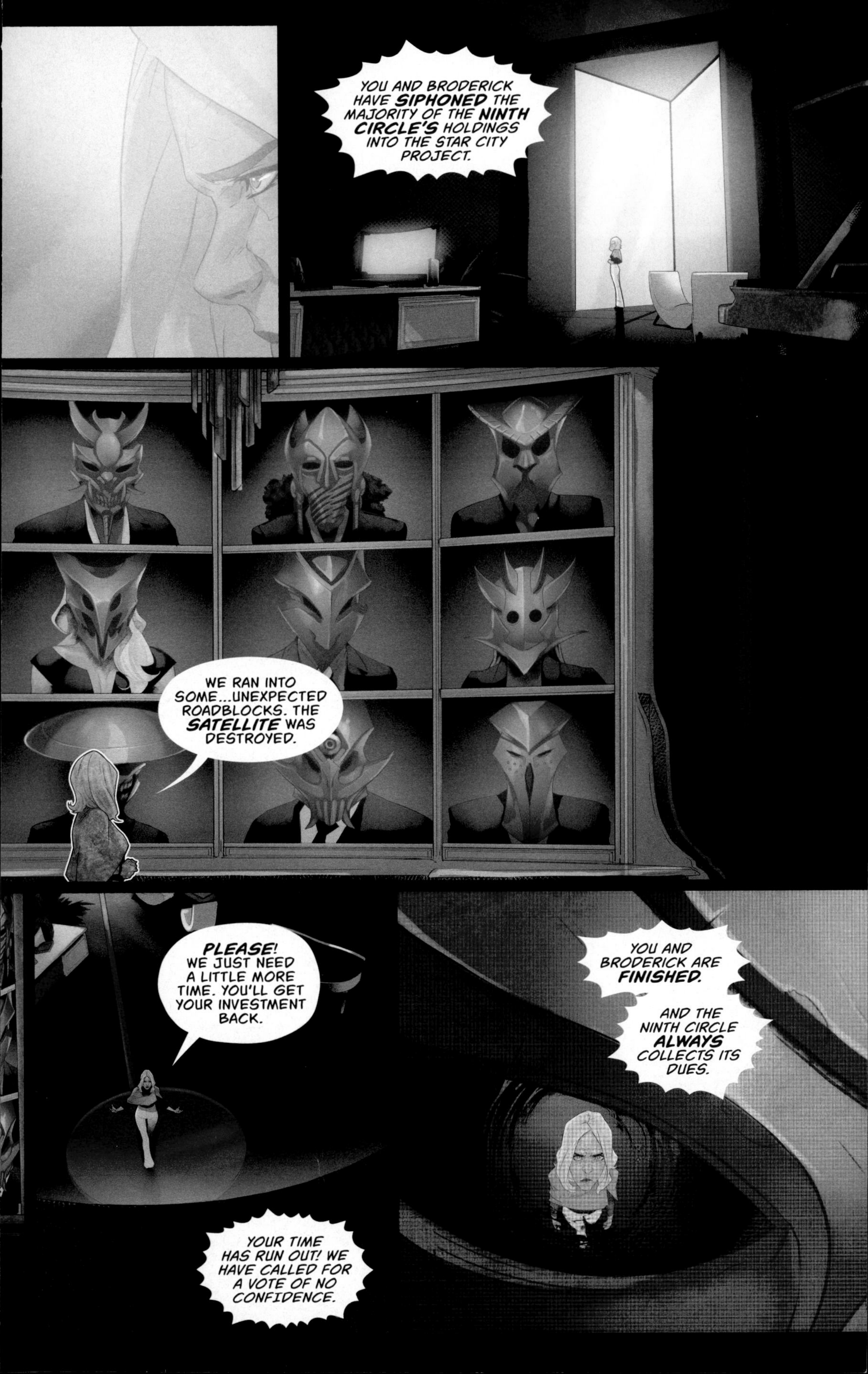

YOU AND BRODERICK HAVE SIPHONED THE MAJORITY OF THE NINTH CIRCLE'S HOLDINGS INTO THE STAR CITY PROJECT.
WE RAN INTO SOME...UNEXPECTED ROADBLOCKS. THE SATELLITE WAS DESTROYED.
PLEASE! WE JUST NEED A LITTLE MORE TIME. YOU'LL GET YOUR INVESTMENT BACK.
YOUR TIME HAS RUN OUT! WE HAVE CALLED FOR A VOTE OF NO CONFIDENCE.
YOU AND BRODERICK ARE FINISHED.
AND THE NINTH CIRCLE ALWAYS COLLECTS ITS DUES.

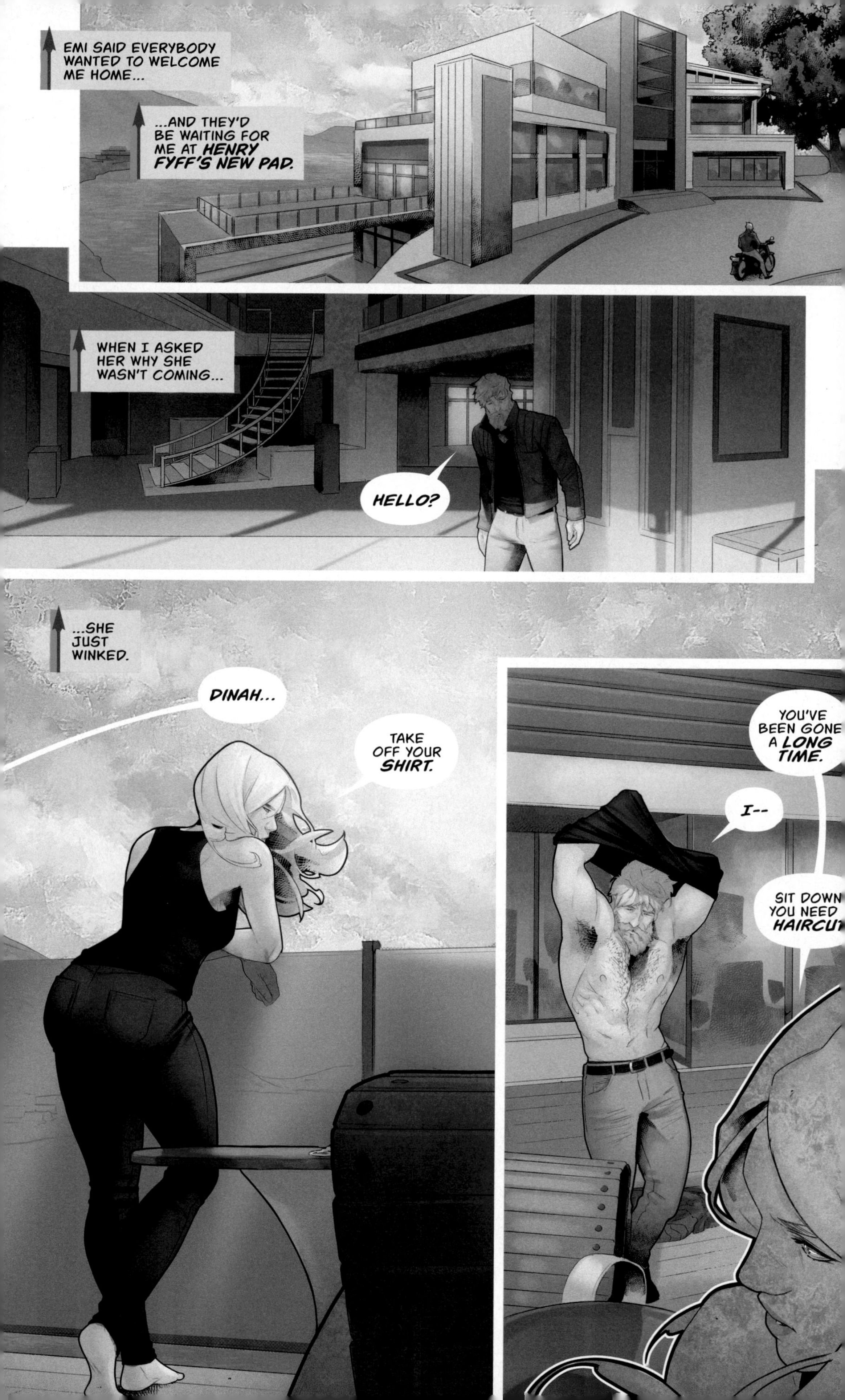
EMI SAID EVERYBODY WANTED TO WELCOME ME HOME...
...AND THEY'D BE WAITING FOR ME AT HENRY FYFF'S NEW PAD.
WHEN I ASKED HER WHY SHE WASN'T COMING...
HELLO?
...SHE JUST WINKED.
DINAH...
TAKE OFF YOUR SHIRT.
YOU'VE BEEN GONE A LONG TIME.
I--
SIT DOWN
YOU NEED
HAIRCU

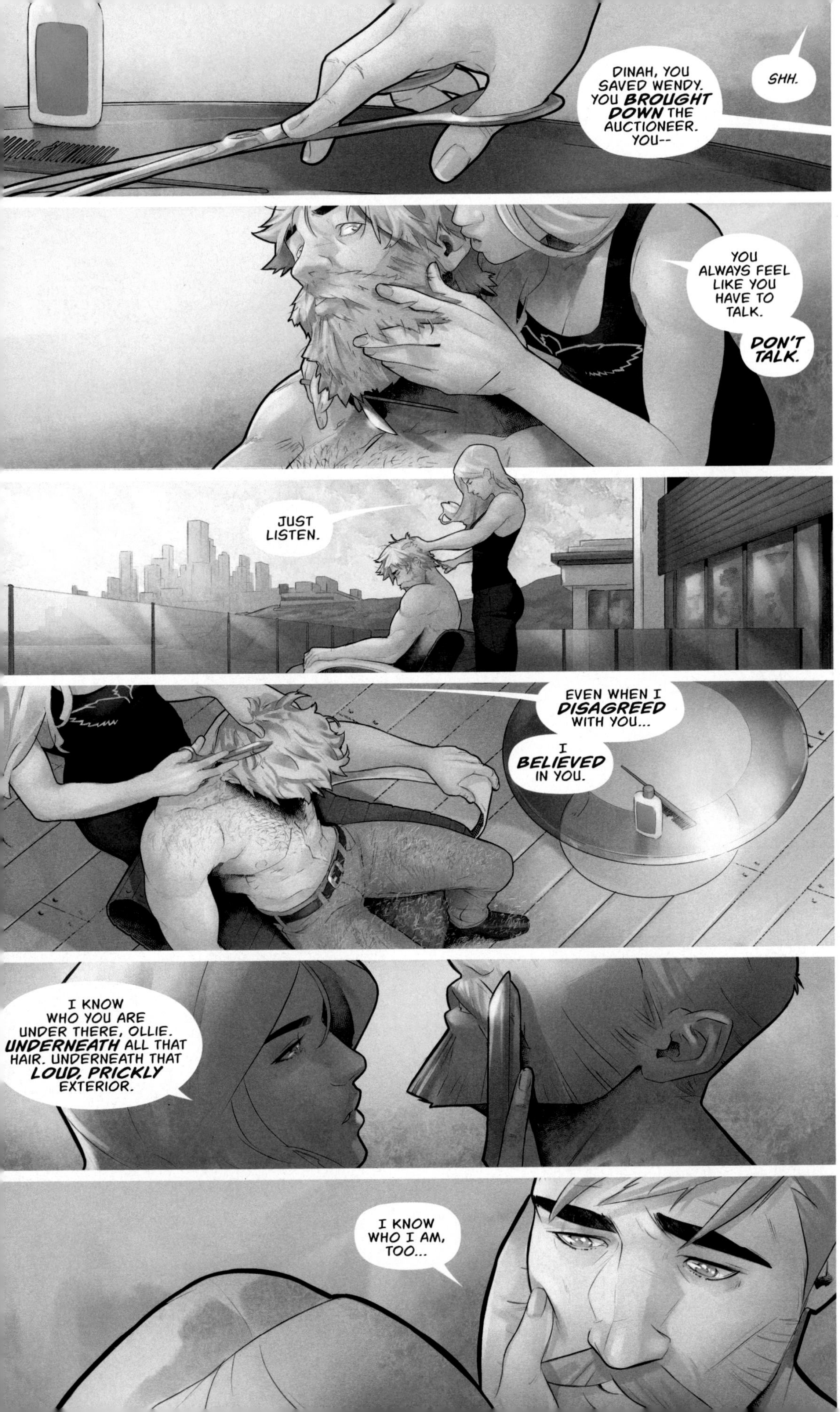

DINAH, YOU SAVED WENDY. YOU BROUGHT DOWN THE AUCTIONEER. YOU--
SHH.
YOU ALWAYS FEEL LIKE YOU HAVE TO TALK.
DON'T TALK.
JUST LISTEN.
EVEN WHEN I DISAGREED WITH YOU...
I BELIEVED IN YOU.
I KNOW WHO YOU ARE UNDER THERE, OLLIE. UNDERNEATH ALL THAT HAIR. UNDERNEATH THAT LOUD, PRICKLY EXTERIOR.
I KNOW WHO I AM, TOO...

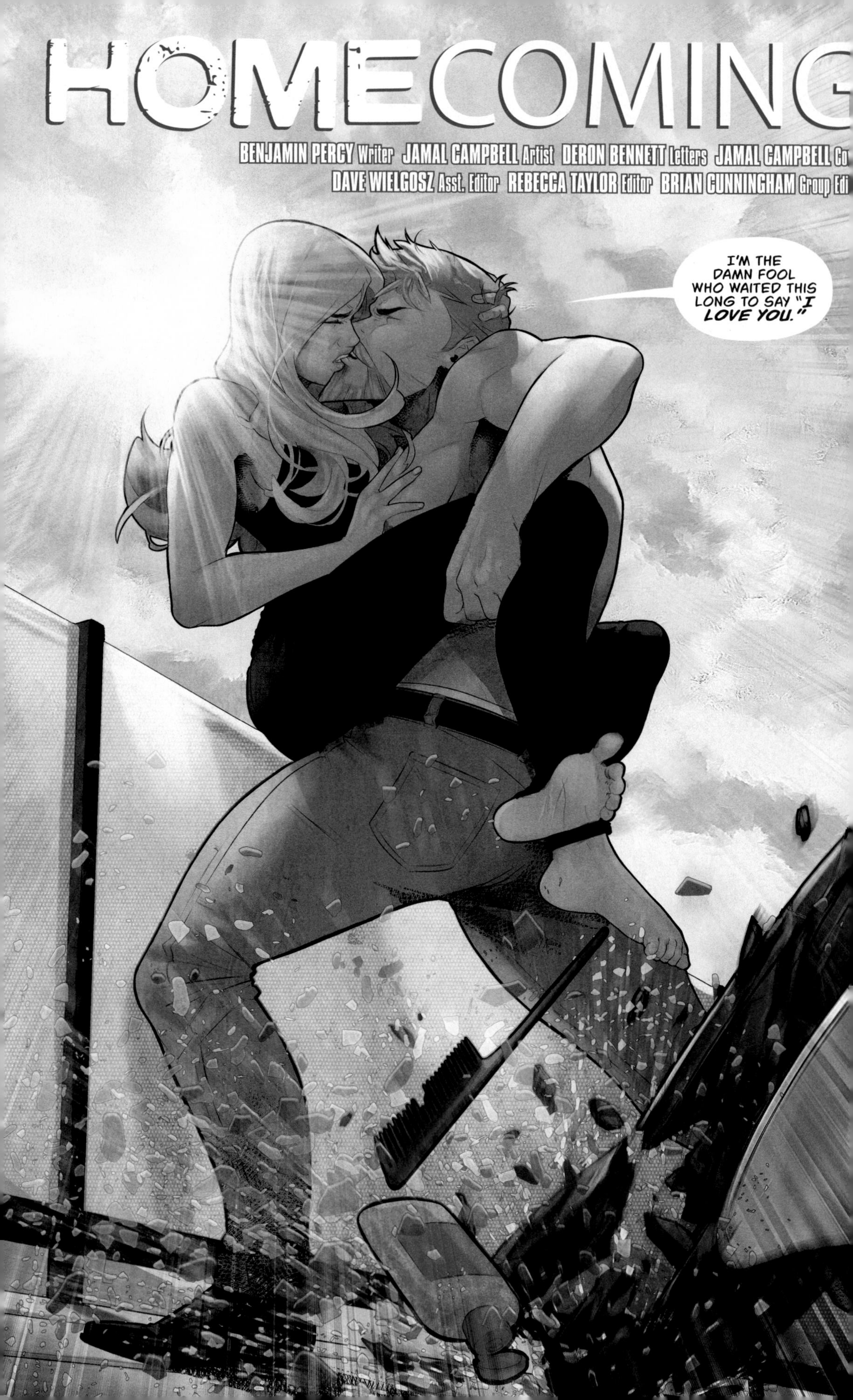
HOMECOMING
BENJAMIN PERCY Writer JAMAL CAMPBELL Artist DERON BENNETT Letters JAMAL CAMPBELL Co
DAVE WIELGOSZ Asst. Editor REBECCA TAYLOR Editor BRIAN CUNNINGHAM Group Edi
I'M THE DAMN FOOL WHO WAITED THIS LONG TO SAY "I LOVE YOU."

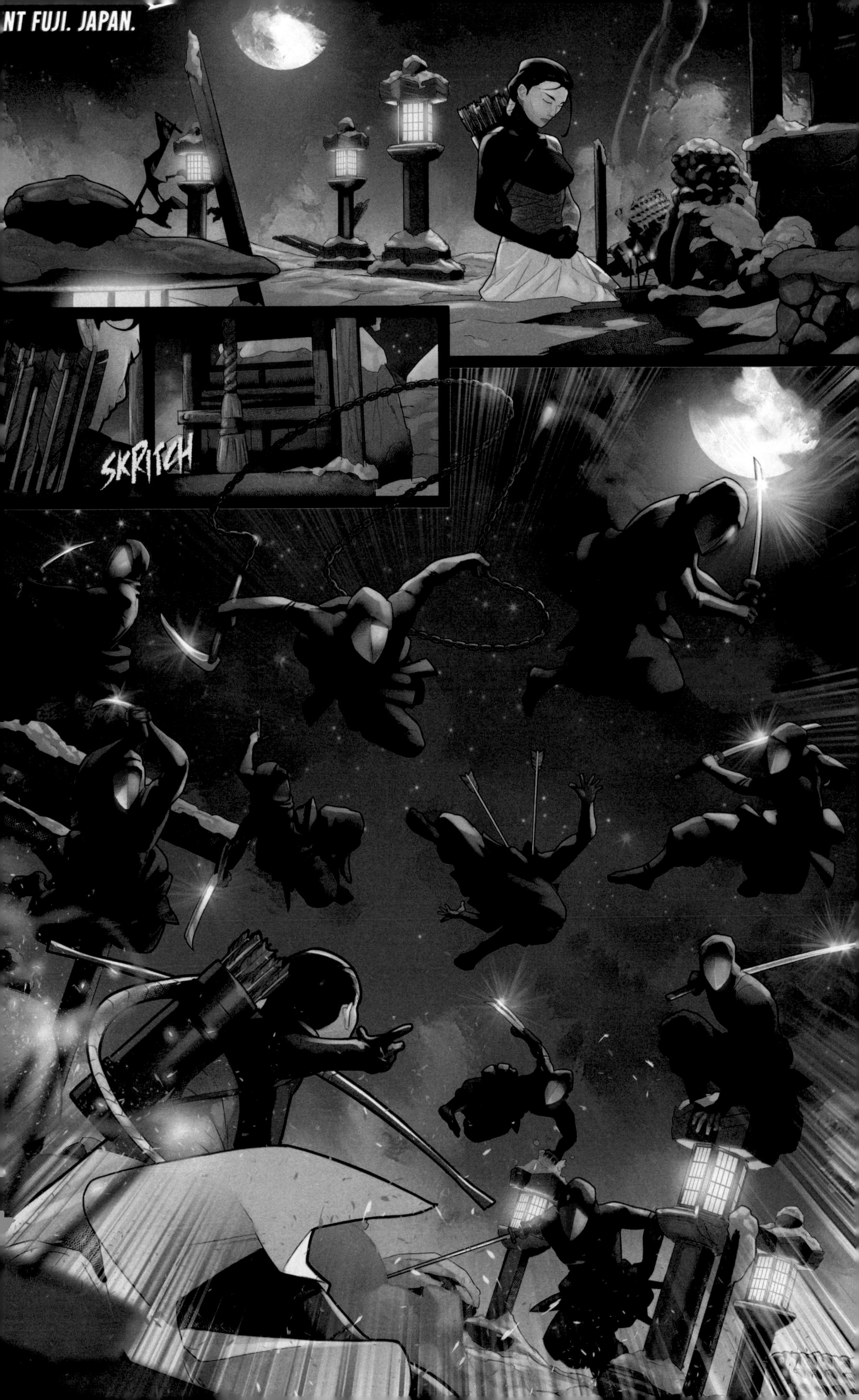

NT FUJI. JAPAN.
SKRITCH

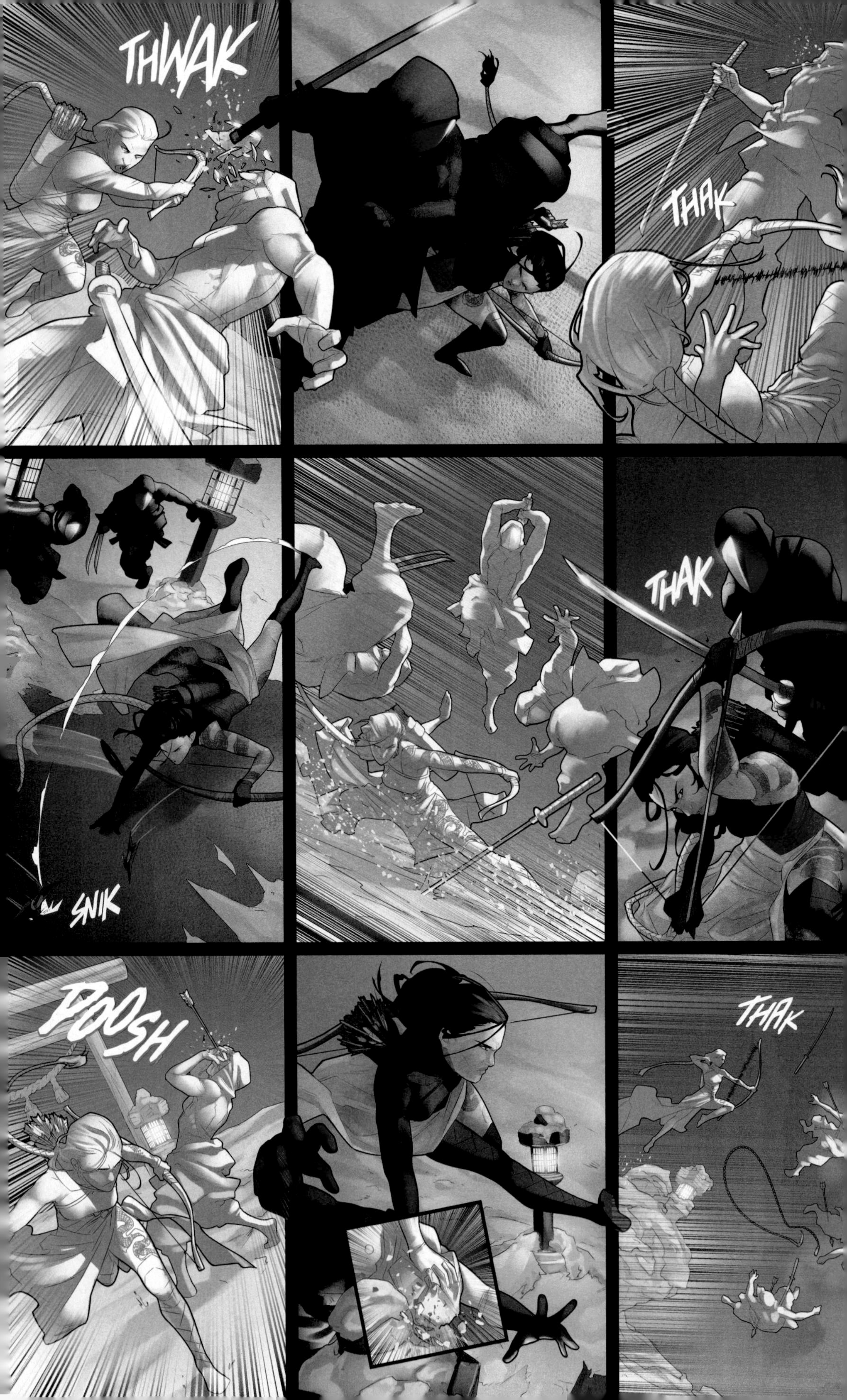
THWAK
THAK
SNIK
THAK
POOSH
THAK

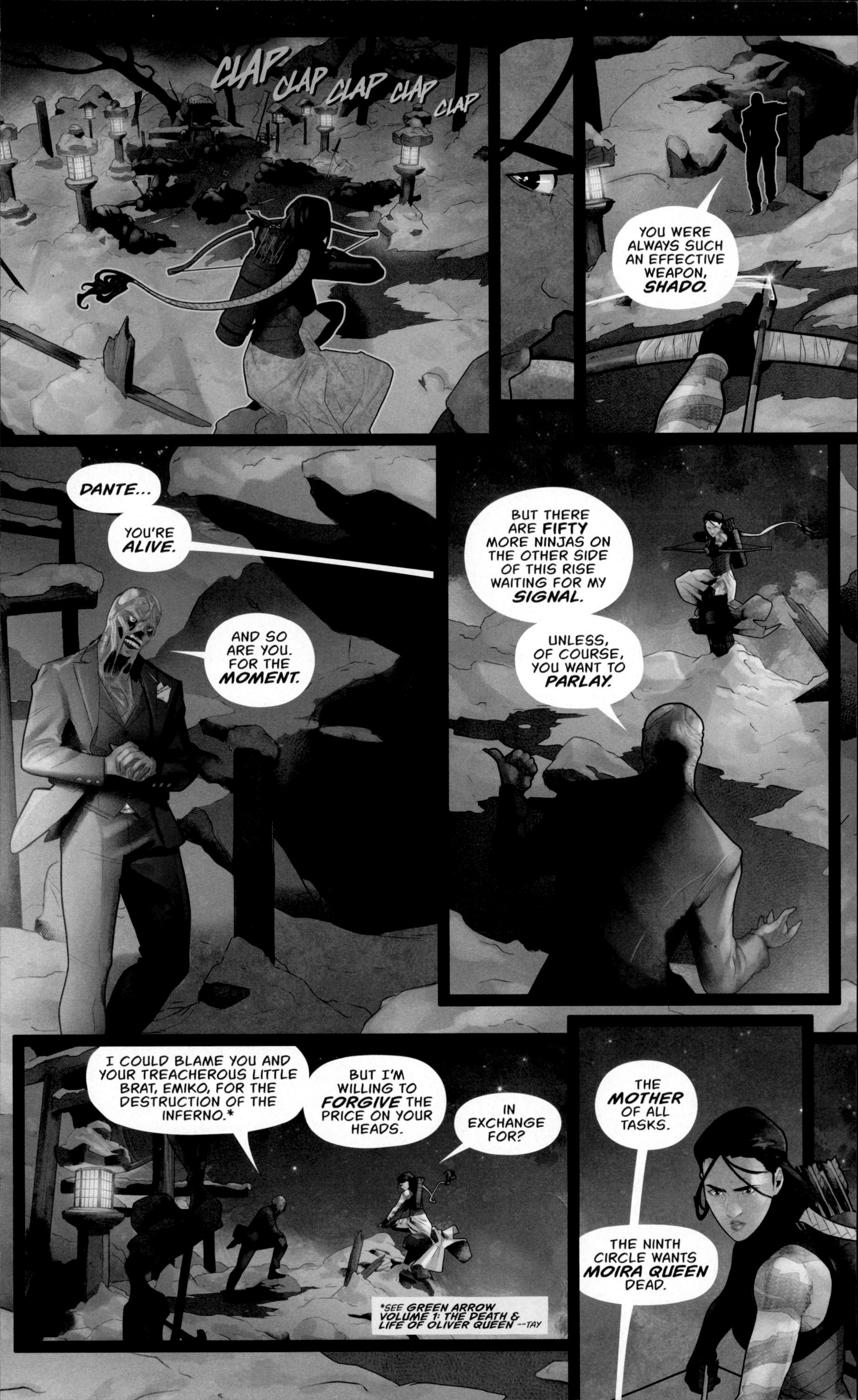

CLAP CLAP CLAP CLAP CLAP
YOU WERE ALWAYS SUCH AN EFFECTIVE WEAPON, **SHADO.**
DANTE...
YOU'RE **ALIVE.**
AND SO ARE YOU. FOR THE **MOMENT.**
BUT THERE ARE **FIFTY** MORE NINJAS ON THE OTHER SIDE OF THIS RISE WAITING FOR MY **SIGNAL.**
UNLESS, OF COURSE, YOU WANT TO **PARLAY.**
I COULD BLAME YOU AND YOUR TREACHEROUS LITTLE BRAT, EMIKO, FOR THE DESTRUCTION OF THE INFERNO.*
BUT I'M WILLING TO **FORGIVE** THE PRICE ON YOUR HEADS.
IN EXCHANGE FOR?
*SEE **GREEN ARROW VOLUME 1: THE DEATH & LIFE OF OLIVER QUEEN** --TAY
THE **MOTHER** OF ALL TASKS.
THE NINTH CIRCLE WANTS **MOIRA QUEEN** DEAD.

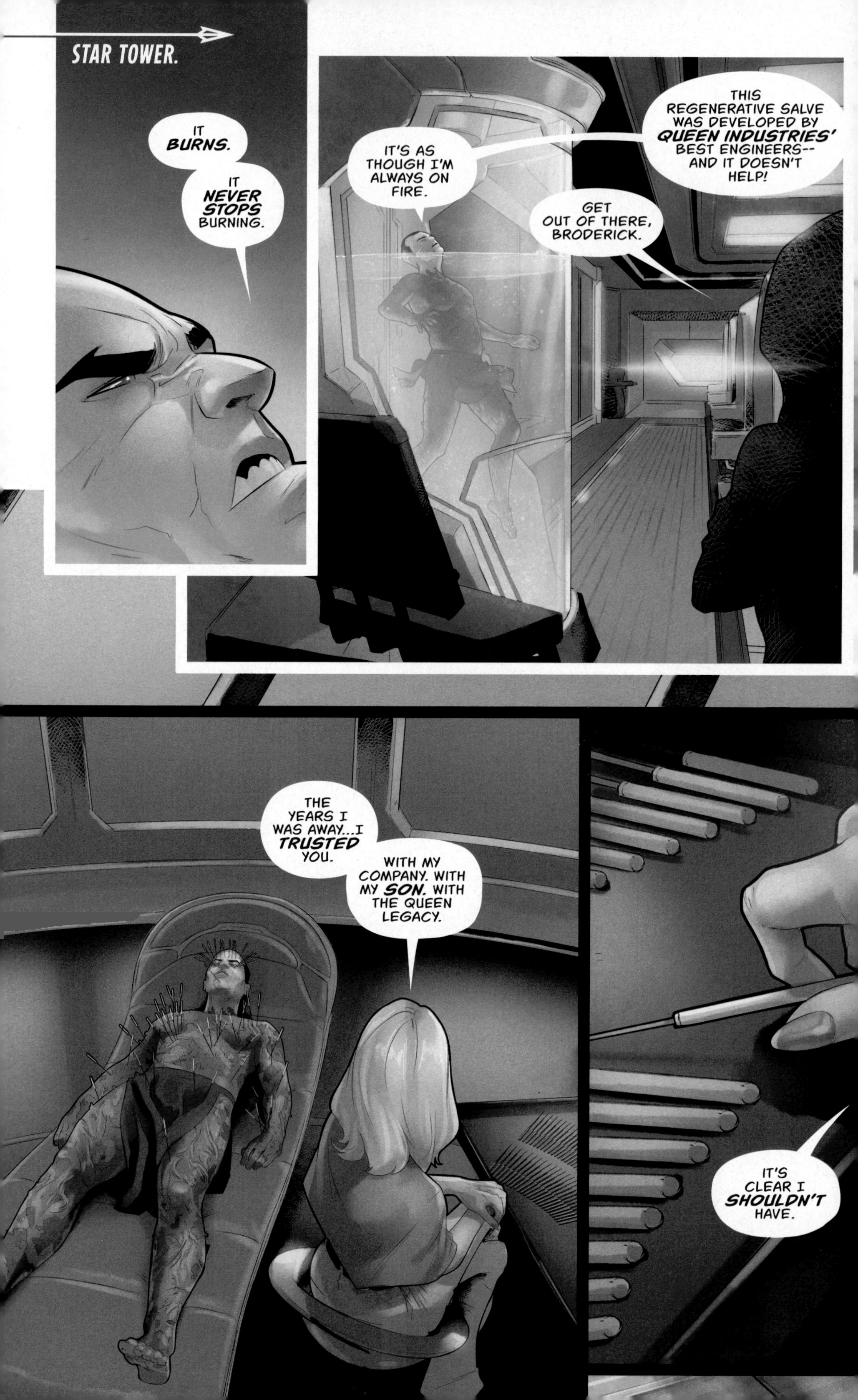
STAR TOWER.
IT BURNS.
IT NEVER STOPS BURNING.
IT'S AS THOUGH I'M ALWAYS ON FIRE.
THIS REGENERATIVE SALVE WAS DEVELOPED BY QUEEN INDUSTRIES' BEST ENGINEERS-- AND IT DOESN'T HELP!
GET OUT OF THERE, BRODERICK.
THE YEARS I WAS AWAY...I TRUSTED YOU.
WITH MY COMPANY. WITH MY SON. WITH THE QUEEN LEGACY.
IT'S CLEAR I SHOULDN'T HAVE.

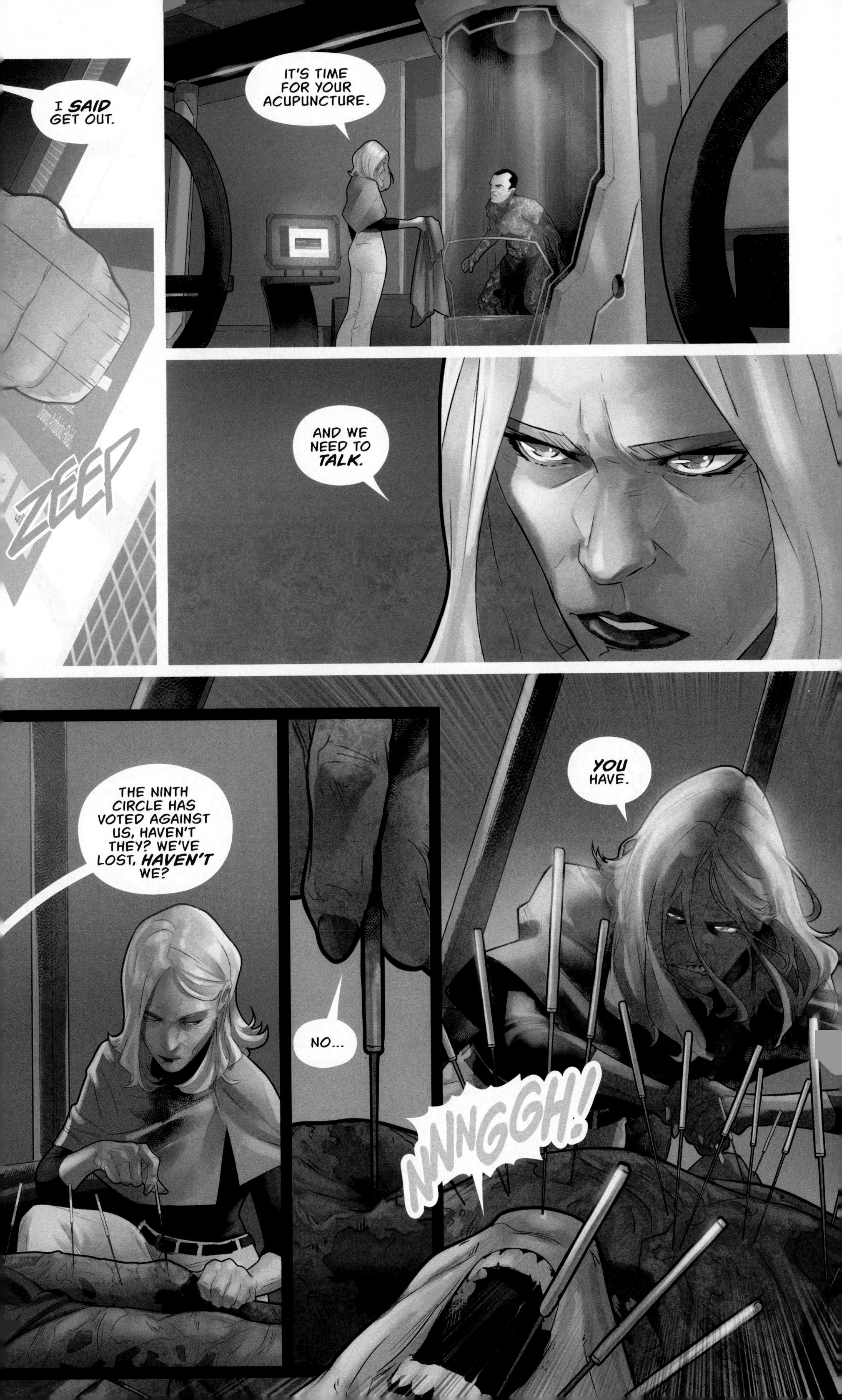
I SAID GET OUT.
IT'S TIME FOR YOUR ACUPUNCTURE.
ZEEP
AND WE NEED TO TALK.
THE NINTH CIRCLE HAS VOTED AGAINST US, HAVEN'T THEY? WE'VE LOST, HAVEN'T WE?
NO...
YOU HAVE.
NNNGGH!

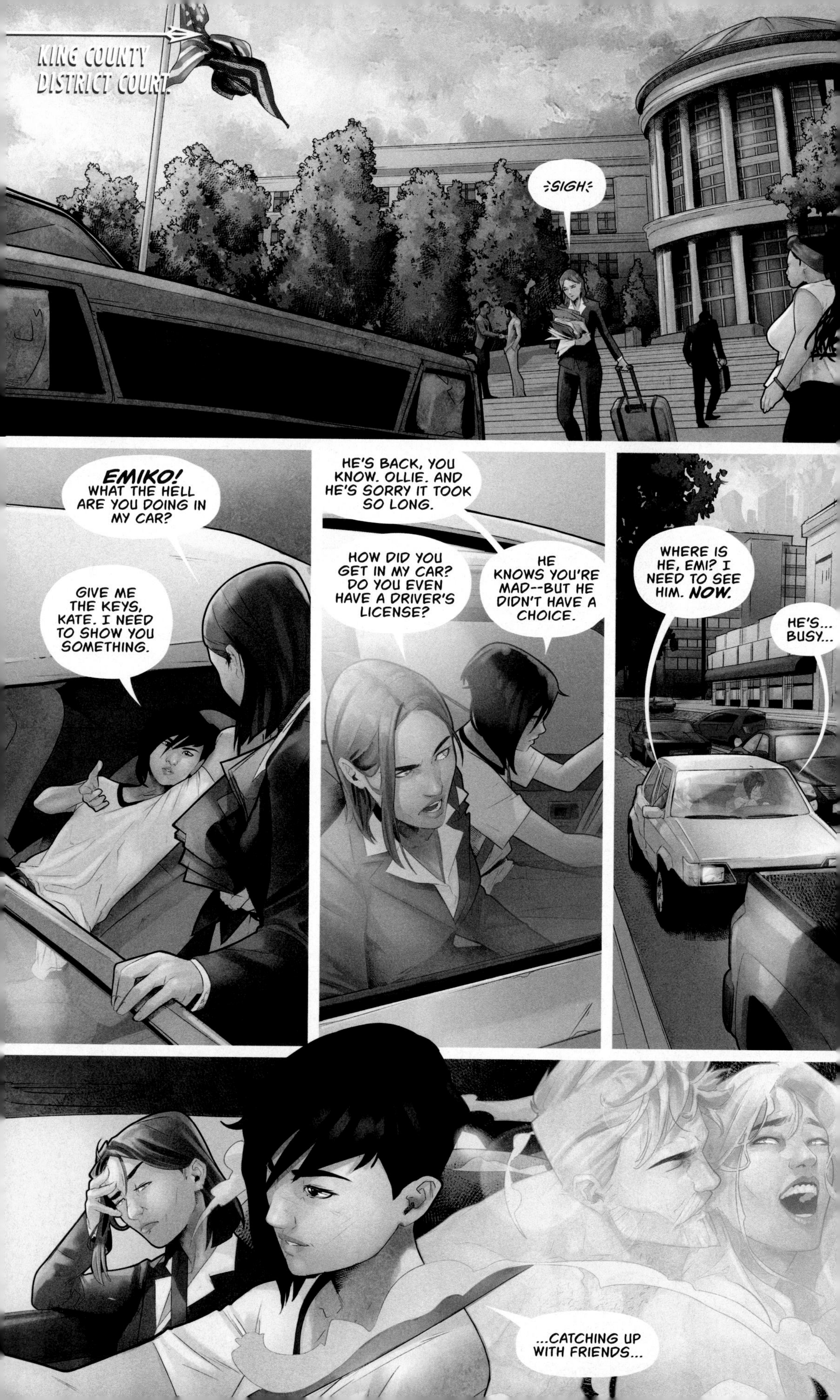

KING COUNTY DISTRICT COURT.
SIGH
EMIKO! WHAT THE HELL ARE YOU DOING IN MY CAR?
GIVE ME THE KEYS, KATE. I NEED TO SHOW YOU SOMETHING.
HE'S BACK, YOU KNOW. OLLIE. AND HE'S SORRY IT TOOK SO LONG.
HOW DID YOU GET IN MY CAR? DO YOU EVEN HAVE A DRIVER'S LICENSE?
HE KNOWS YOU'RE MAD--BUT HE DIDN'T HAVE A CHOICE.
WHERE IS HE, EMI? I NEED TO SEE HIM. NOW.
HE'S... BUSY...
...CATCHING UP WITH FRIENDS...

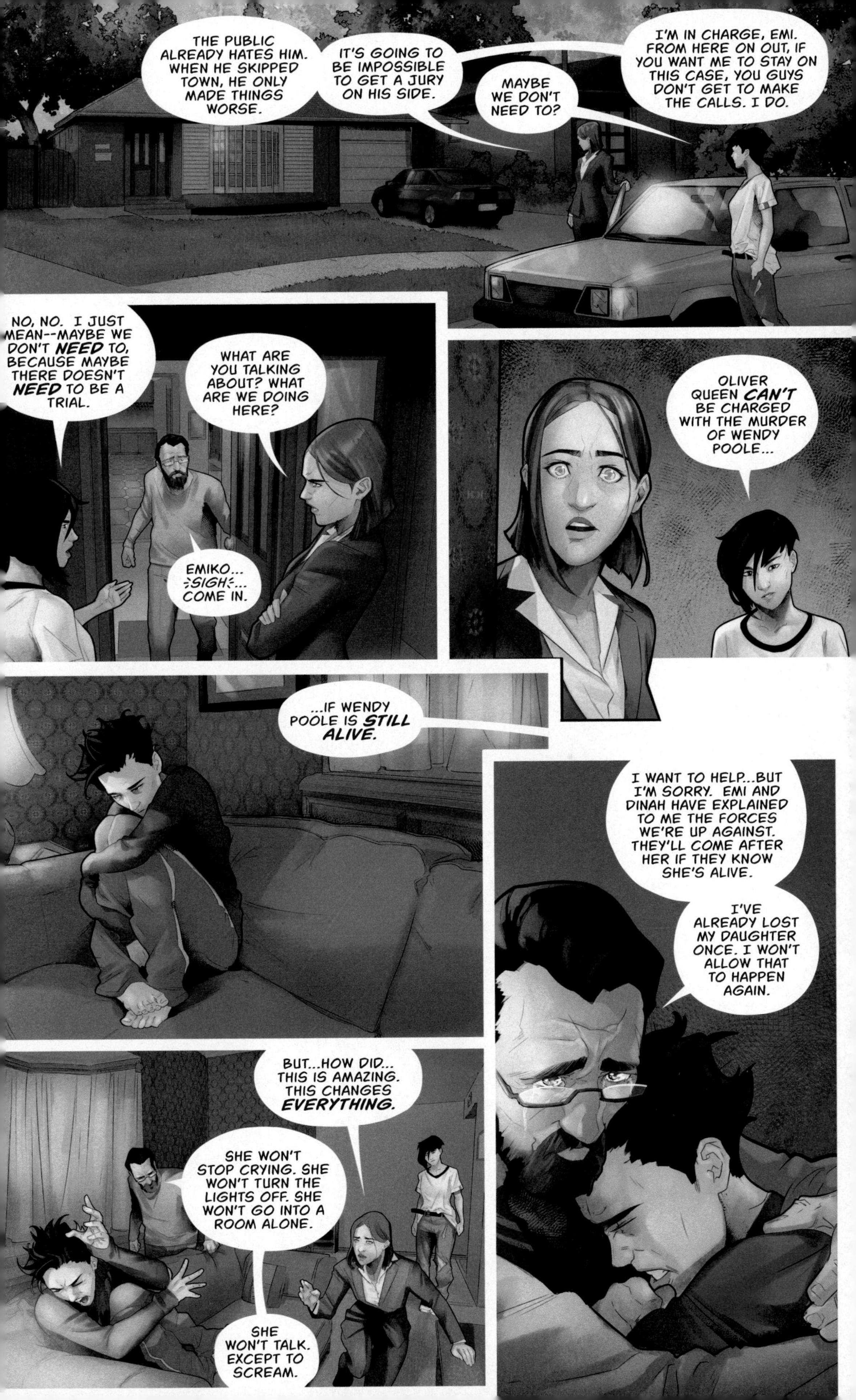
THE PUBLIC ALREADY HATES HIM. WHEN HE SKIPPED TOWN, HE ONLY MADE THINGS WORSE.
IT'S GOING TO BE IMPOSSIBLE TO GET A JURY ON HIS SIDE.
MAYBE WE DON'T NEED TO?
I'M IN CHARGE, EMI. FROM HERE ON OUT, IF YOU WANT ME TO STAY ON THIS CASE, YOU GUYS DON'T GET TO MAKE THE CALLS. I DO.
NO, NO. I JUST MEAN--MAYBE WE DON'T NEED TO, BECAUSE MAYBE THERE DOESN'T NEED TO BE A TRIAL.
WHAT ARE YOU TALKING ABOUT? WHAT ARE WE DOING HERE?
EMIKO... ⁝SIGH⁝... COME IN.
OLIVER QUEEN CAN'T BE CHARGED WITH THE MURDER OF WENDY POOLE...
...IF WENDY POOLE IS STILL ALIVE.
I WANT TO HELP...BUT I'M SORRY. EMI AND DINAH HAVE EXPLAINED TO ME THE FORCES WE'RE UP AGAINST. THEY'LL COME AFTER HER IF THEY KNOW SHE'S ALIVE.
I'VE ALREADY LOST MY DAUGHTER ONCE. I WON'T ALLOW THAT TO HAPPEN AGAIN.
BUT...HOW DID... THIS IS AMAZING. THIS CHANGES EVERYTHING.
SHE WON'T STOP CRYING. SHE WON'T TURN THE LIGHTS OFF. SHE WON'T GO INTO A ROOM ALONE.
SHE WON'T TALK. EXCEPT TO SCREAM.

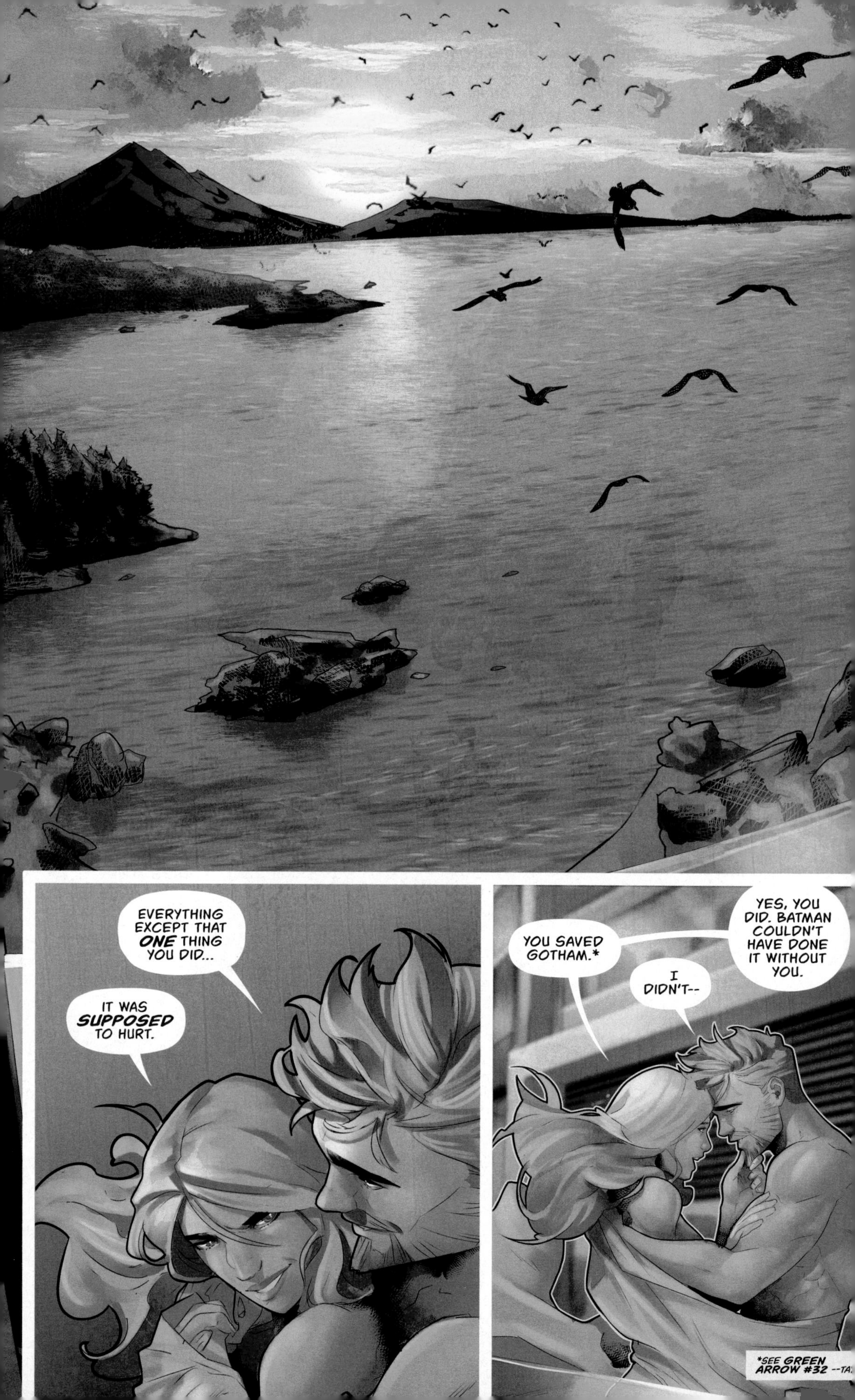
EVERYTHING EXCEPT THAT ONE THING YOU DID...
IT WAS SUPPOSED TO HURT.
YOU SAVED GOTHAM.*
I DIDN'T--
YES, YOU DID. BATMAN COULDN'T HAVE DONE IT WITHOUT YOU.
*SEE GREEN ARROW #32 --TA

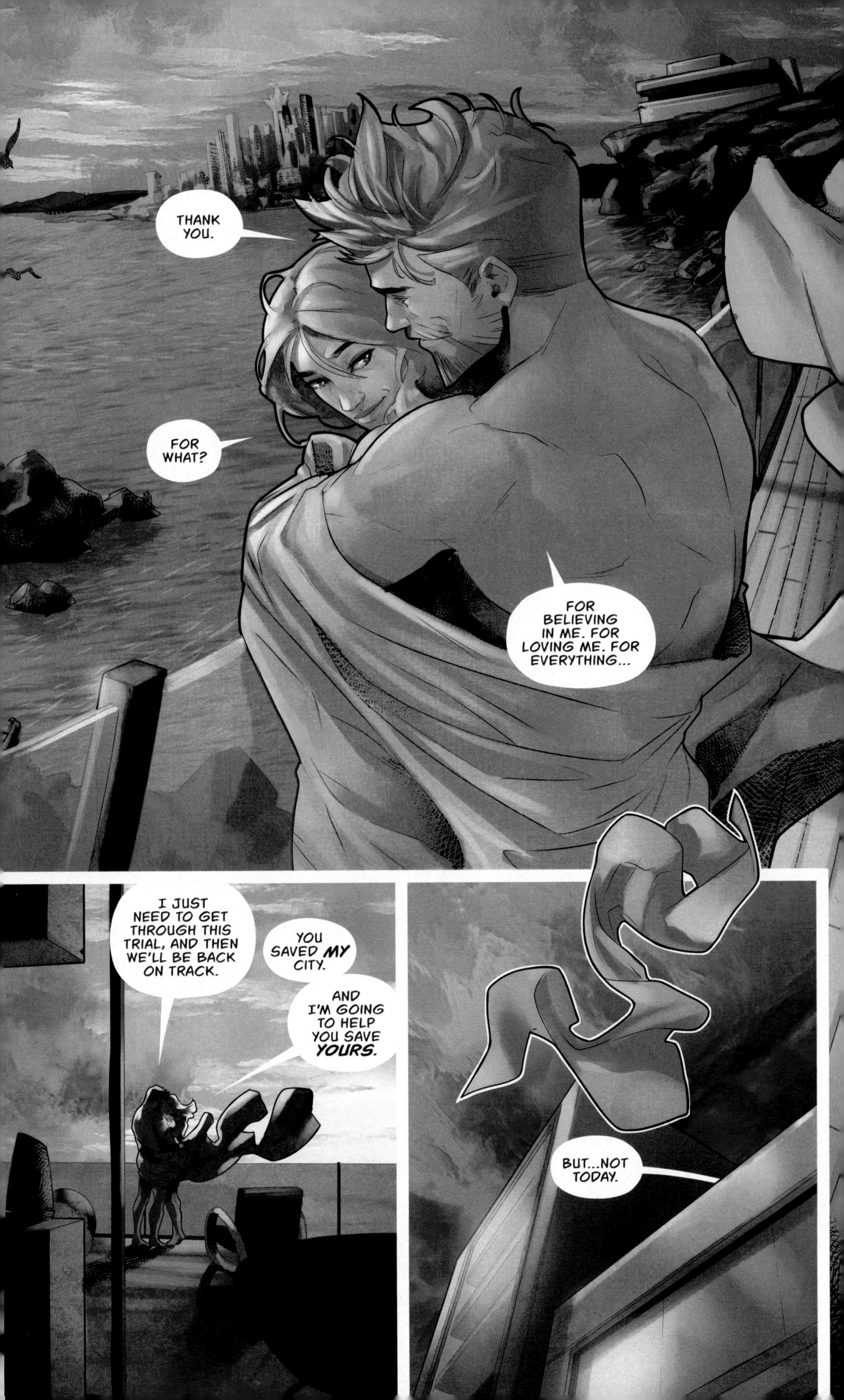
THANK YOU.
FOR WHAT?
FOR BELIEVING IN ME. FOR LOVING ME. FOR EVERYTHING...
I JUST NEED TO GET THROUGH THIS TRIAL, AND THEN WE'LL BE BACK ON TRACK.
YOU SAVED MY CITY.
AND I'M GOING TO HELP YOU SAVE YOURS.
BUT...NOT TODAY.

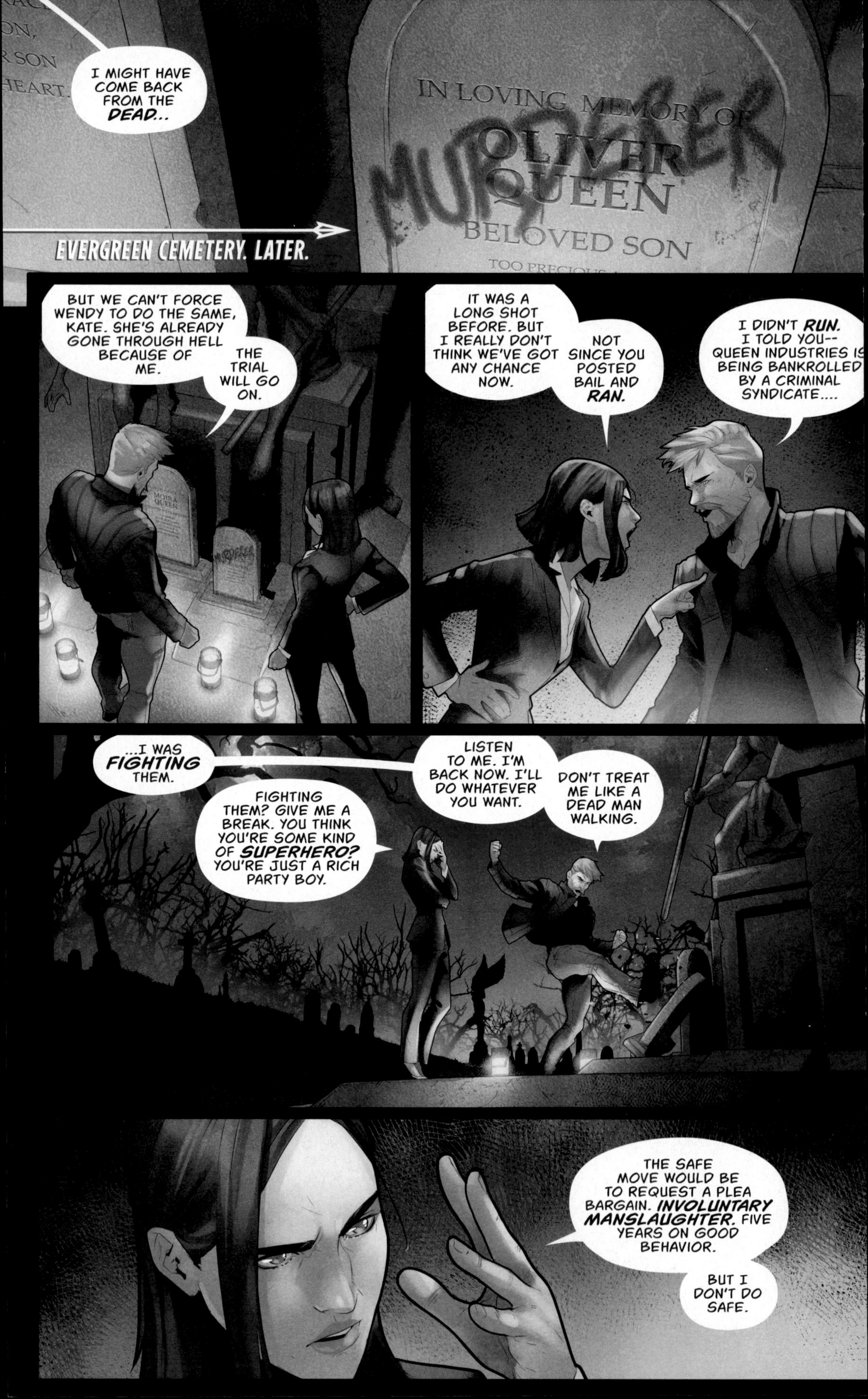

I MIGHT HAVE COME BACK FROM THE DEAD...
IN LOVING MEMORY OF OLIVER QUEEN BELOVED SON
MURDERER
EVERGREEN CEMETERY. LATER.
BUT WE CAN'T FORCE WENDY TO DO THE SAME, KATE. SHE'S ALREADY GONE THROUGH HELL BECAUSE OF ME.
THE TRIAL WILL GO ON.
MOIRA QUEEN
IT WAS A LONG SHOT BEFORE. BUT I REALLY DON'T THINK WE'VE GOT ANY CHANCE NOW.
NOT SINCE YOU POSTED BAIL AND RAN.
I DIDN'T RUN. I TOLD YOU-- QUEEN INDUSTRIES IS BEING BANKROLLED BY A CRIMINAL SYNDICATE....
...I WAS FIGHTING THEM.
FIGHTING THEM? GIVE ME A BREAK. YOU THINK YOU'RE SOME KIND OF SUPERHERO? YOU'RE JUST A RICH PARTY BOY.
LISTEN TO ME. I'M BACK NOW. I'LL DO WHATEVER YOU WANT.
DON'T TREAT ME LIKE A DEAD MAN WALKING.
THE SAFE MOVE WOULD BE TO REQUEST A PLEA BARGAIN. INVOLUNTARY MANSLAUGHTER. FIVE YEARS ON GOOD BEHAVIOR.
BUT I DON'T DO SAFE.

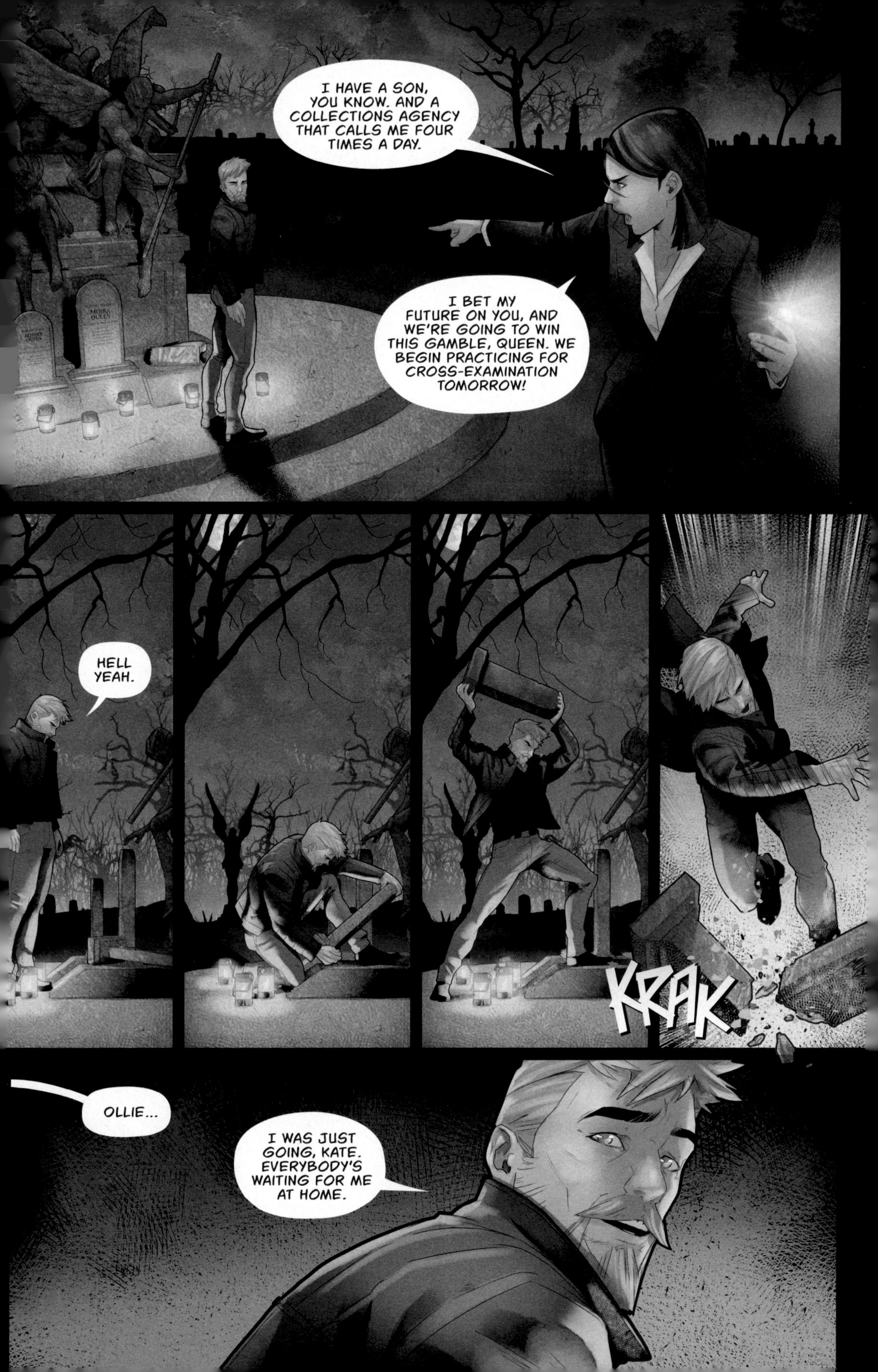
I HAVE A SON, YOU KNOW. AND A COLLECTIONS AGENCY THAT CALLS ME FOUR TIMES A DAY.
I BET MY FUTURE ON YOU, AND WE'RE GOING TO WIN THIS GAMBLE, QUEEN. WE BEGIN PRACTICING FOR CROSS-EXAMINATION TOMORROW!
HELL YEAH.
KRAK
OLLIE...
I WAS JUST GOING, KATE. EVERYBODY'S WAITING FOR ME AT HOME.

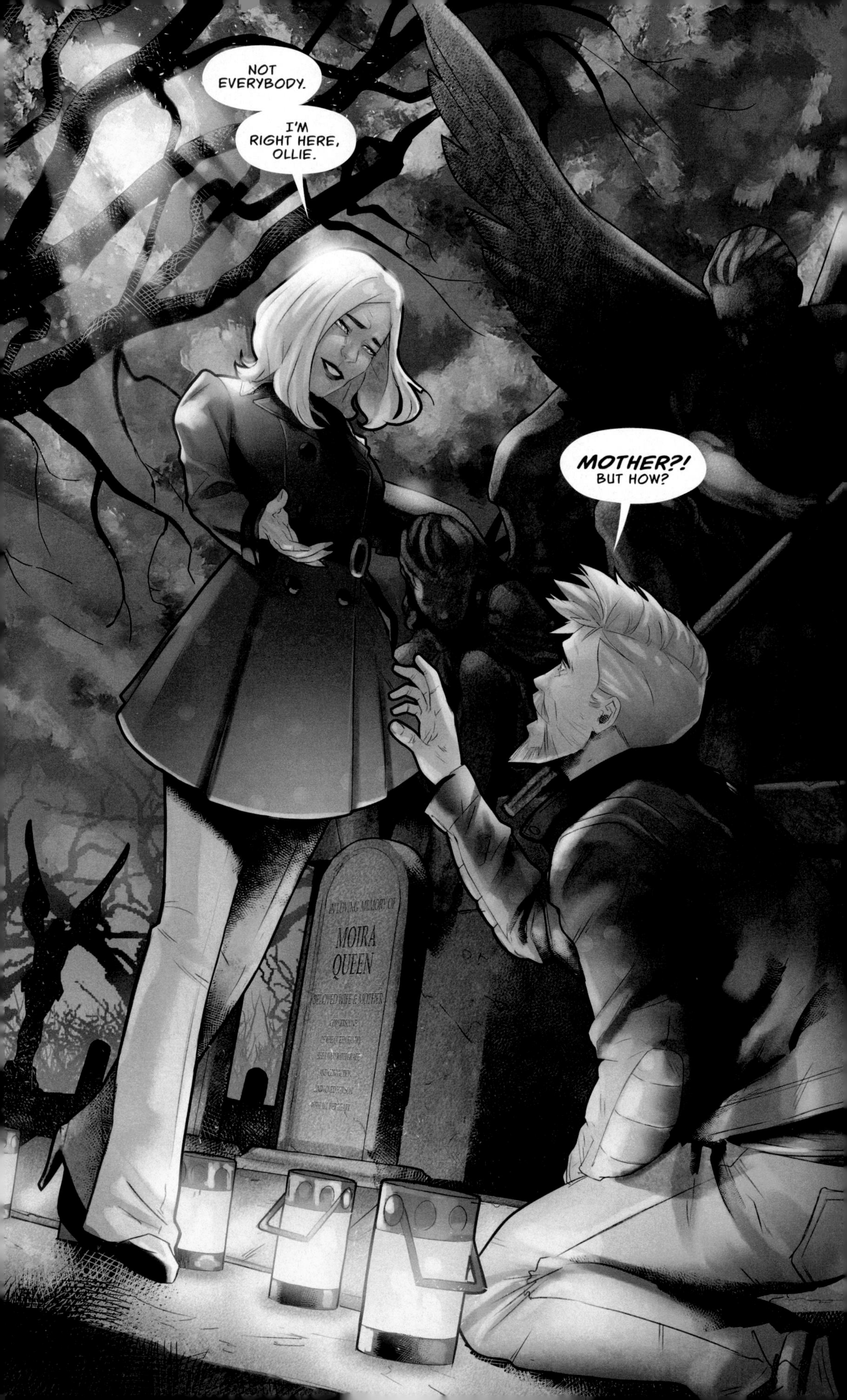
NOT EVERYBODY.
I'M RIGHT HERE, OLLIE.
MOTHER?! BUT HOW?
IN LOVING MEMORY OF
MOIRA QUEEN
BELOVED WIFE & MOTHER

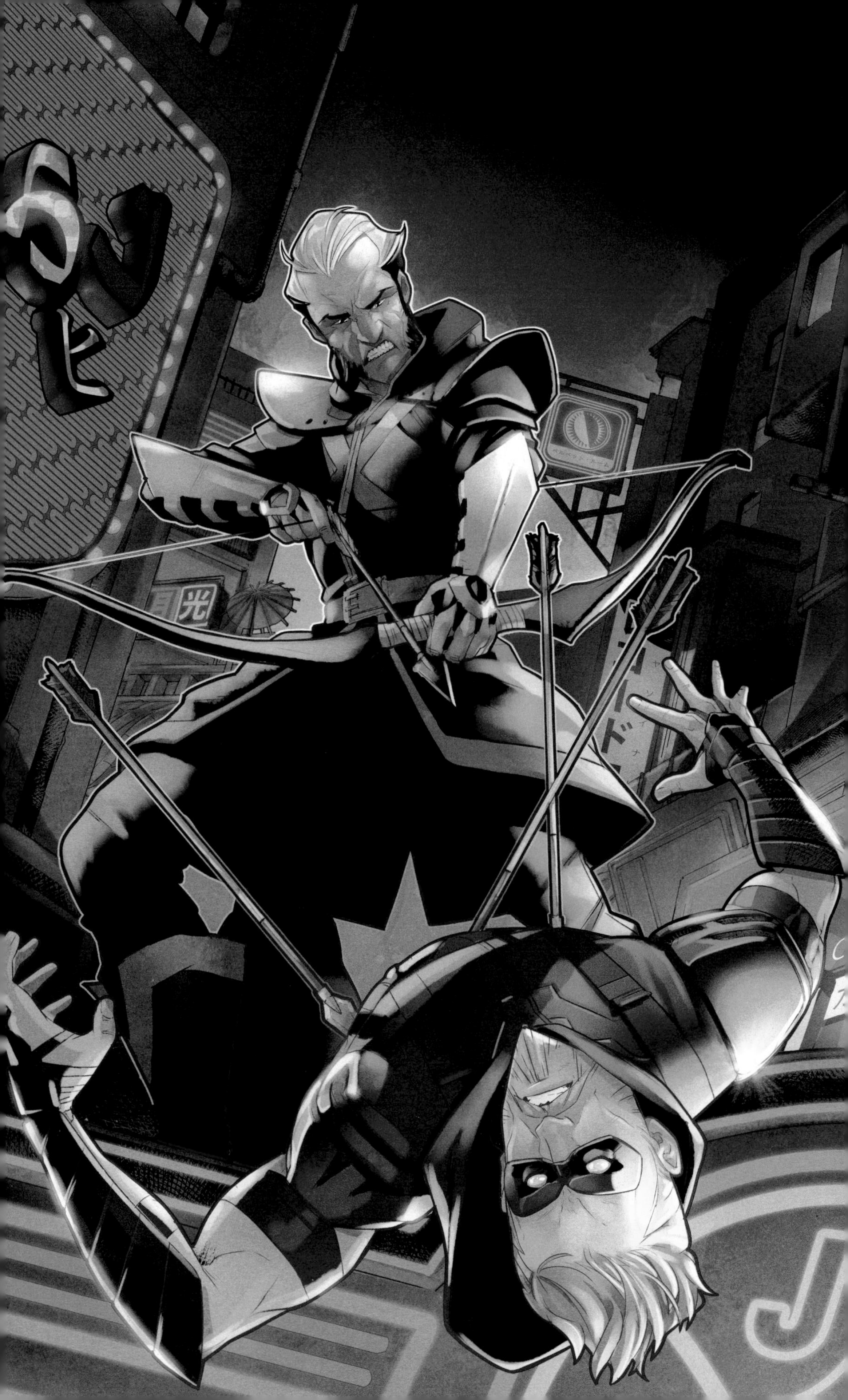

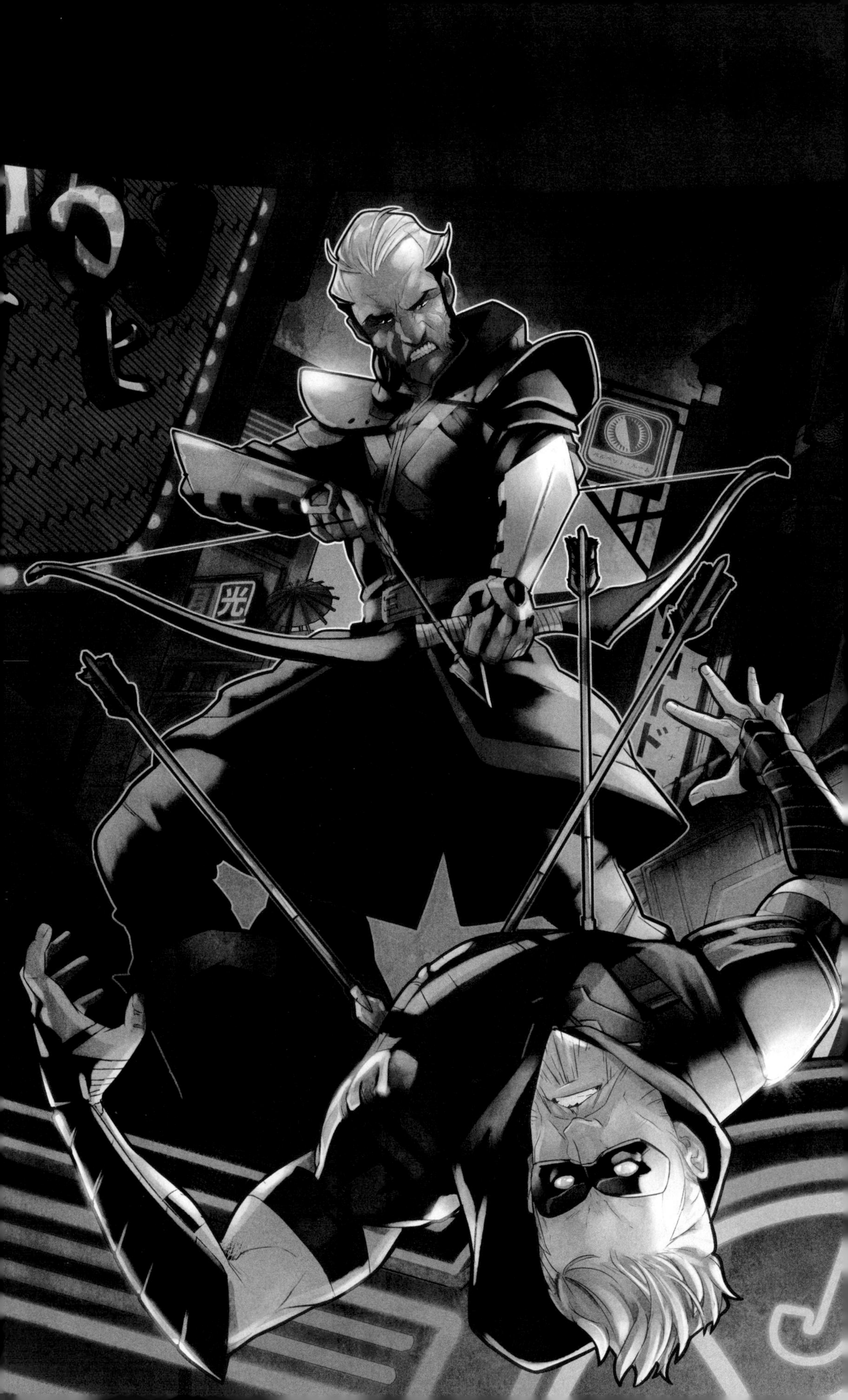
光

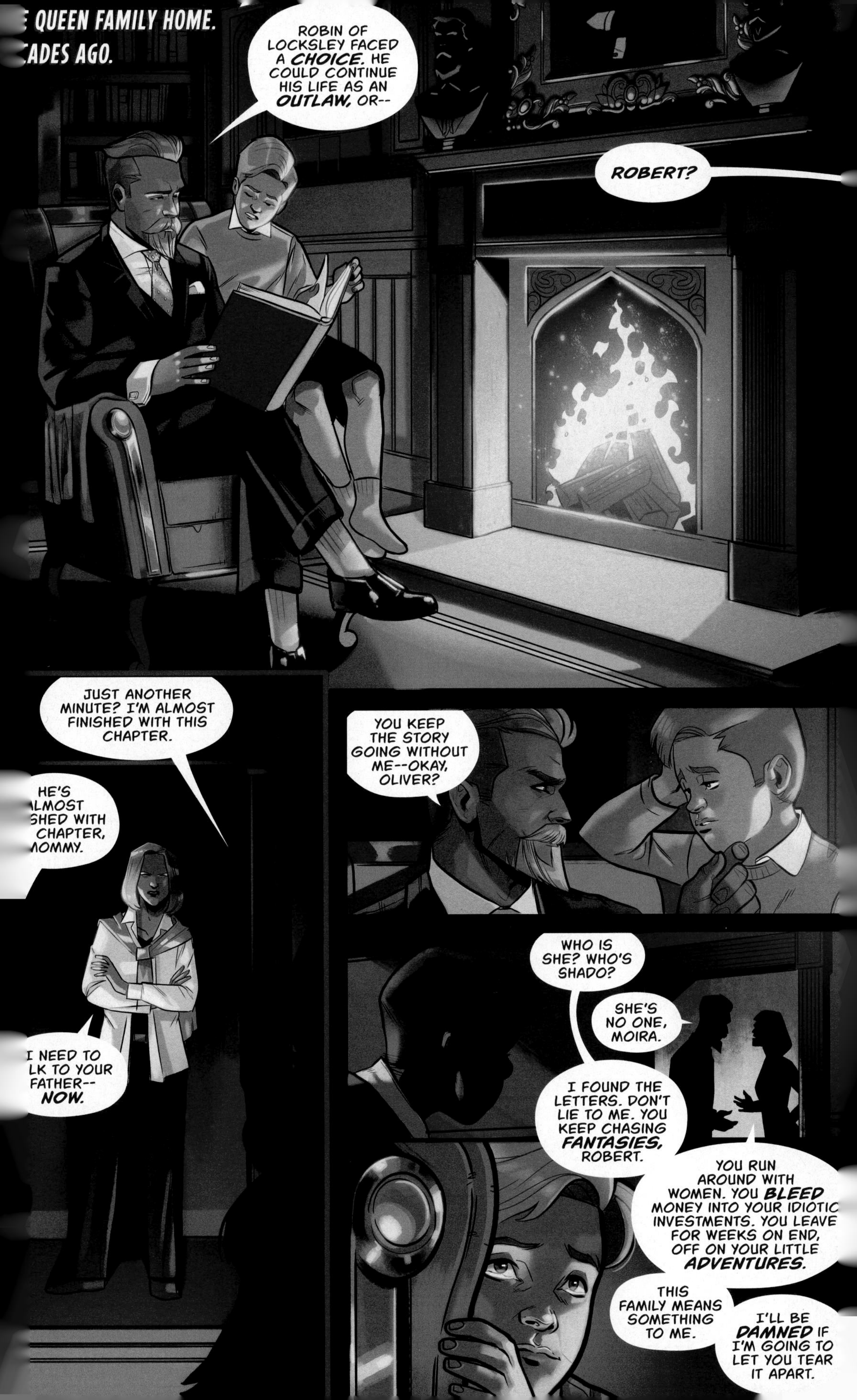

E QUEEN FAMILY HOME.
CADES AGO.
ROBIN OF LOCKSLEY FACED A CHOICE. HE COULD CONTINUE HIS LIFE AS AN OUTLAW, OR--
ROBERT?
JUST ANOTHER MINUTE? I'M ALMOST FINISHED WITH THIS CHAPTER.
HE'S LMOST SHED WITH CHAPTER, MOMMY.
YOU KEEP THE STORY GOING WITHOUT ME--OKAY, OLIVER?
I NEED TO LK TO YOUR FATHER-- NOW.
WHO IS SHE? WHO'S SHADO?
SHE'S NO ONE, MOIRA.
I FOUND THE LETTERS. DON'T LIE TO ME. YOU KEEP CHASING FANTASIES, ROBERT.
YOU RUN AROUND WITH WOMEN. YOU BLEED MONEY INTO YOUR IDIOTIC INVESTMENTS. YOU LEAVE FOR WEEKS ON END, OFF ON YOUR LITTLE ADVENTURES.
THIS FAMILY MEANS SOMETHING TO ME.
I'LL BE DAMNED IF I'M GOING TO LET YOU TEAR IT APART.

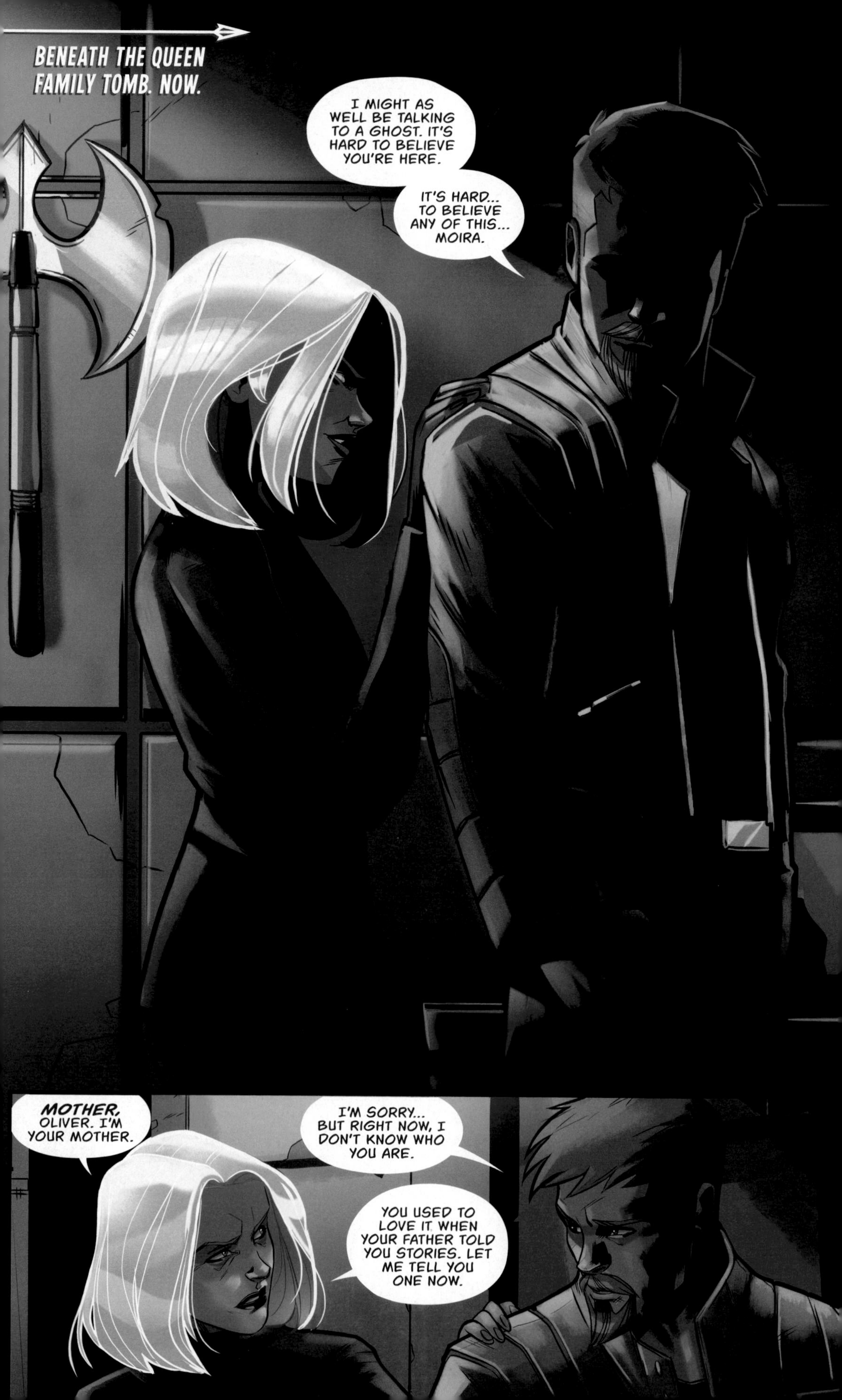
BENEATH THE QUEEN FAMILY TOMB. NOW.
I MIGHT AS WELL BE TALKING TO A GHOST. IT'S HARD TO BELIEVE YOU'RE HERE.
IT'S HARD... TO BELIEVE ANY OF THIS... MOIRA.
MOTHER, OLIVER. I'M YOUR MOTHER.
I'M SORRY... BUT RIGHT NOW, I DON'T KNOW WHO YOU ARE.
YOU USED TO LOVE IT WHEN YOUR FATHER TOLD YOU STORIES. LET ME TELL YOU ONE NOW.

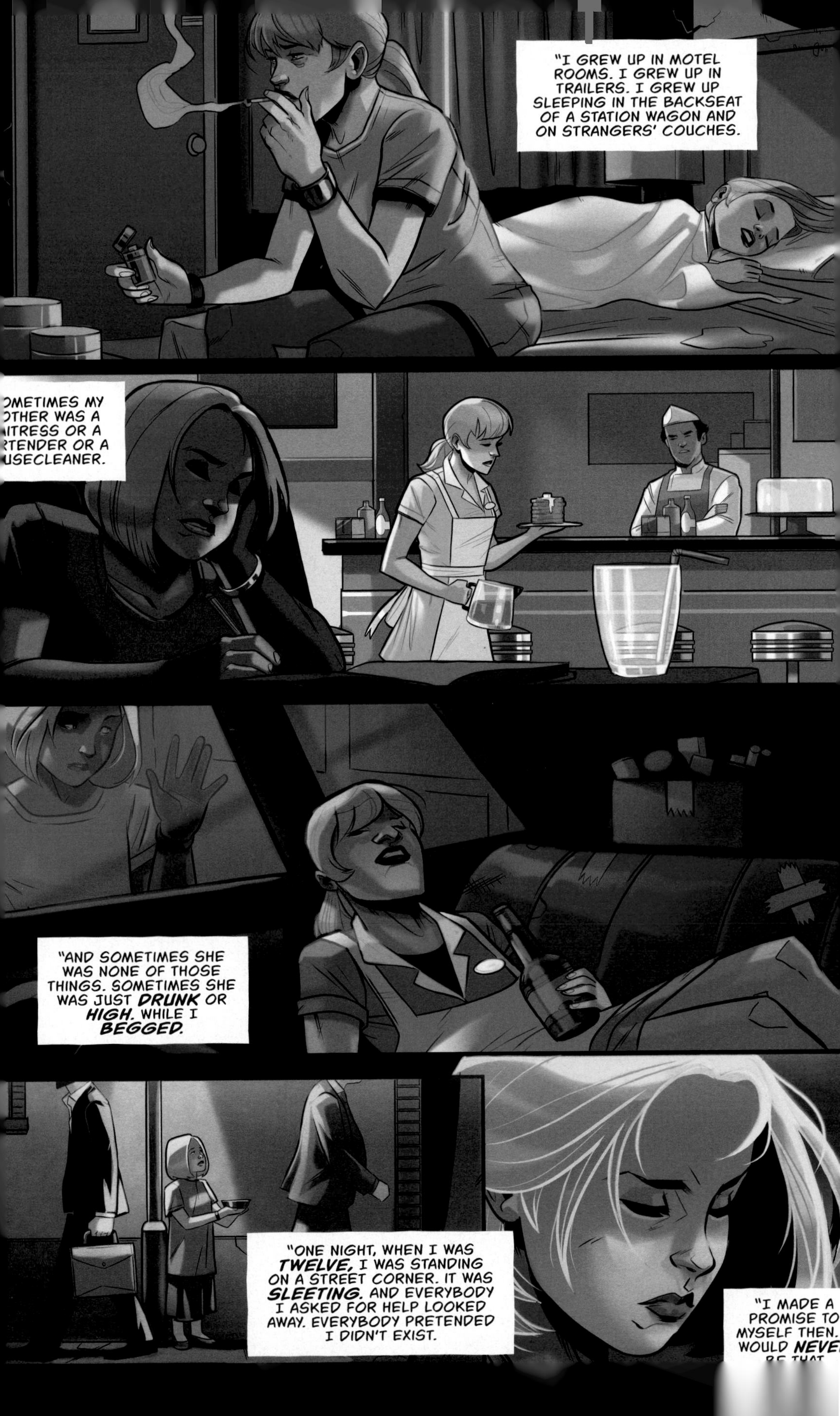
"I GREW UP IN MOTEL ROOMS. I GREW UP IN TRAILERS. I GREW UP SLEEPING IN THE BACKSEAT OF A STATION WAGON AND ON STRANGERS' COUCHES.
OMETIMES MY OTHER WAS A AITRESS OR A RTENDER OR A USECLEANER.
"AND SOMETIMES SHE WAS NONE OF THOSE THINGS. SOMETIMES SHE WAS JUST DRUNK OR HIGH. WHILE I BEGGED.
"ONE NIGHT, WHEN I WAS TWELVE, I WAS STANDING ON A STREET CORNER. IT WAS SLEETING. AND EVERYBODY I ASKED FOR HELP LOOKED AWAY. EVERYBODY PRETENDED I DIDN'T EXIST.
"I MADE A PROMISE TO MYSELF THEN. WOULD NEVE

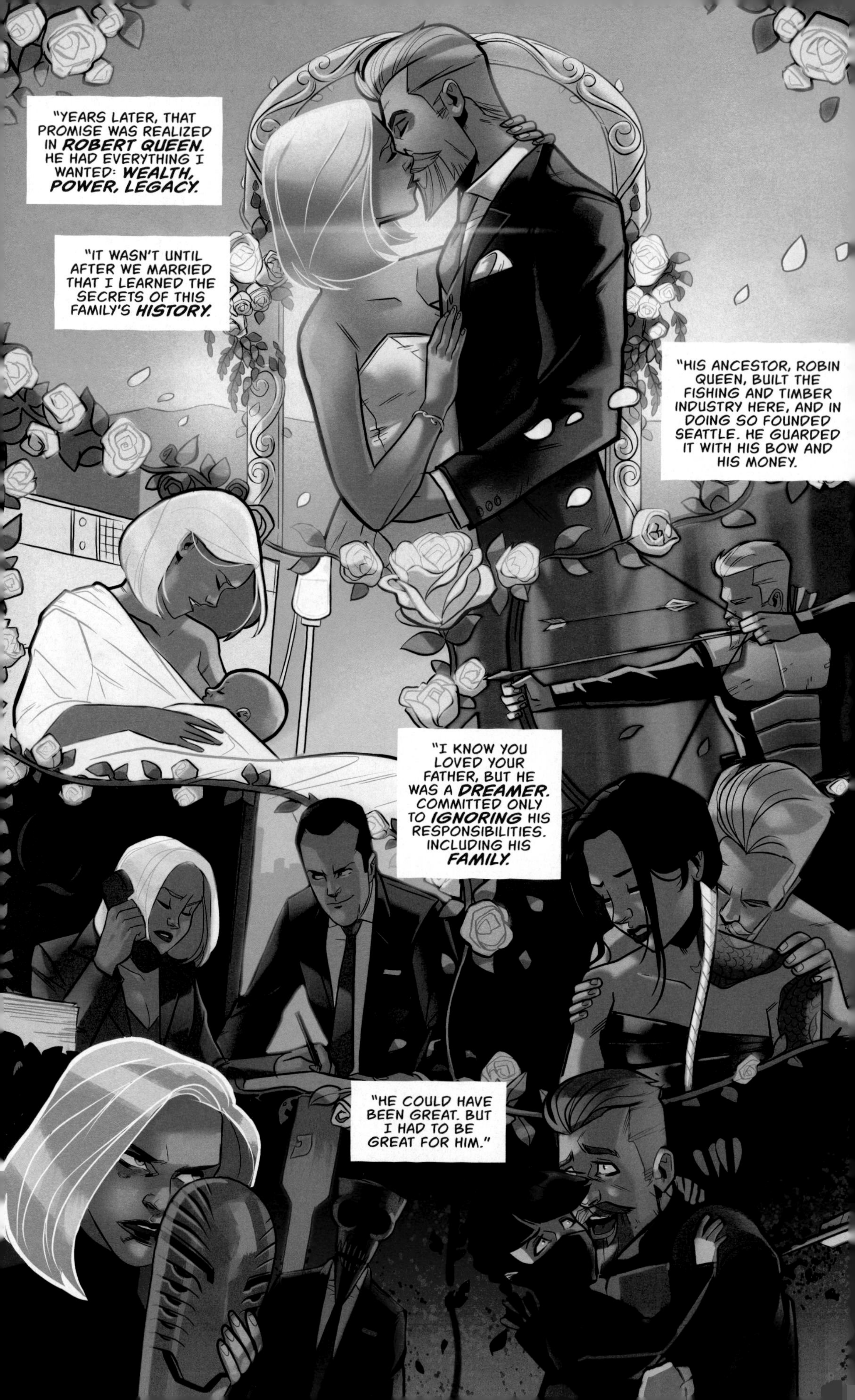
"YEARS LATER, THAT PROMISE WAS REALIZED IN ROBERT QUEEN. HE HAD EVERYTHING I WANTED: WEALTH, POWER, LEGACY.
"IT WASN'T UNTIL AFTER WE MARRIED THAT I LEARNED THE SECRETS OF THIS FAMILY'S HISTORY.
"HIS ANCESTOR, ROBIN QUEEN, BUILT THE FISHING AND TIMBER INDUSTRY HERE, AND IN DOING SO FOUNDED SEATTLE. HE GUARDED IT WITH HIS BOW AND HIS MONEY.
"I KNOW YOU LOVED YOUR FATHER, BUT HE WAS A DREAMER. COMMITTED ONLY TO IGNORING HIS RESPONSIBILITIES. INCLUDING HIS FAMILY.
"HE COULD HAVE BEEN GREAT. BUT I HAD TO BE GREAT FOR HIM."

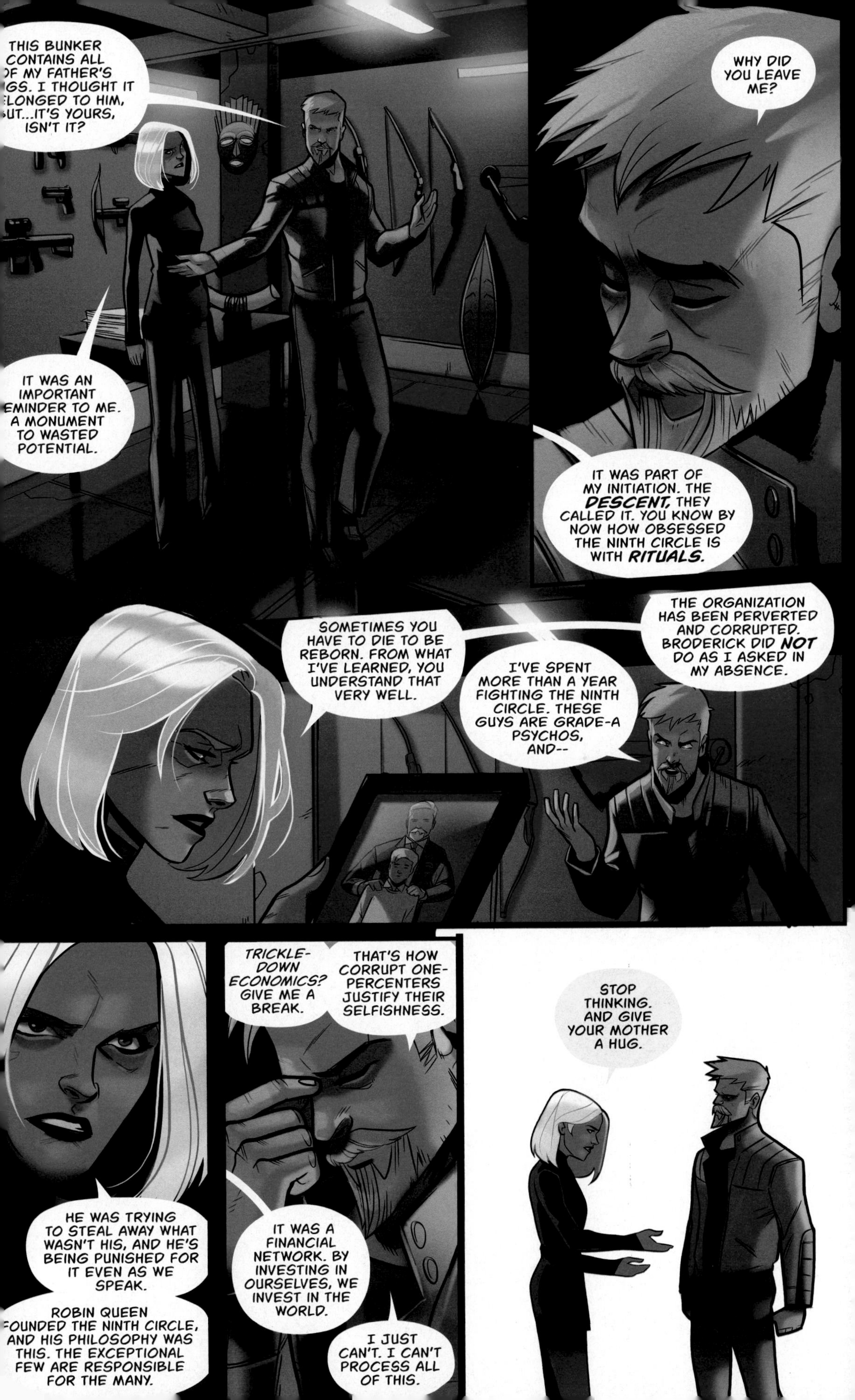
THIS BUNKER CONTAINS ALL OF MY FATHER'S THINGS. I THOUGHT IT BELONGED TO HIM, BUT...IT'S YOURS, ISN'T IT?
IT WAS AN IMPORTANT REMINDER TO ME. A MONUMENT TO WASTED POTENTIAL.
WHY DID YOU LEAVE ME?
IT WAS PART OF MY INITIATION. THE *DESCENT,* THEY CALLED IT. YOU KNOW BY NOW HOW OBSESSED THE NINTH CIRCLE IS WITH *RITUALS.*
SOMETIMES YOU HAVE TO DIE TO BE REBORN. FROM WHAT I'VE LEARNED, YOU UNDERSTAND THAT VERY WELL.
THE ORGANIZATION HAS BEEN PERVERTED AND CORRUPTED. BRODERICK DID *NOT* DO AS I ASKED IN MY ABSENCE.
I'VE SPENT MORE THAN A YEAR FIGHTING THE NINTH CIRCLE. THESE GUYS ARE GRADE-A PSYCHOS, AND--
HE WAS TRYING TO STEAL AWAY WHAT WASN'T HIS, AND HE'S BEING PUNISHED FOR IT EVEN AS WE SPEAK.
ROBIN QUEEN FOUNDED THE NINTH CIRCLE, AND HIS PHILOSOPHY WAS THIS. THE EXCEPTIONAL FEW ARE RESPONSIBLE FOR THE MANY.
IT WAS A FINANCIAL NETWORK. BY INVESTING IN OURSELVES, WE INVEST IN THE WORLD.
TRICKLE-DOWN ECONOMICS? GIVE ME A BREAK.
THAT'S HOW CORRUPT ONE-PERCENTERS JUSTIFY THEIR SELFISHNESS.
I JUST CAN'T. I CAN'T PROCESS ALL OF THIS.
STOP THINKING. AND GIVE YOUR MOTHER A HUG.

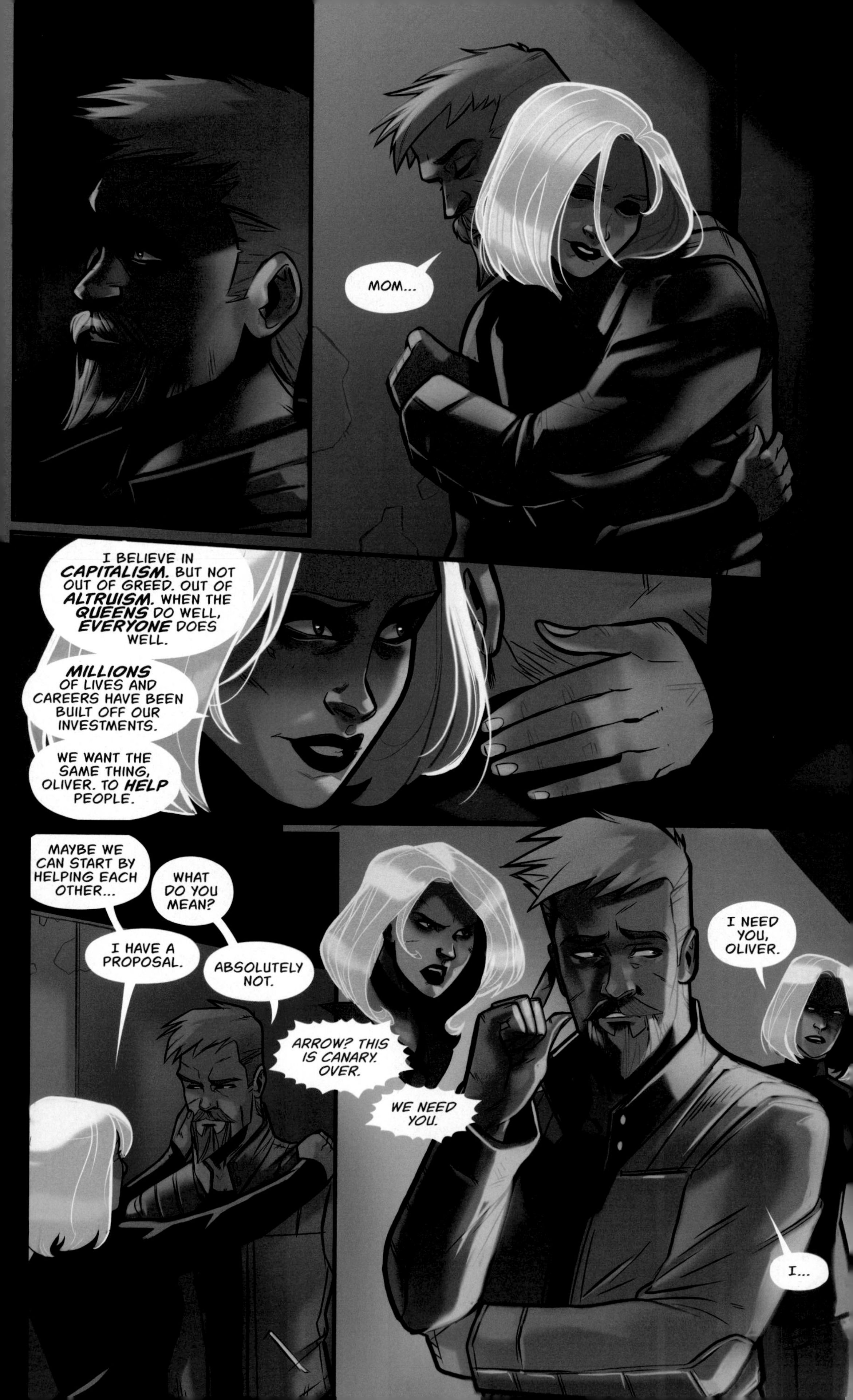
MOM...
I BELIEVE IN CAPITALISM. BUT NOT OUT OF GREED. OUT OF ALTRUISM. WHEN THE QUEENS DO WELL, EVERYONE DOES WELL.
MILLIONS OF LIVES AND CAREERS HAVE BEEN BUILT OFF OUR INVESTMENTS.
WE WANT THE SAME THING, OLIVER. TO HELP PEOPLE.
MAYBE WE CAN START BY HELPING EACH OTHER...
WHAT DO YOU MEAN?
I HAVE A PROPOSAL.
ABSOLUTELY NOT.
ARROW? THIS IS CANARY. OVER.
WE NEED YOU.
I NEED YOU, OLIVER.
I...

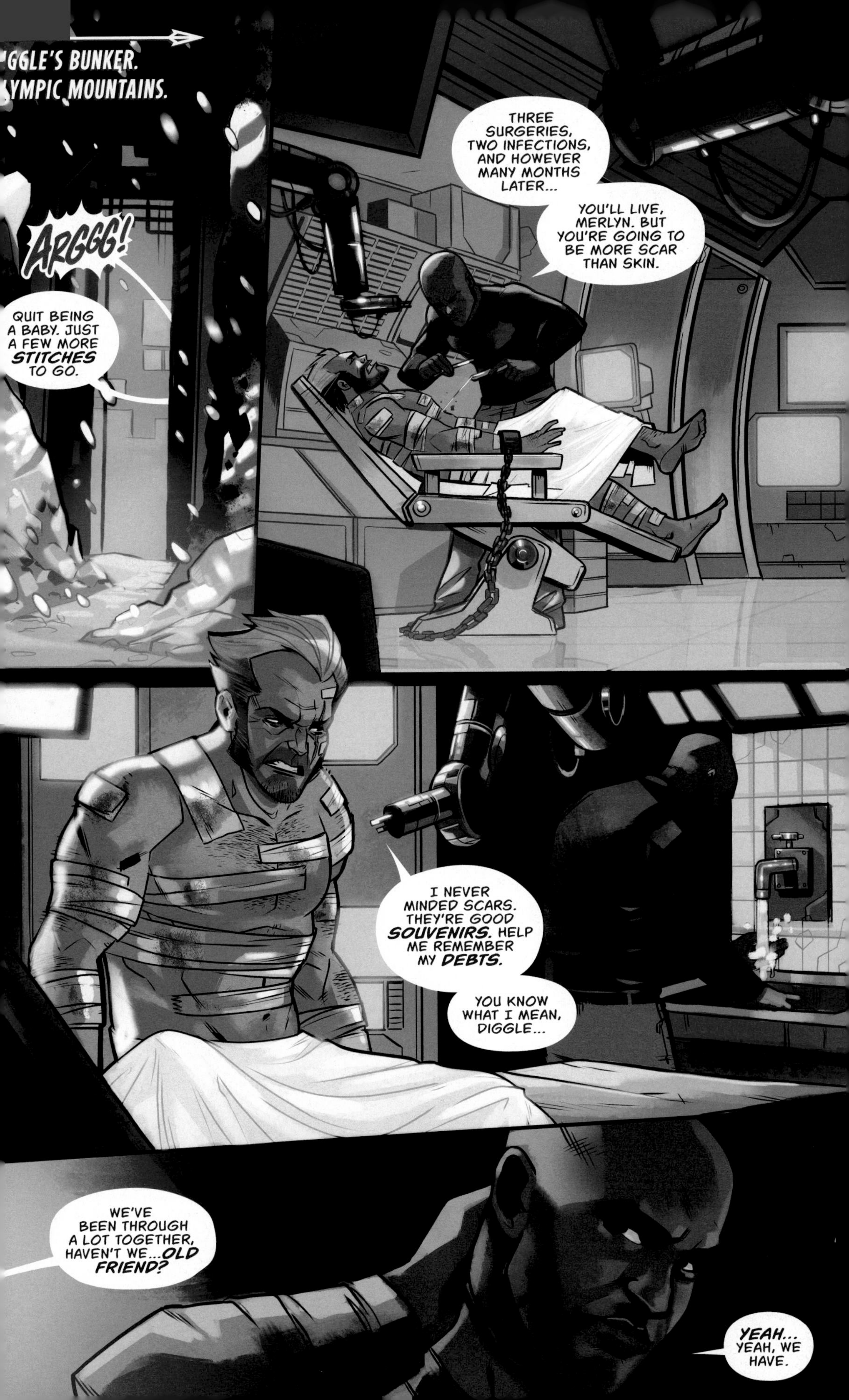
GGLE'S BUNKER.
YMPIC MOUNTAINS.
ARGGG!
QUIT BEING A BABY. JUST A FEW MORE STITCHES TO GO.
THREE SURGERIES, TWO INFECTIONS, AND HOWEVER MANY MONTHS LATER...
YOU'LL LIVE, MERLYN. BUT YOU'RE GOING TO BE MORE SCAR THAN SKIN.
I NEVER MINDED SCARS. THEY'RE GOOD SOUVENIRS. HELP ME REMEMBER MY DEBTS.
YOU KNOW WHAT I MEAN, DIGGLE...
WE'VE BEEN THROUGH A LOT TOGETHER, HAVEN'T WE...OLD FRIEND?
YEAH... YEAH, WE HAVE.

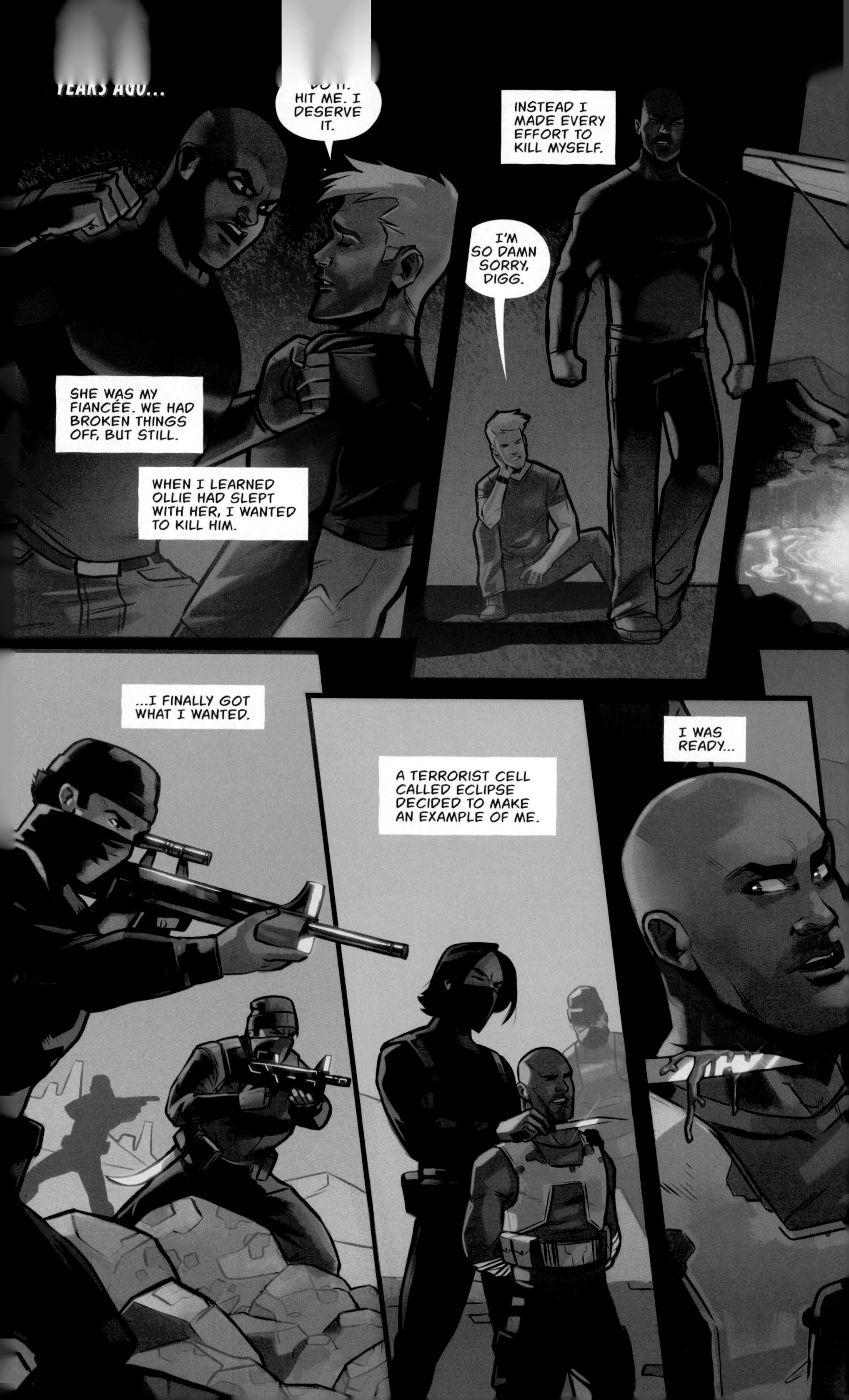
HIT ME. I DESERVE IT.
SHE WAS MY FIANCÉE. WE HAD BROKEN THINGS OFF, BUT STILL.
WHEN I LEARNED OLLIE HAD SLEPT WITH HER, I WANTED TO KILL HIM.
INSTEAD I MADE EVERY EFFORT TO KILL MYSELF.
I'M SO DAMN SORRY, DIGG.
...I FINALLY GOT WHAT I WANTED.
A TERRORIST CELL CALLED ECLIPSE DECIDED TO MAKE AN EXAMPLE OF ME.
I WAS READY...

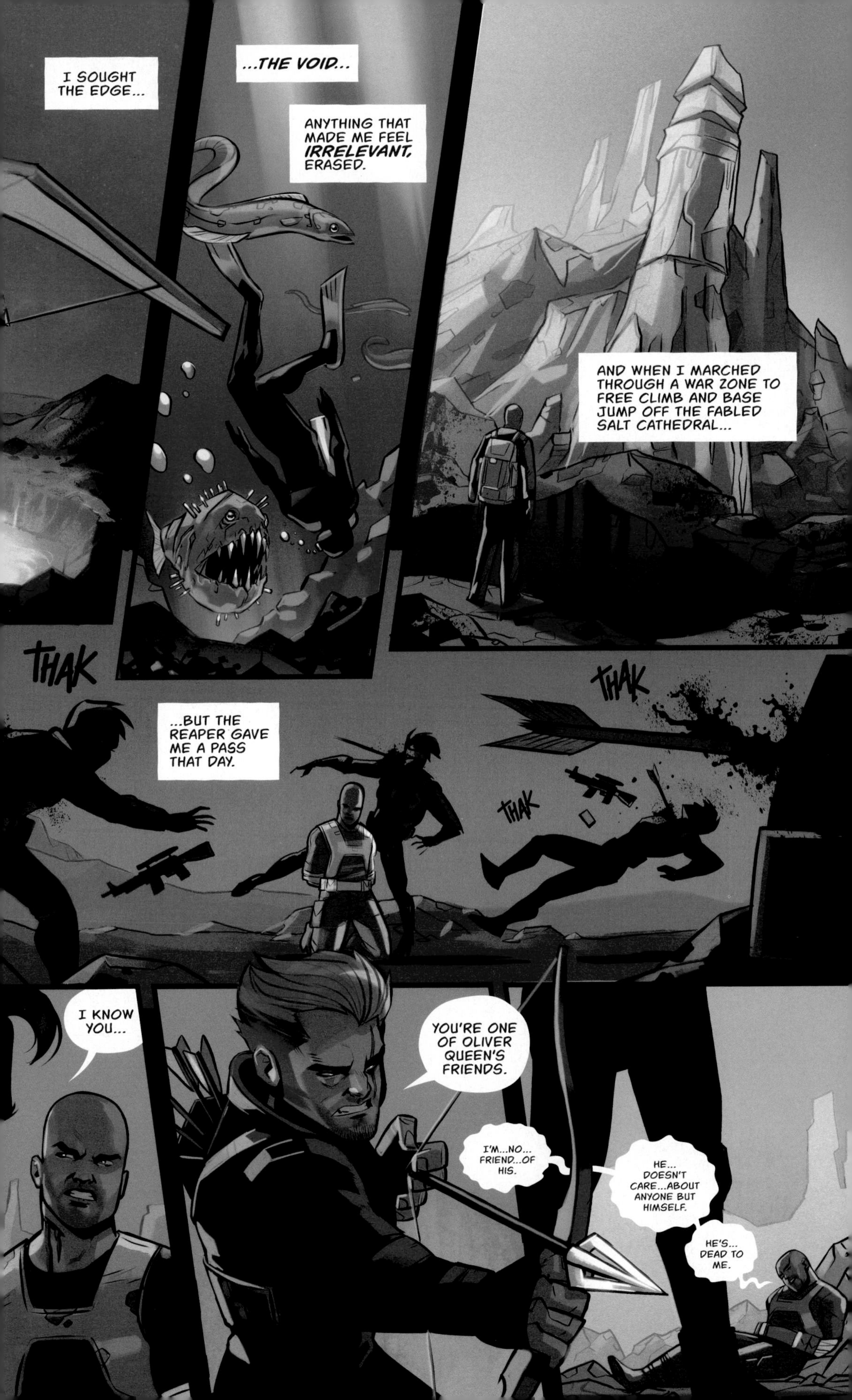
I SOUGHT THE EDGE...
...THE VOID...
ANYTHING THAT MADE ME FEEL *IRRELEVANT,* ERASED.
AND WHEN I MARCHED THROUGH A WAR ZONE TO FREE CLIMB AND BASE JUMP OFF THE FABLED SALT CATHEDRAL...
THAK
...BUT THE REAPER GAVE ME A PASS THAT DAY.
THAK
THAK
I KNOW YOU...
YOU'RE ONE OF OLIVER QUEEN'S FRIENDS.
I'M...NO... FRIEND...OF HIS.
HE... DOESN'T CARE...ABOUT ANYONE BUT HIMSELF.
HE'S... DEAD TO ME.

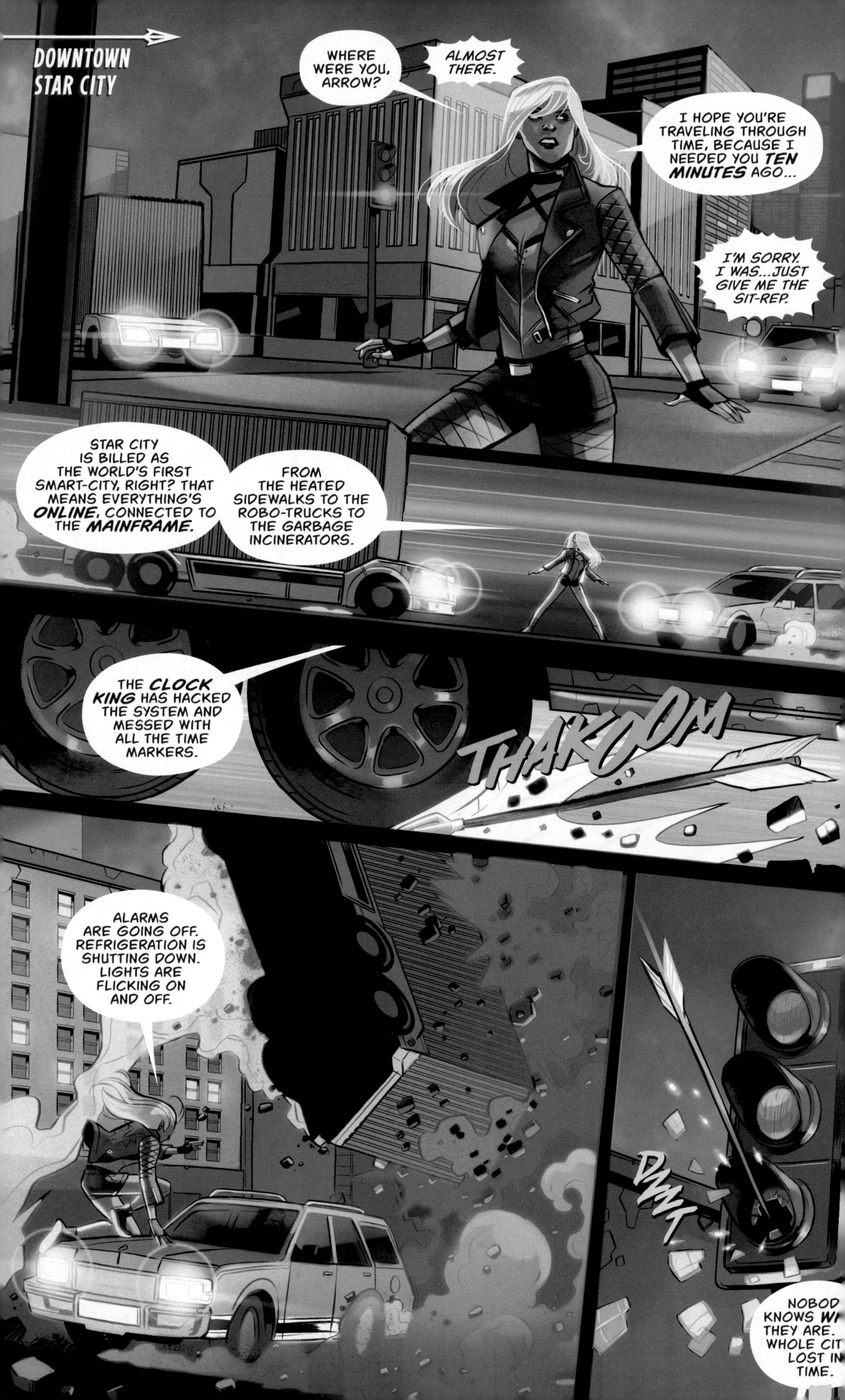
DOWNTOWN STAR CITY
WHERE WERE YOU, ARROW?
ALMOST THERE.
I HOPE YOU'RE TRAVELING THROUGH TIME, BECAUSE I NEEDED YOU TEN MINUTES AGO...
I'M SORRY. I WAS...JUST GIVE ME THE SIT-REP.
STAR CITY IS BILLED AS THE WORLD'S FIRST SMART-CITY, RIGHT? THAT MEANS EVERYTHING'S ONLINE, CONNECTED TO THE MAINFRAME.
FROM THE HEATED SIDEWALKS TO THE ROBO-TRUCKS TO THE GARBAGE INCINERATORS.
THE CLOCK KING HAS HACKED THE SYSTEM AND MESSED WITH ALL THE TIME MARKERS.
THAKOOM
ALARMS ARE GOING OFF. REFRIGERATION IS SHUTTING DOWN. LIGHTS ARE FLICKING ON AND OFF.
DWNT
NOBOD KNOWS WI THEY ARE. WHOLE CIT LOST IN TIME.

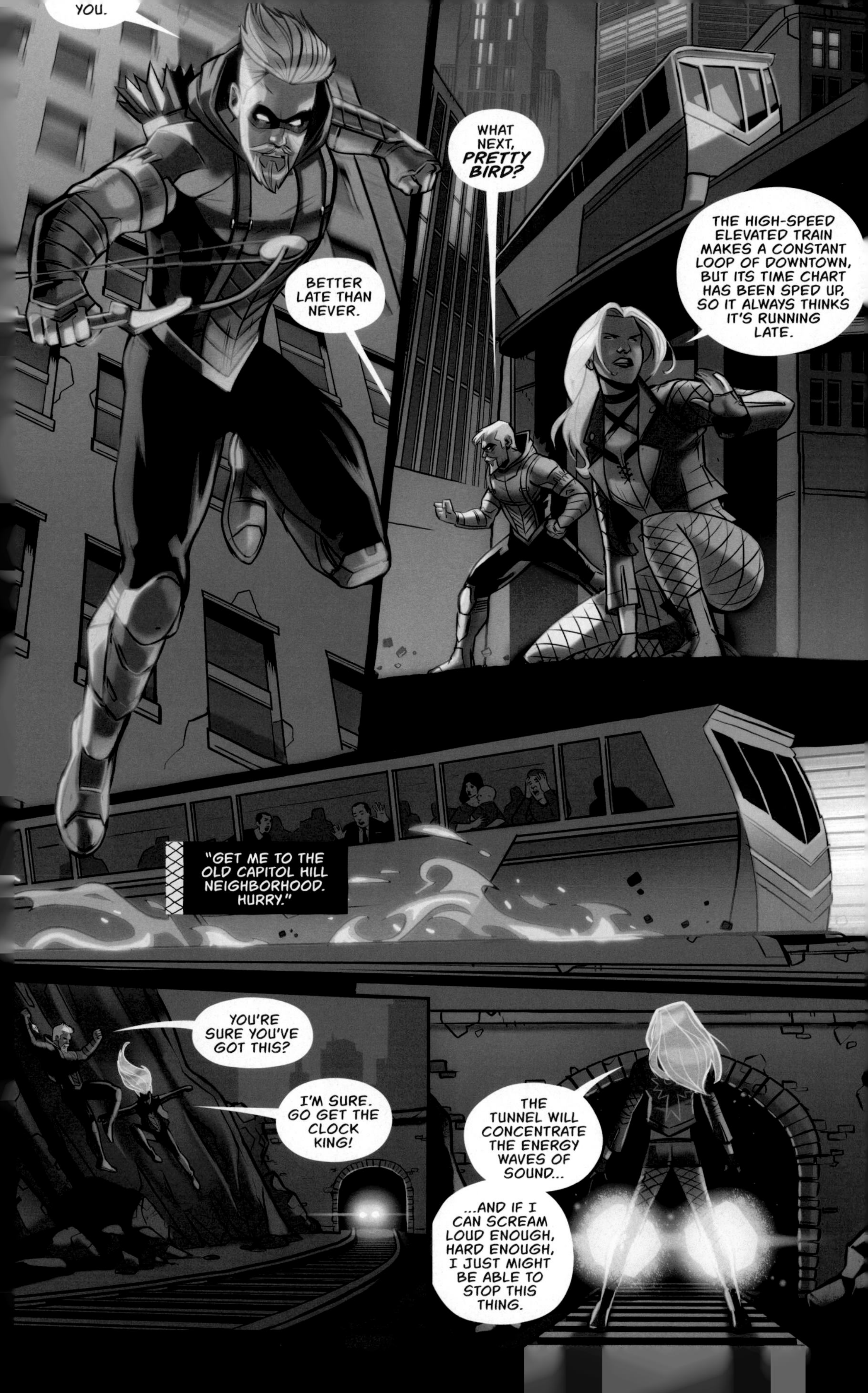
YOU.
BETTER LATE THAN NEVER.
WHAT NEXT, *PRETTY BIRD?*
THE HIGH-SPEED ELEVATED TRAIN MAKES A CONSTANT LOOP OF DOWNTOWN, BUT ITS TIME CHART HAS BEEN SPED UP, SO IT ALWAYS THINKS IT'S RUNNING LATE.
"GET ME TO THE OLD CAPITOL HILL NEIGHBORHOOD. HURRY."
YOU'RE SURE YOU'VE GOT THIS?
I'M SURE. GO GET THE CLOCK KING!
THE TUNNEL WILL CONCENTRATE THE ENERGY WAVES OF SOUND...
...AND IF I CAN SCREAM LOUD ENOUGH, HARD ENOUGH, I JUST MIGHT BE ABLE TO STOP THIS THING.

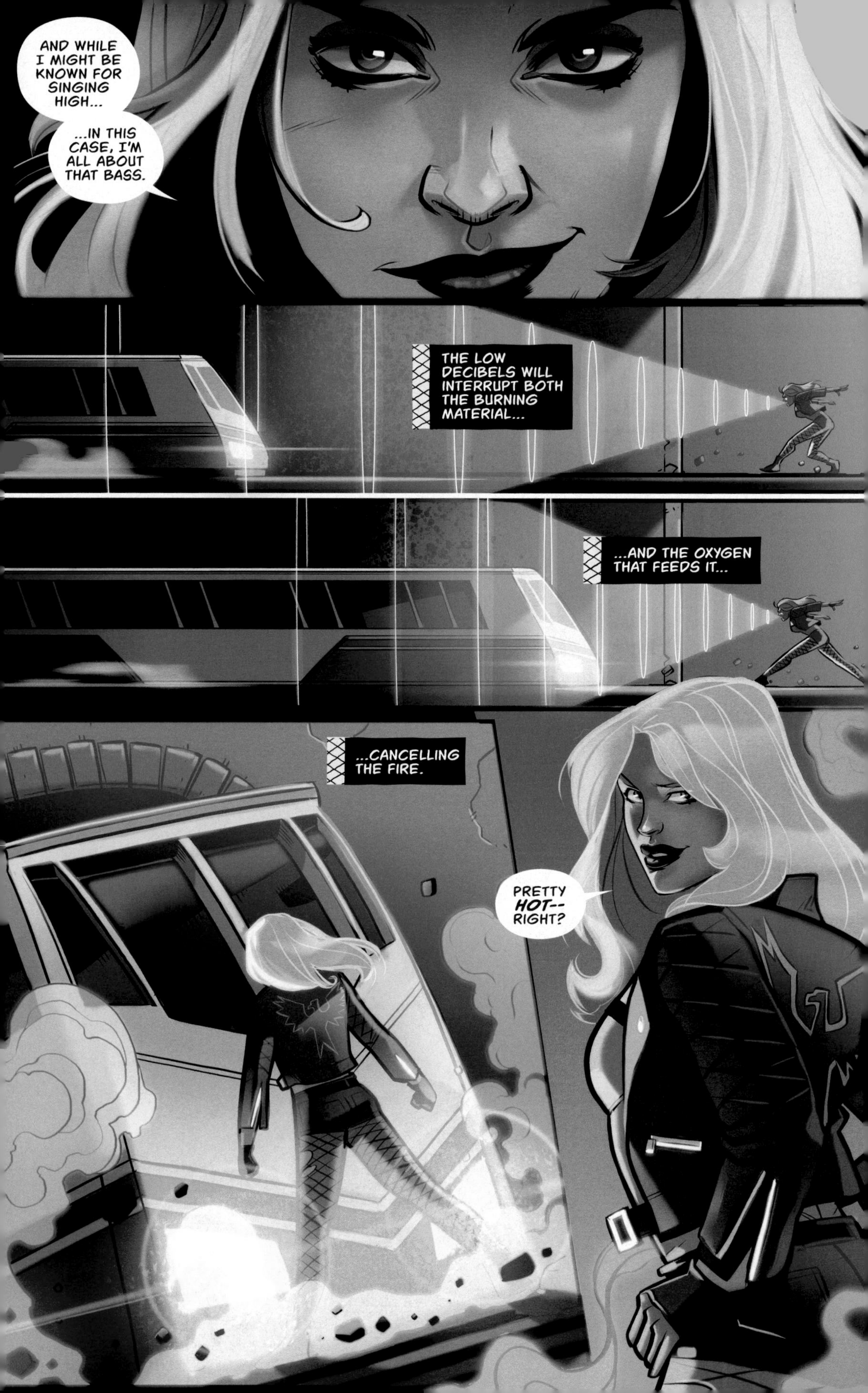
AND WHILE I MIGHT BE KNOWN FOR SINGING HIGH...
...IN THIS CASE, I'M ALL ABOUT THAT BASS.
THE LOW DECIBELS WILL INTERRUPT BOTH THE BURNING MATERIAL...
...AND THE OXYGEN THAT FEEDS IT...
...CANCELLING THE FIRE.
PRETTY *HOT*-- RIGHT?

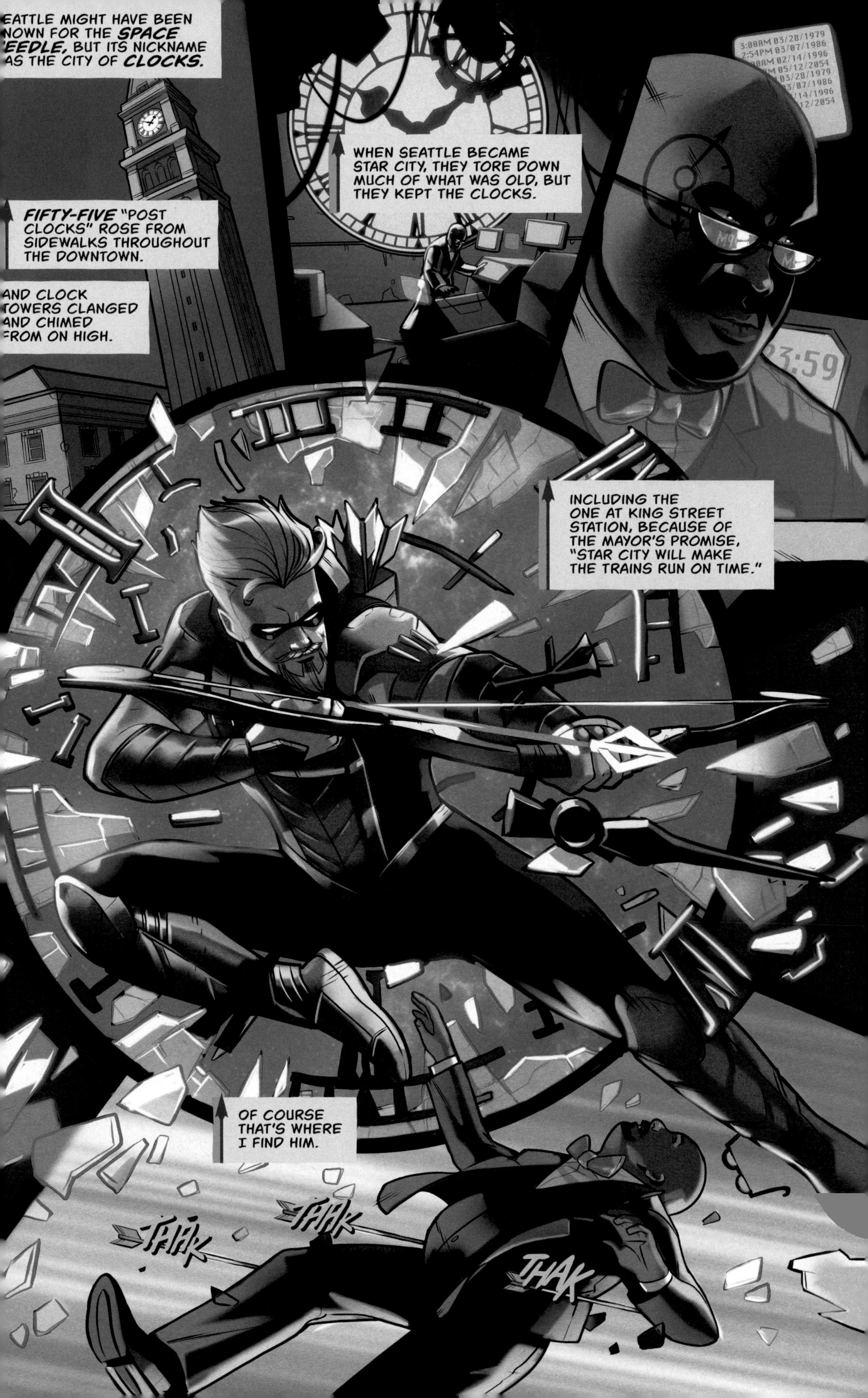
EATTLE MIGHT HAVE BEEN NOWN FOR THE SPACE EEDLE, BUT ITS NICKNAME AS THE CITY OF CLOCKS.
WHEN SEATTLE BECAME STAR CITY, THEY TORE DOWN MUCH OF WHAT WAS OLD, BUT THEY KEPT THE CLOCKS.
FIFTY-FIVE "POST CLOCKS" ROSE FROM SIDEWALKS THROUGHOUT THE DOWNTOWN.
AND CLOCK TOWERS CLANGED AND CHIMED FROM ON HIGH.
INCLUDING THE ONE AT KING STREET STATION, BECAUSE OF THE MAYOR'S PROMISE, "STAR CITY WILL MAKE THE TRAINS RUN ON TIME."
OF COURSE THAT'S WHERE I FIND HIM.
THAK
THAK
THAK

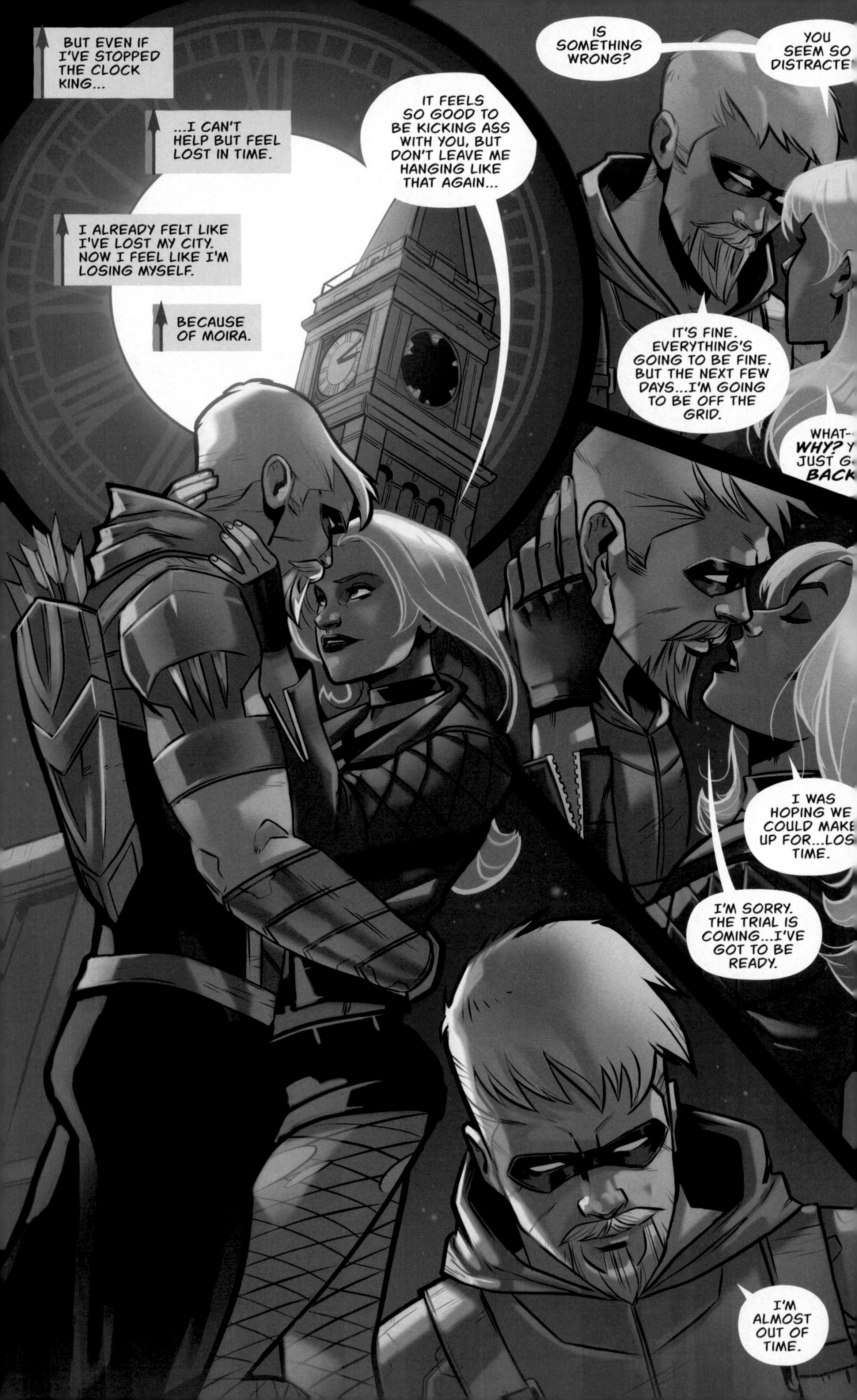
BUT EVEN IF I'VE STOPPED THE CLOCK KING...
...I CAN'T HELP BUT FEEL LOST IN TIME.
I ALREADY FELT LIKE I'VE LOST MY CITY. NOW I FEEL LIKE I'M LOSING MYSELF.
BECAUSE OF MOIRA.
IT FEELS SO GOOD TO BE KICKING ASS WITH YOU, BUT DON'T LEAVE ME HANGING LIKE THAT AGAIN...
IS SOMETHING WRONG?
YOU SEEM SO DISTRACTE
IT'S FINE. EVERYTHING'S GOING TO BE FINE. BUT THE NEXT FEW DAYS...I'M GOING TO BE OFF THE GRID.
WHAT-- WHY?
I WAS HOPING WE COULD MAKE UP FOR...LOS TIME.
I'M SORRY. THE TRIAL IS COMING...I'VE GOT TO BE READY.
I'M ALMOST OUT OF TIME.

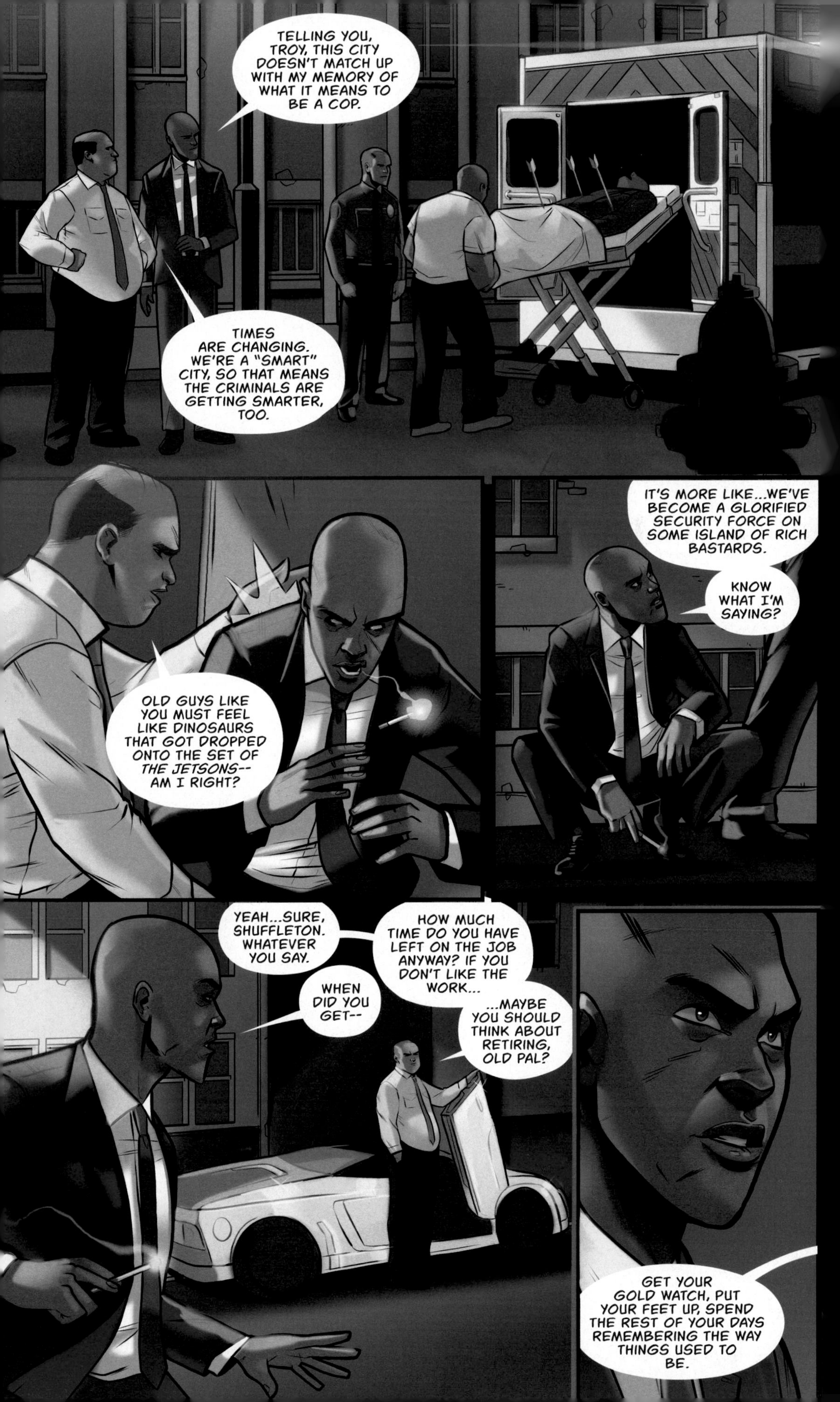

TELLING YOU, TROY, THIS CITY DOESN'T MATCH UP WITH MY MEMORY OF WHAT IT MEANS TO BE A COP.
TIMES ARE CHANGING. WE'RE A "SMART" CITY, SO THAT MEANS THE CRIMINALS ARE GETTING SMARTER, TOO.
OLD GUYS LIKE YOU MUST FEEL LIKE DINOSAURS THAT GOT DROPPED ONTO THE SET OF *THE JETSONS*-- AM I RIGHT?
IT'S MORE LIKE...WE'VE BECOME A GLORIFIED SECURITY FORCE ON SOME ISLAND OF RICH BASTARDS.
KNOW WHAT I'M SAYING?
YEAH...SURE, SHUFFLETON. WHATEVER YOU SAY.
WHEN DID YOU GET--
HOW MUCH TIME DO YOU HAVE LEFT ON THE JOB ANYWAY? IF YOU DON'T LIKE THE WORK...
...MAYBE YOU SHOULD THINK ABOUT RETIRING, OLD PAL?
GET YOUR GOLD WATCH, PUT YOUR FEET UP, SPEND THE REST OF YOUR DAYS REMEMBERING THE WAY THINGS USED TO BE.

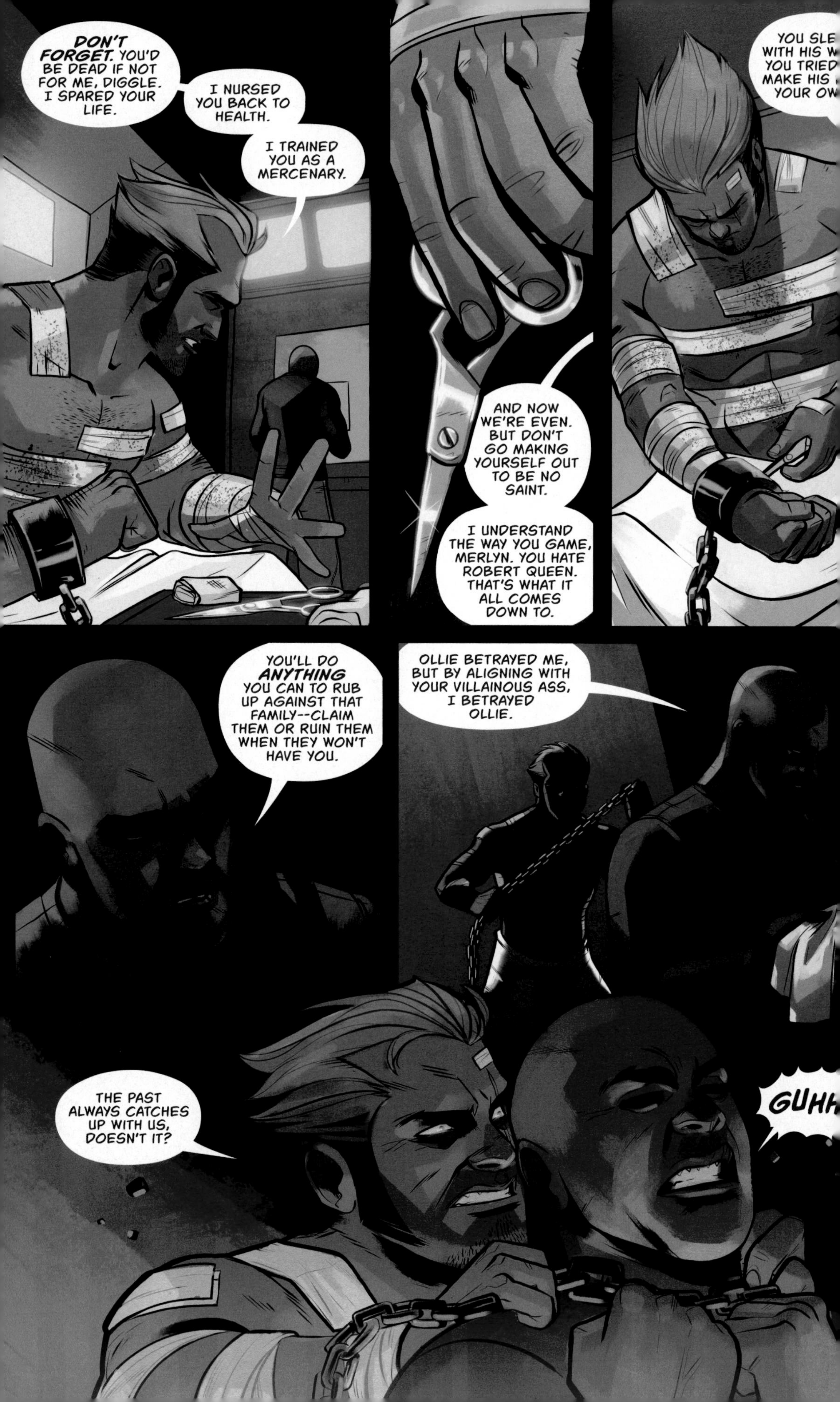
DON'T FORGET. YOU'D BE DEAD IF NOT FOR ME, DIGGLE. I SPARED YOUR LIFE.
I NURSED YOU BACK TO HEALTH.
I TRAINED YOU AS A MERCENARY.
AND NOW WE'RE EVEN. BUT DON'T GO MAKING YOURSELF OUT TO BE NO SAINT.
I UNDERSTAND THE WAY YOU GAME, MERLYN. YOU HATE ROBERT QUEEN. THAT'S WHAT IT ALL COMES DOWN TO.
YOU SLE WITH HIS W YOU TRIED MAKE HIS YOUR OW
YOU'LL DO ANYTHING YOU CAN TO RUB UP AGAINST THAT FAMILY--CLAIM THEM OR RUIN THEM WHEN THEY WON'T HAVE YOU.
OLLIE BETRAYED ME, BUT BY ALIGNING WITH YOUR VILLAINOUS ASS, I BETRAYED OLLIE.
THE PAST ALWAYS CATCHES UP WITH US, DOESN'T IT?
GUHH

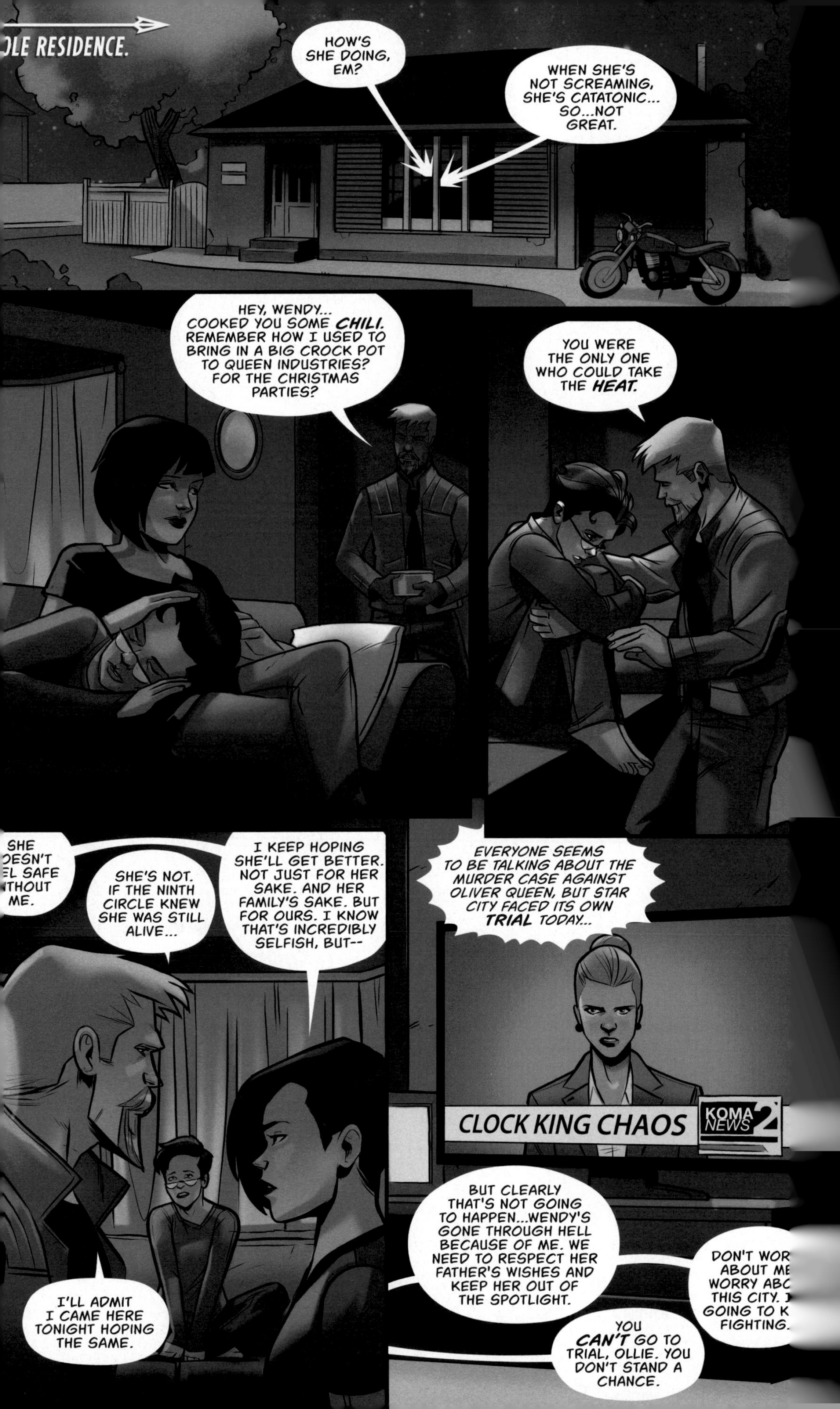

OLE RESIDENCE.
HOW'S SHE DOING, EM?
WHEN SHE'S NOT SCREAMING, SHE'S CATATONIC... SO...NOT GREAT.
HEY, WENDY... COOKED YOU SOME CHILI. REMEMBER HOW I USED TO BRING IN A BIG CROCK POT TO QUEEN INDUSTRIES? FOR THE CHRISTMAS PARTIES?
YOU WERE THE ONLY ONE WHO COULD TAKE THE HEAT.
SHE OESN'T EL SAFE THOUT ME.
SHE'S NOT. IF THE NINTH CIRCLE KNEW SHE WAS STILL ALIVE...
I KEEP HOPING SHE'LL GET BETTER. NOT JUST FOR HER SAKE. AND HER FAMILY'S SAKE. BUT FOR OURS. I KNOW THAT'S INCREDIBLY SELFISH, BUT--
I'LL ADMIT I CAME HERE TONIGHT HOPING THE SAME.
EVERYONE SEEMS TO BE TALKING ABOUT THE MURDER CASE AGAINST OLIVER QUEEN, BUT STAR CITY FACED ITS OWN TRIAL TODAY...
CLOCK KING CHAOS
KOMA NEWS 2
BUT CLEARLY THAT'S NOT GOING TO HAPPEN...WENDY'S GONE THROUGH HELL BECAUSE OF ME. WE NEED TO RESPECT HER FATHER'S WISHES AND KEEP HER OUT OF THE SPOTLIGHT.
DON'T WOR ABOUT ME WORRY ABO THIS CITY. I GOING TO K FIGHTING.
YOU CAN'T GO TO TRIAL, OLLIE. YOU DON'T STAND A CHANCE.

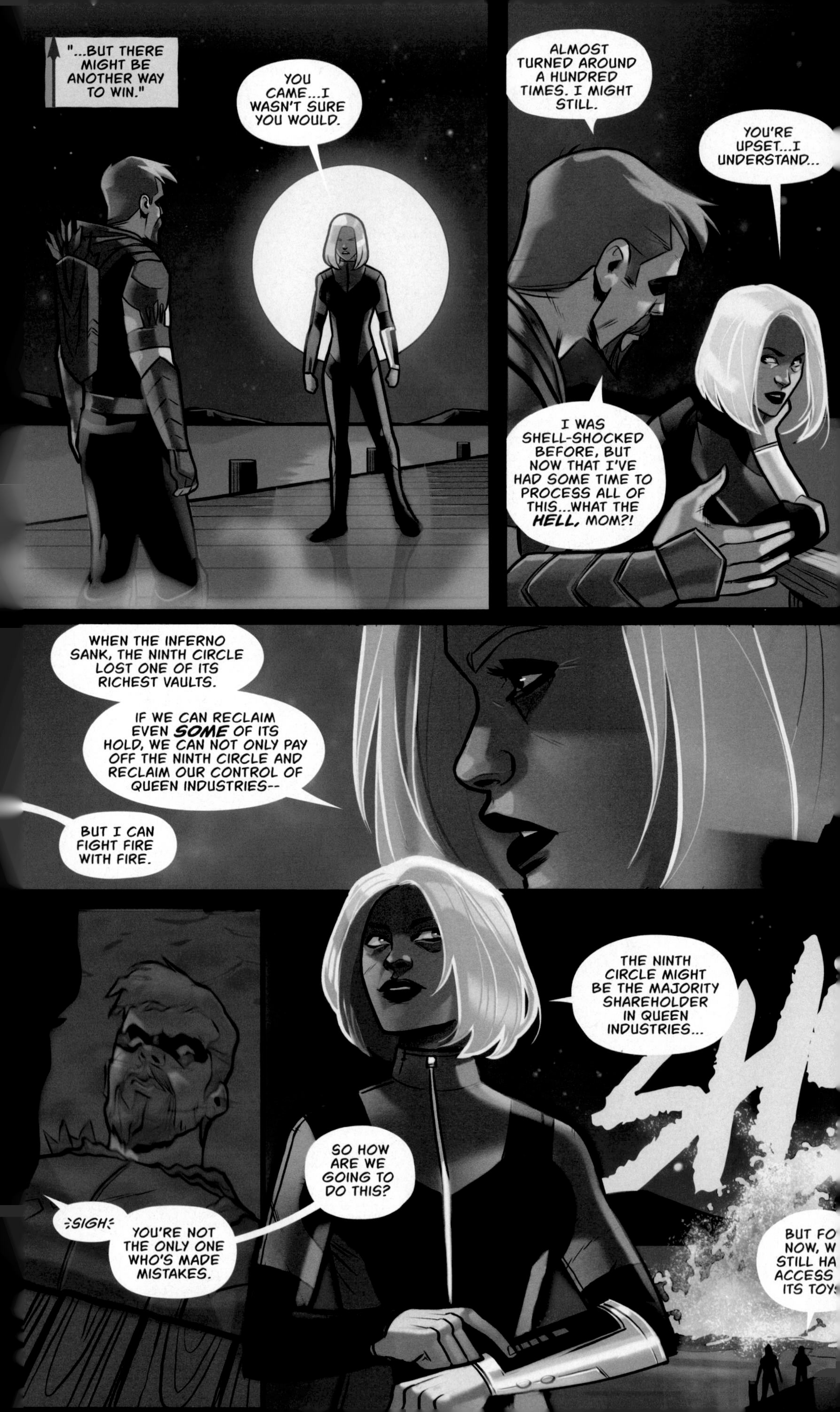
"...BUT THERE MIGHT BE ANOTHER WAY TO WIN."
YOU CAME...I WASN'T SURE YOU WOULD.
ALMOST TURNED AROUND A HUNDRED TIMES. I MIGHT STILL.
YOU'RE UPSET...I UNDERSTAND...
I WAS SHELL-SHOCKED BEFORE, BUT NOW THAT I'VE HAD SOME TIME TO PROCESS ALL OF THIS...WHAT THE *HELL,* MOM?!
WHEN THE INFERNO SANK, THE NINTH CIRCLE LOST ONE OF ITS RICHEST VAULTS.
IF WE CAN RECLAIM EVEN *SOME* OF ITS HOLD, WE CAN NOT ONLY PAY OFF THE NINTH CIRCLE AND RECLAIM OUR CONTROL OF QUEEN INDUSTRIES--
BUT I CAN FIGHT FIRE WITH FIRE.
THE NINTH CIRCLE MIGHT BE THE MAJORITY SHAREHOLDER IN QUEEN INDUSTRIES...
SO HOW ARE WE GOING TO DO THIS?
SIGH
YOU'RE NOT THE ONLY ONE WHO'S MADE MISTAKES.

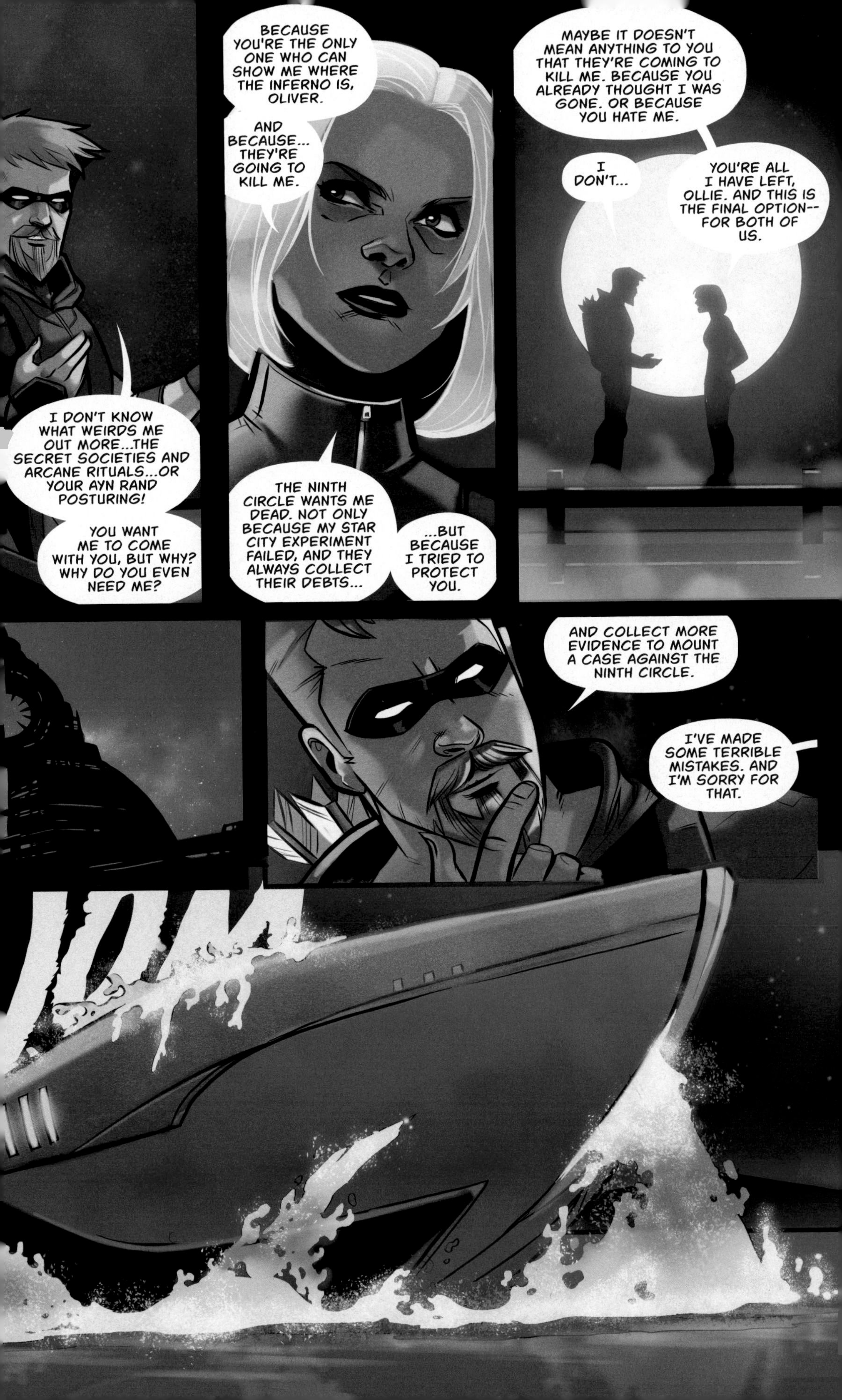

BECAUSE YOU'RE THE ONLY ONE WHO CAN SHOW ME WHERE THE INFERNO IS, OLIVER.
AND BECAUSE... THEY'RE GOING TO KILL ME.
I DON'T KNOW WHAT WEIRDS ME OUT MORE...THE SECRET SOCIETIES AND ARCANE RITUALS...OR YOUR AYN RAND POSTURING!
YOU WANT ME TO COME WITH YOU, BUT WHY? WHY DO YOU EVEN NEED ME?
THE NINTH CIRCLE WANTS ME DEAD. NOT ONLY BECAUSE MY STAR CITY EXPERIMENT FAILED, AND THEY ALWAYS COLLECT THEIR DEBTS...
...BUT BECAUSE I TRIED TO PROTECT YOU.
MAYBE IT DOESN'T MEAN ANYTHING TO YOU THAT THEY'RE COMING TO KILL ME. BECAUSE YOU ALREADY THOUGHT I WAS GONE. OR BECAUSE YOU HATE ME.
I DON'T...
YOU'RE ALL I HAVE LEFT, OLLIE. AND THIS IS THE FINAL OPTION-- FOR BOTH OF US.
AND COLLECT MORE EVIDENCE TO MOUNT A CASE AGAINST THE NINTH CIRCLE.
I'VE MADE SOME TERRIBLE MISTAKES. AND I'M SORRY FOR THAT.

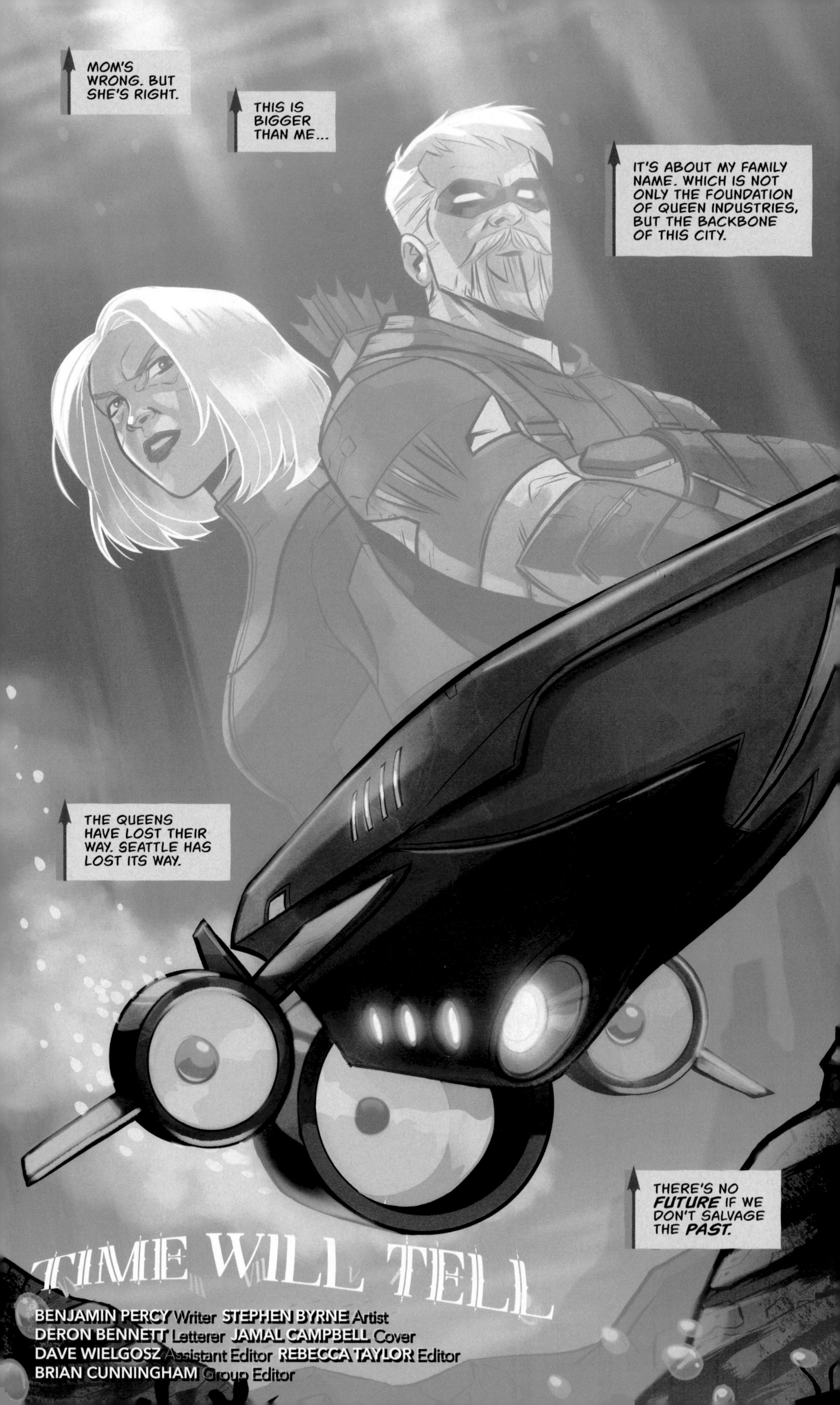

MOM'S WRONG. BUT SHE'S RIGHT.
THIS IS BIGGER THAN ME...
IT'S ABOUT MY FAMILY NAME. WHICH IS NOT ONLY THE FOUNDATION OF QUEEN INDUSTRIES, BUT THE BACKBONE OF THIS CITY.
THE QUEENS HAVE LOST THEIR WAY. SEATTLE HAS LOST ITS WAY.
THERE'S NO *FUTURE* IF WE DON'T SALVAGE THE *PAST.*
TIME WILL TELL
BENJAMIN PERCY Writer STEPHEN BYRNE Artist
DERON BENNETT Letterer JAMAL CAMPBELL Cover
DAVE WIELGOSZ Assistant Editor REBECCA TAYLOR Editor
BRIAN CUNNINGHAM Group Editor

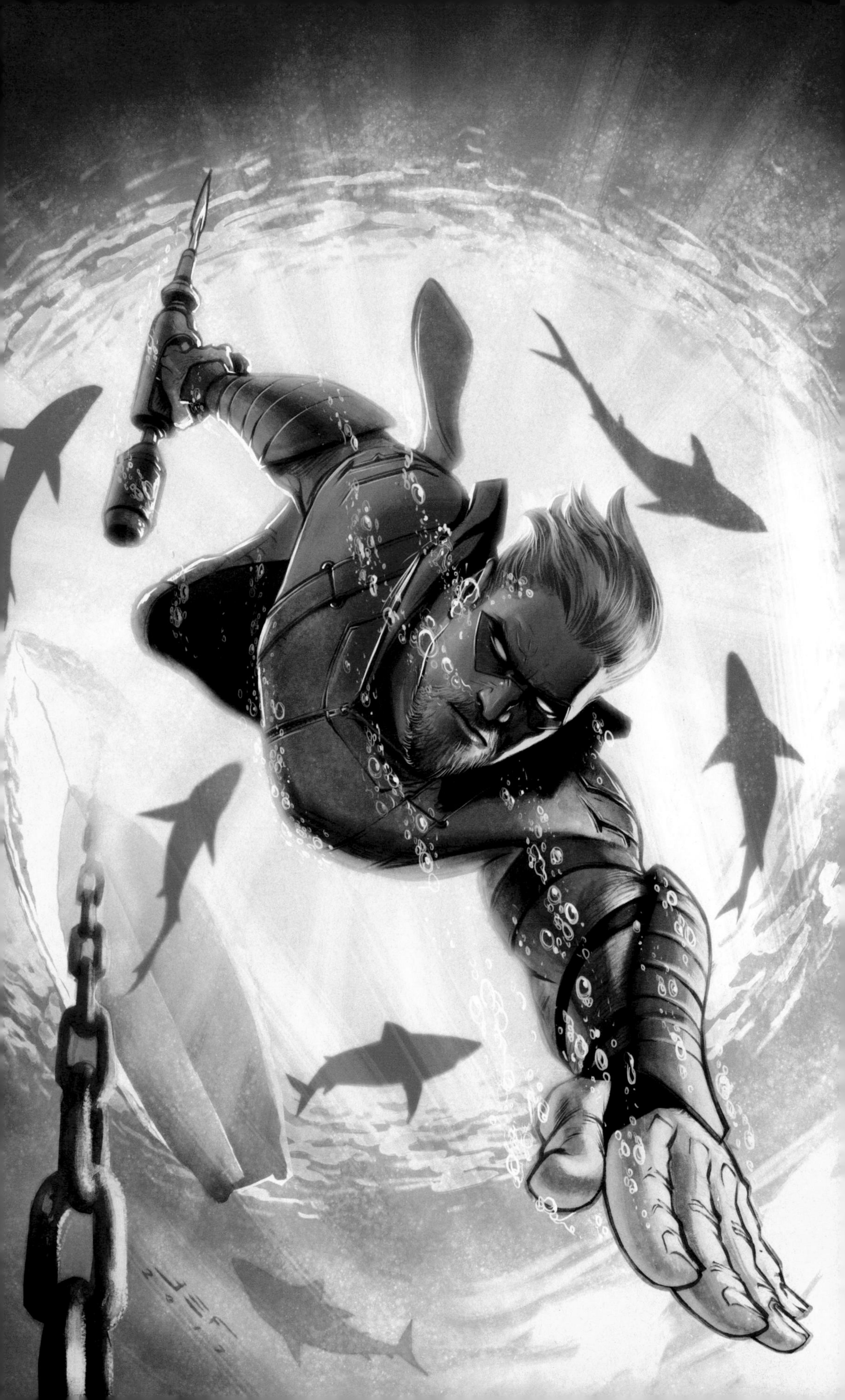

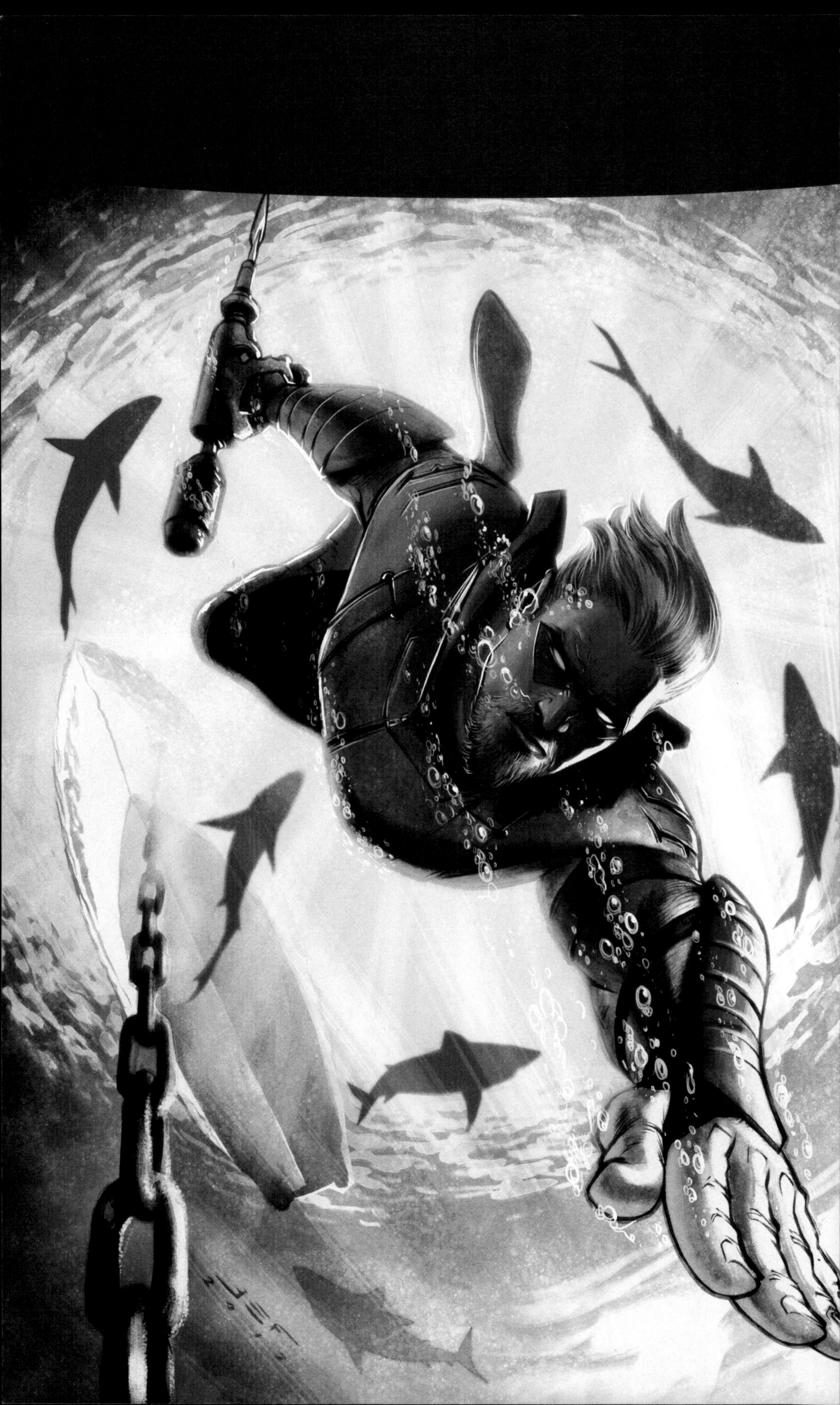

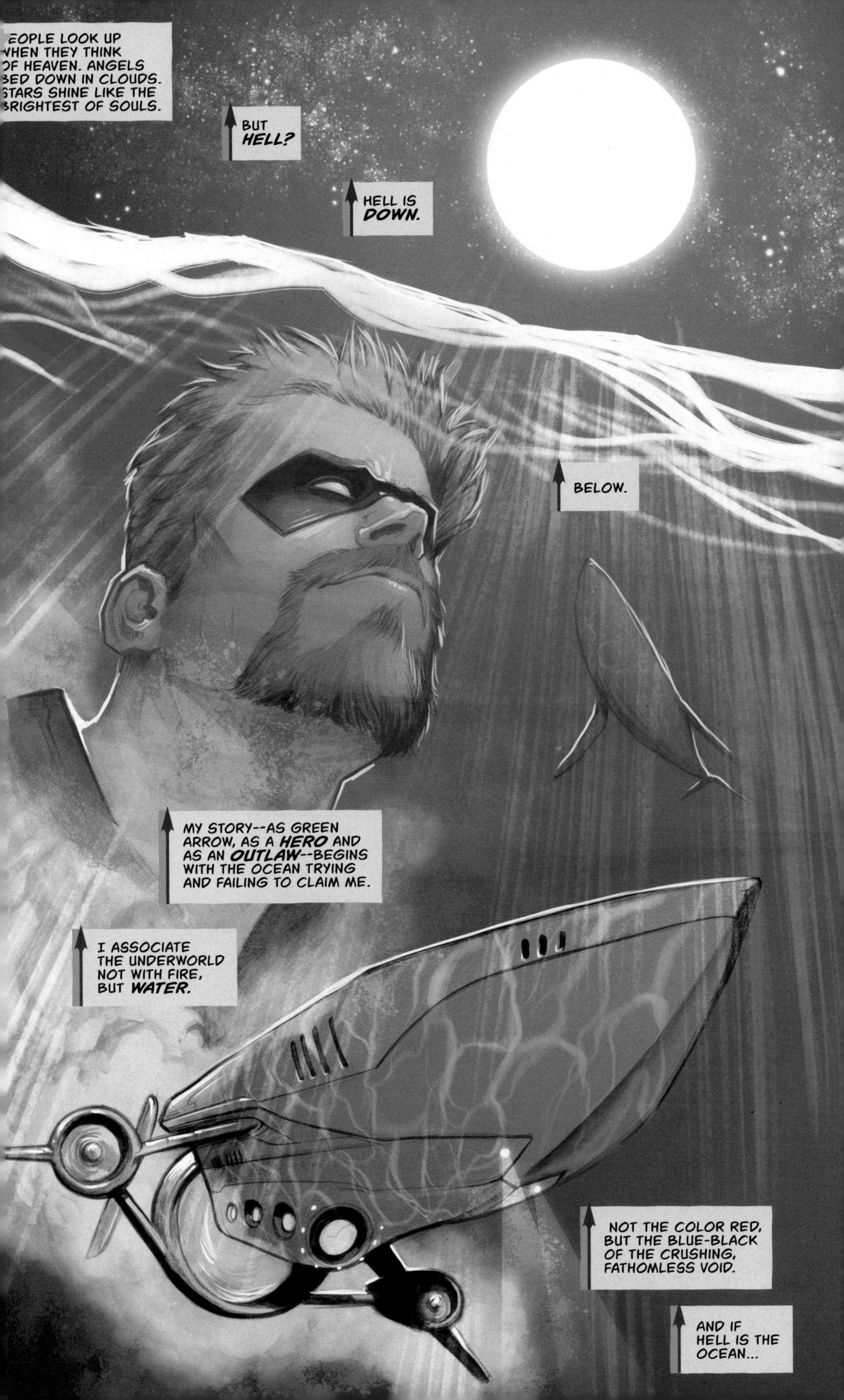
EOPLE LOOK UP WHEN THEY THINK OF HEAVEN. ANGELS BED DOWN IN CLOUDS. STARS SHINE LIKE THE BRIGHTEST OF SOULS.
BUT *HELL?*
HELL IS *DOWN.*
BELOW.
MY STORY--AS GREEN ARROW, AS A *HERO* AND AS AN *OUTLAW*--BEGINS WITH THE OCEAN TRYING AND FAILING TO CLAIM ME.
I ASSOCIATE THE UNDERWORLD NOT WITH FIRE, BUT *WATER.*
NOT THE COLOR RED, BUT THE BLUE-BLACK OF THE CRUSHING, FATHOMLESS VOID.
AND IF HELL IS THE OCEAN...

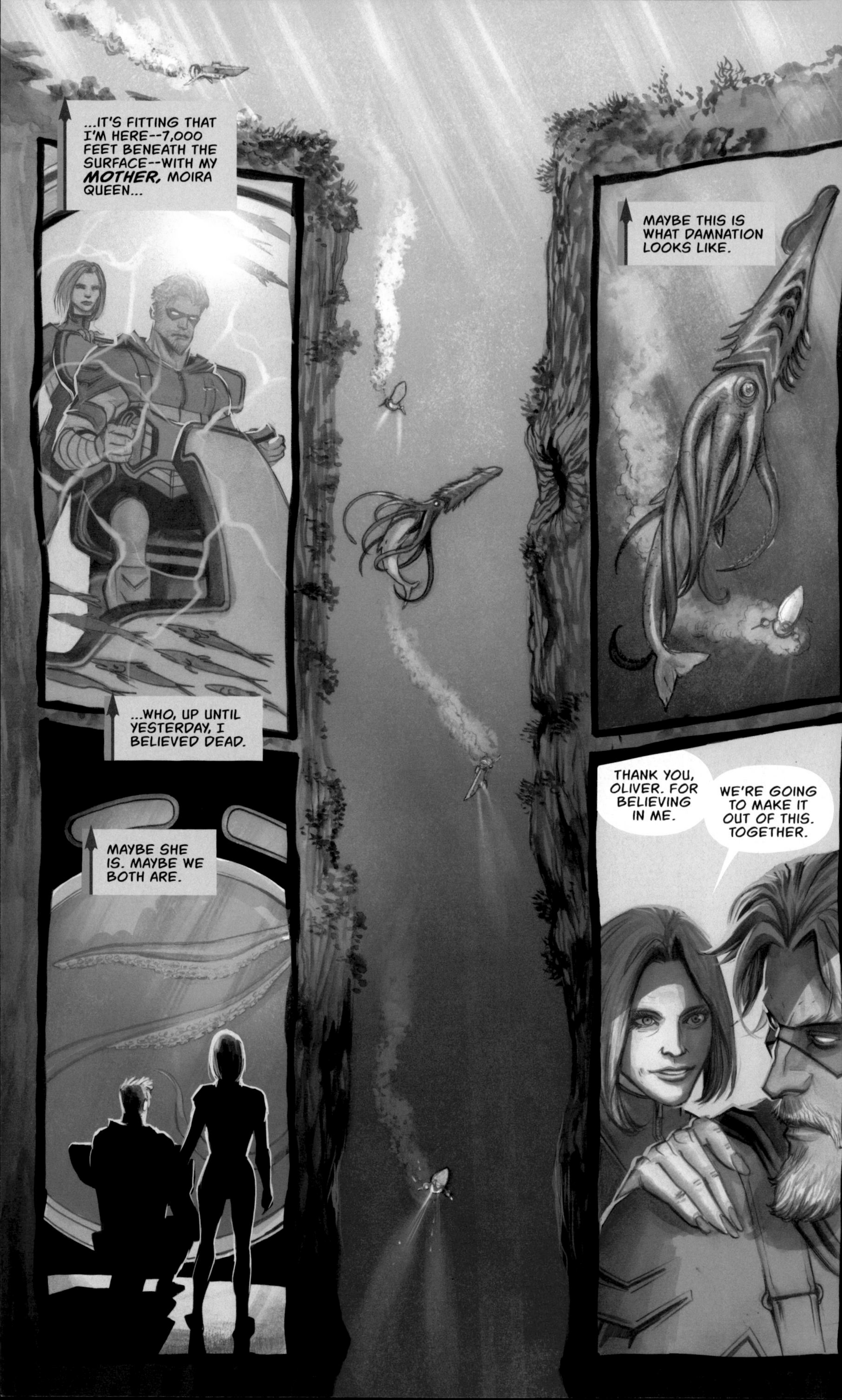
...IT'S FITTING THAT I'M HERE--7,000 FEET BENEATH THE SURFACE--WITH MY MOTHER, MOIRA QUEEN...
...WHO, UP UNTIL YESTERDAY, I BELIEVED DEAD.
MAYBE SHE IS. MAYBE WE BOTH ARE.
MAYBE THIS IS WHAT DAMNATION LOOKS LIKE.
THANK YOU, OLIVER. FOR BELIEVING IN ME.
WE'RE GOING TO MAKE IT OUT OF THIS. TOGETHER.

EVIL IS EXPENSIVE, AND THE *NINTH CIRCLE* IS A SAVINGS-AND-LOAN INSTITUTION THAT SERVES THE CRIMINAL UNDERWORLD.

THEIR CLIENTS DON'T WANT TO BE TRACKED, SO THEIR VAULTS NEVER STOP MOVING...

...BATTLESHIP BANKS THAT CUT THROUGH INTERNATIONAL WATERS.

MORE THAN A YEAR AGO, I *DESTROYED* ONE OF THEM.

ITS RUINS SANK INTO ONE OF THE DEEPEST, DEADLIEST TRENCHES IN THE PACIFIC.

AND NOW MY SALVATION--AND MY MOTHER'S SURVIVAL-- DEPENDS ON...

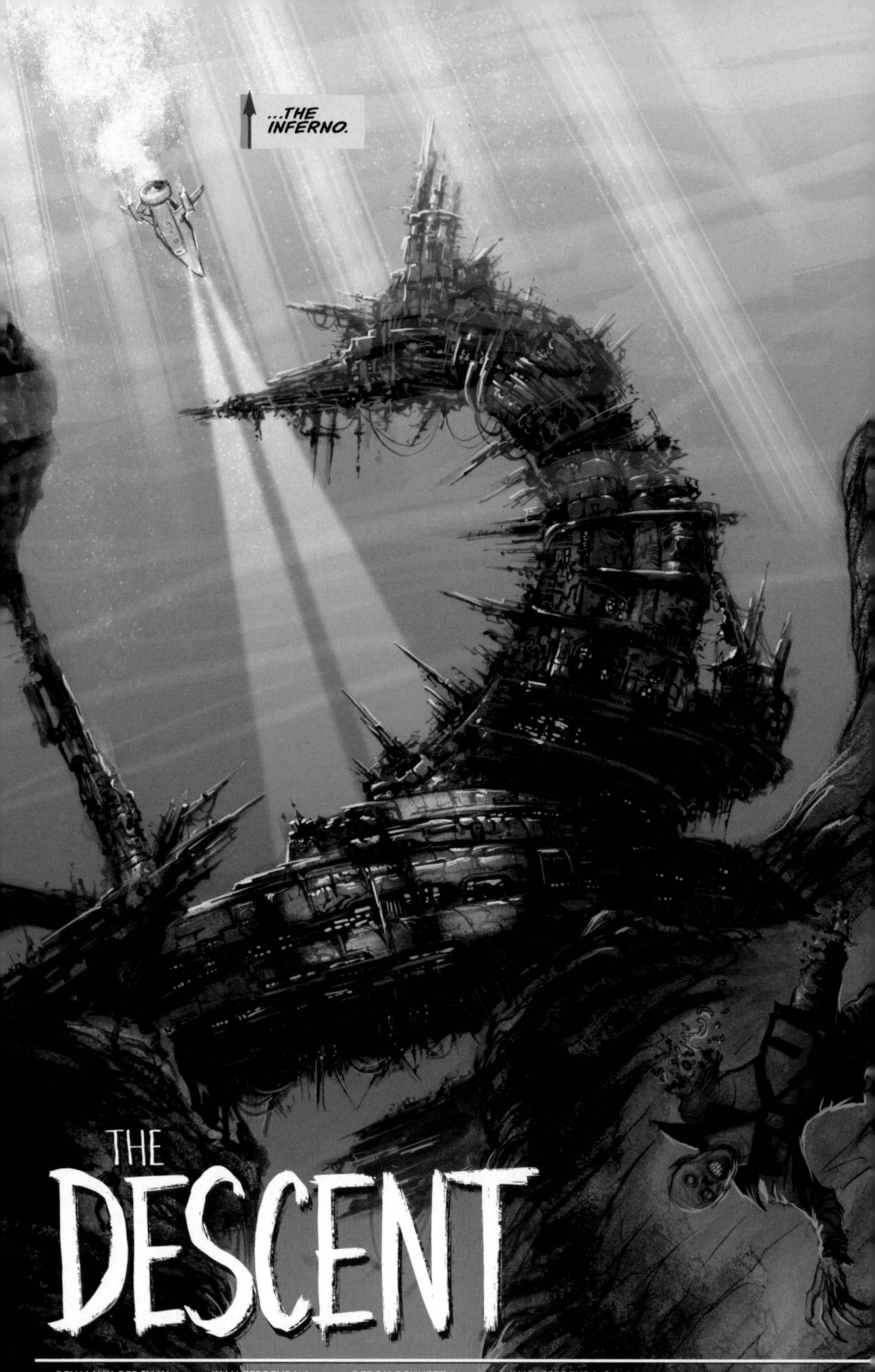
...THE INFERNO.

THE DESCENT

BENJAMIN PERCY Writer JUAN FERREYRA Artist DERON BENNETT Letters JUAN FERREYRA Cover
DAVE WIELGOSZ Asst. Editor REBECCA TAYLOR Editor BRIAN CUNNINGHAM Group Editor

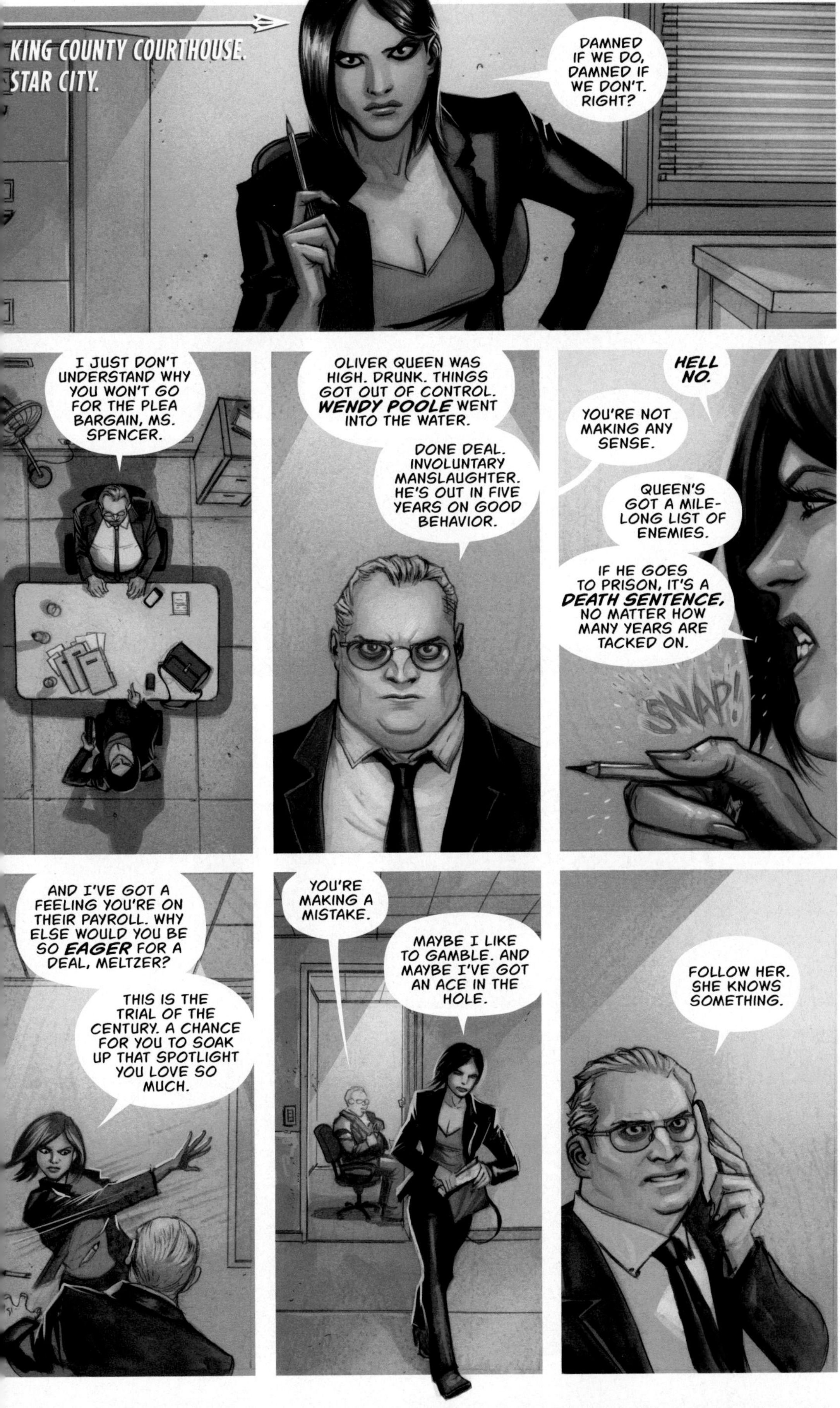
KING COUNTY COURTHOUSE.
STAR CITY.
DAMNED IF WE DO, DAMNED IF WE DON'T. RIGHT?
I JUST DON'T UNDERSTAND WHY YOU WON'T GO FOR THE PLEA BARGAIN, MS. SPENCER.
OLIVER QUEEN WAS HIGH. DRUNK. THINGS GOT OUT OF CONTROL. WENDY POOLE WENT INTO THE WATER.
DONE DEAL. INVOLUNTARY MANSLAUGHTER. HE'S OUT IN FIVE YEARS ON GOOD BEHAVIOR.
HELL NO.
YOU'RE NOT MAKING ANY SENSE.
QUEEN'S GOT A MILE-LONG LIST OF ENEMIES.
IF HE GOES TO PRISON, IT'S A DEATH SENTENCE, NO MATTER HOW MANY YEARS ARE TACKED ON.
SNAP!
AND I'VE GOT A FEELING YOU'RE ON THEIR PAYROLL. WHY ELSE WOULD YOU BE SO EAGER FOR A DEAL, MELTZER?
THIS IS THE TRIAL OF THE CENTURY. A CHANCE FOR YOU TO SOAK UP THAT SPOTLIGHT YOU LOVE SO MUCH.
YOU'RE MAKING A MISTAKE.
MAYBE I LIKE TO GAMBLE. AND MAYBE I'VE GOT AN ACE IN THE HOLE.
FOLLOW HER. SHE KNOWS SOMETHING.

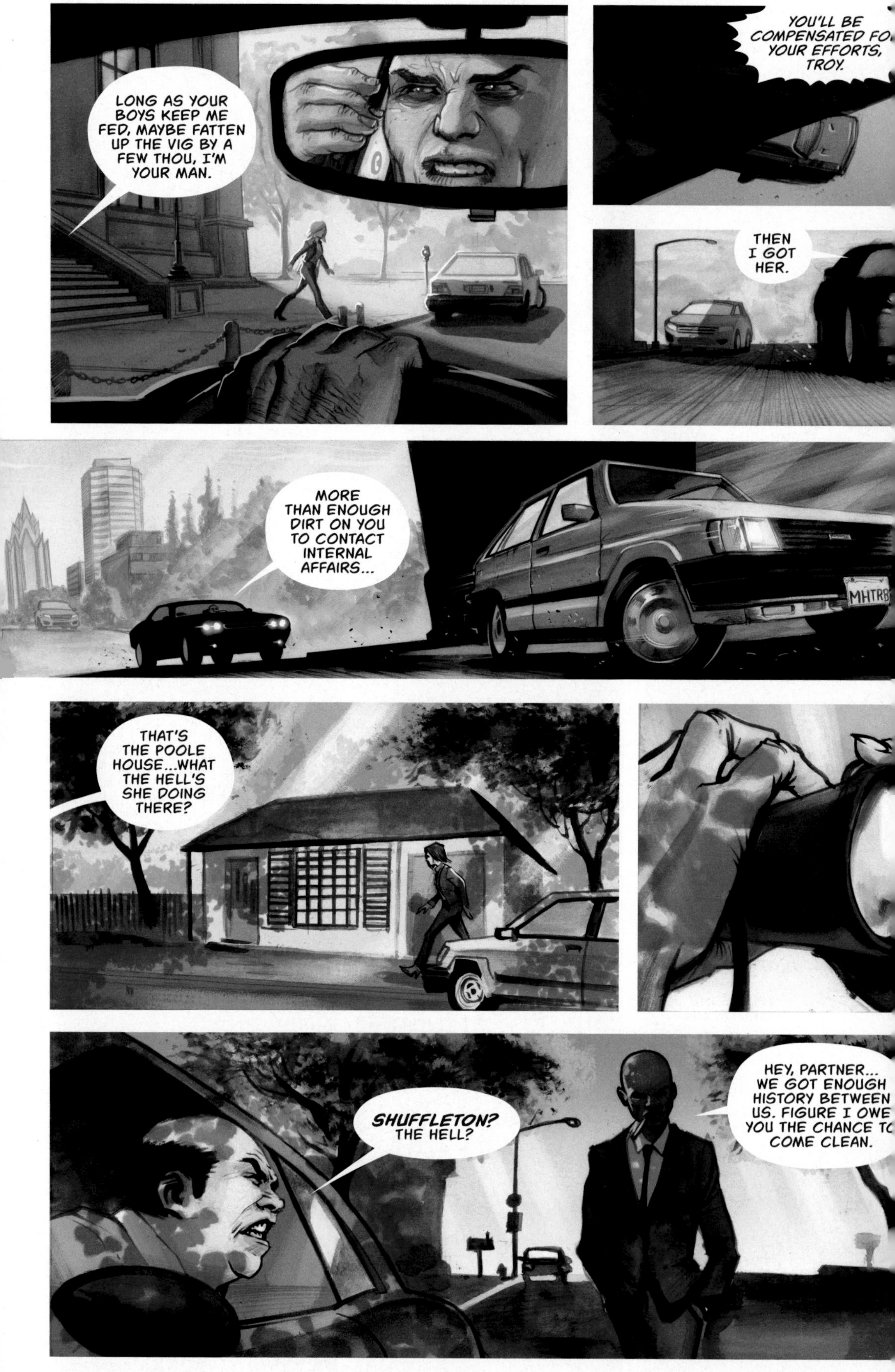
LONG AS YOUR BOYS KEEP ME FED, MAYBE FATTEN UP THE VIG BY A FEW THOU, I'M YOUR MAN.
YOU'LL BE COMPENSATED FO YOUR EFFORTS, TROY.
THEN I GOT HER.
MORE THAN ENOUGH DIRT ON YOU TO CONTACT INTERNAL AFFAIRS...
MHTRB
THAT'S THE POOLE HOUSE...WHAT THE HELL'S SHE DOING THERE?
SHUFFLETON? THE HELL?
HEY, PARTNER... WE GOT ENOUGH HISTORY BETWEEN US. FIGURE I OWE YOU THE CHANCE T
COME CLEAN.

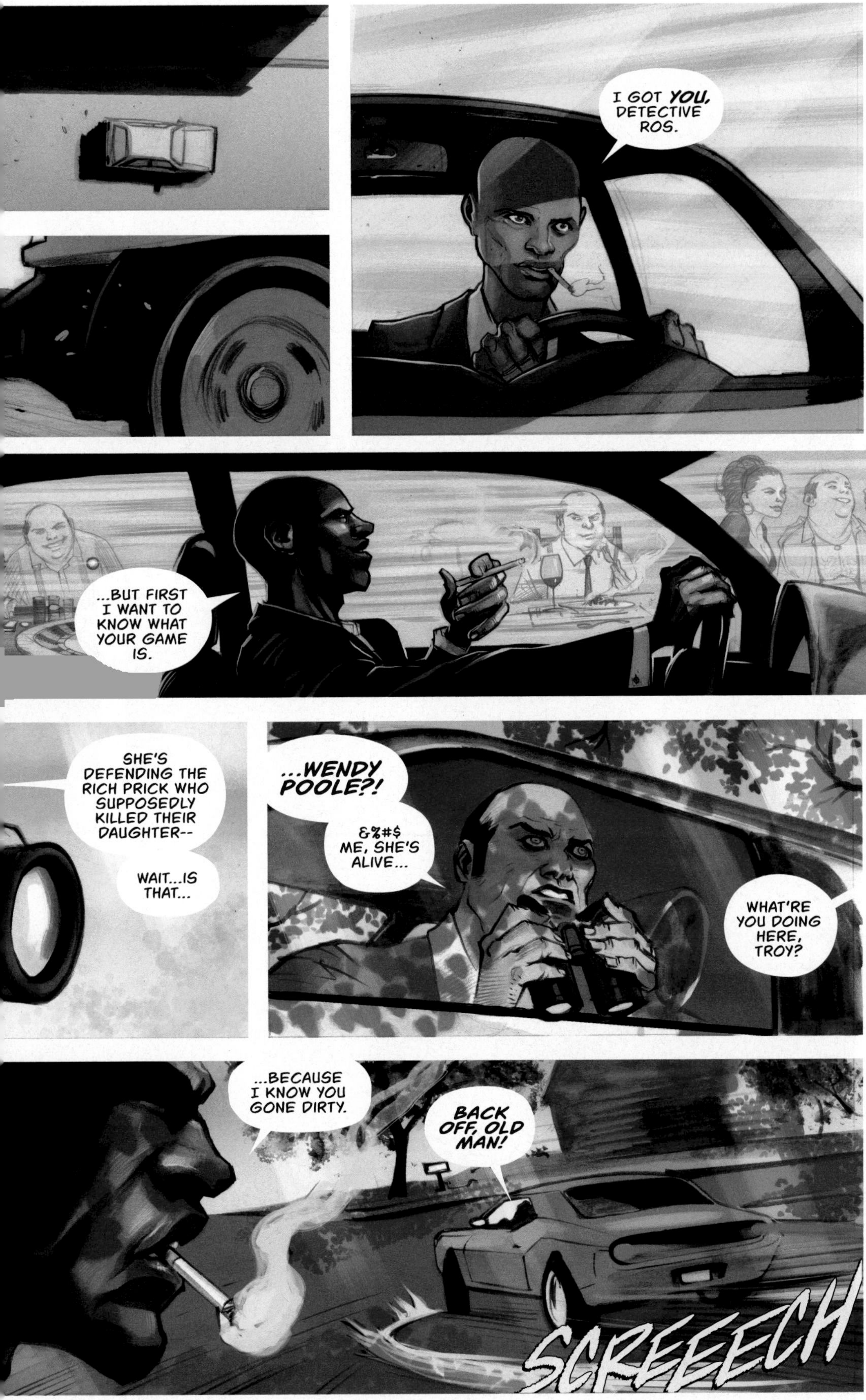
I GOT YOU, DETECTIVE ROS.
...BUT FIRST I WANT TO KNOW WHAT YOUR GAME IS.
SHE'S DEFENDING THE RICH PRICK WHO SUPPOSEDLY KILLED THEIR DAUGHTER--
WAIT...IS THAT...
...WENDY POOLE?!
&%#$ ME, SHE'S ALIVE...
WHAT'RE YOU DOING HERE, TROY?
...BECAUSE I KNOW YOU GONE DIRTY.
BACK OFF, OLD MAN!
SCREEECH

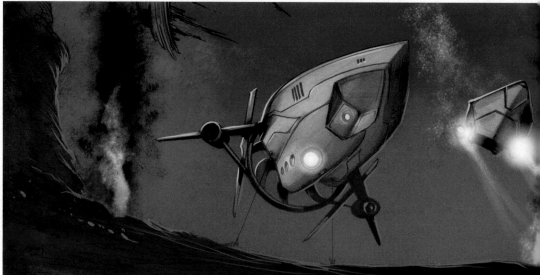

AND IF THERE'S ONE CRACKED LENS OR LEAKY VALVE--A SINGLE MISCALCULATION IN THE DESIGN--WE'LL BE *DEAD* IN SECONDS.

...BUT IF YOU CONSIDER YOUR DEPTH GAUGE READINGS...

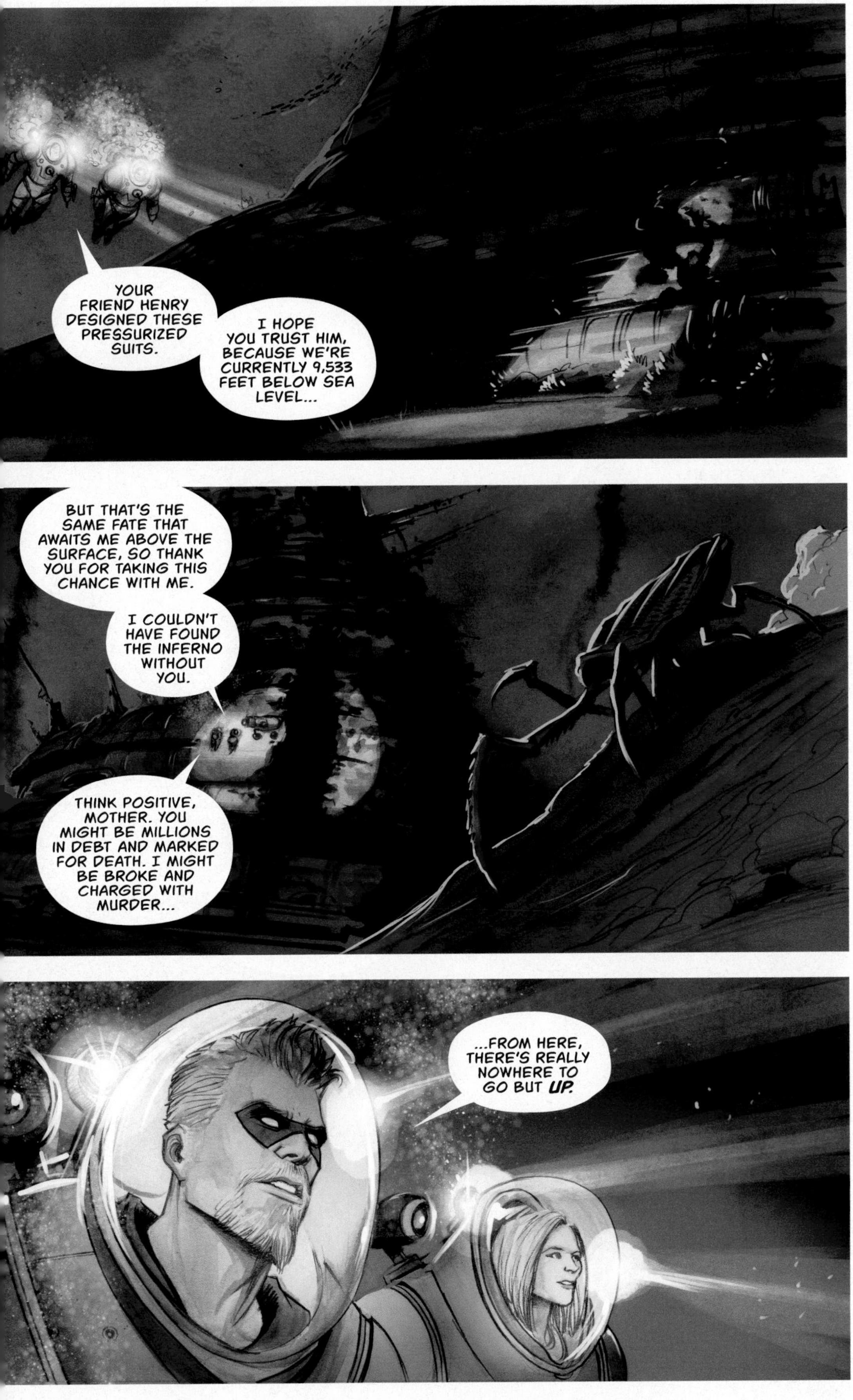
YOUR FRIEND HENRY DESIGNED THESE PRESSURIZED SUITS.
I HOPE YOU TRUST HIM, BECAUSE WE'RE CURRENTLY 9,533 FEET BELOW SEA LEVEL...
BUT THAT'S THE SAME FATE THAT AWAITS ME ABOVE THE SURFACE, SO THANK YOU FOR TAKING THIS CHANCE WITH ME.
I COULDN'T HAVE FOUND THE INFERNO WITHOUT YOU.
THINK POSITIVE, MOTHER. YOU MIGHT BE MILLIONS IN DEBT AND MARKED FOR DEATH. I MIGHT BE BROKE AND CHARGED WITH MURDER...
...FROM HERE, THERE'S REALLY NOWHERE TO GO BUT *UP*.

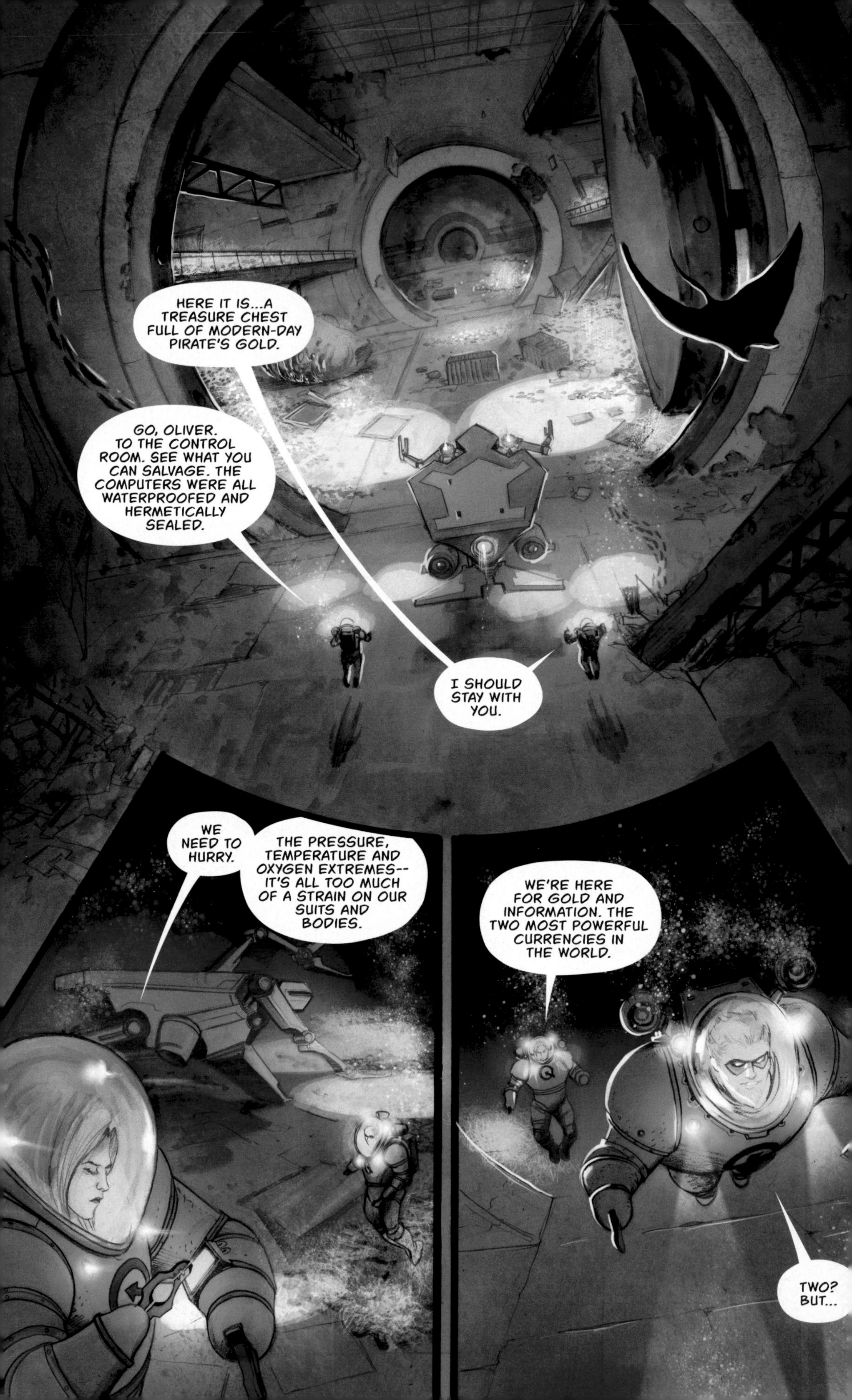
HERE IT IS...A TREASURE CHEST FULL OF MODERN-DAY PIRATE'S GOLD.
GO, OLIVER. TO THE CONTROL ROOM. SEE WHAT YOU CAN SALVAGE. THE COMPUTERS WERE ALL WATERPROOFED AND HERMETICALLY SEALED.
I SHOULD STAY WITH YOU.
WE NEED TO HURRY.
THE PRESSURE, TEMPERATURE AND OXYGEN EXTREMES-- IT'S ALL TOO MUCH OF A STRAIN ON OUR SUITS AND BODIES.
WE'RE HERE FOR GOLD AND INFORMATION. THE TWO MOST POWERFUL CURRENCIES IN THE WORLD.
TWO? BUT...

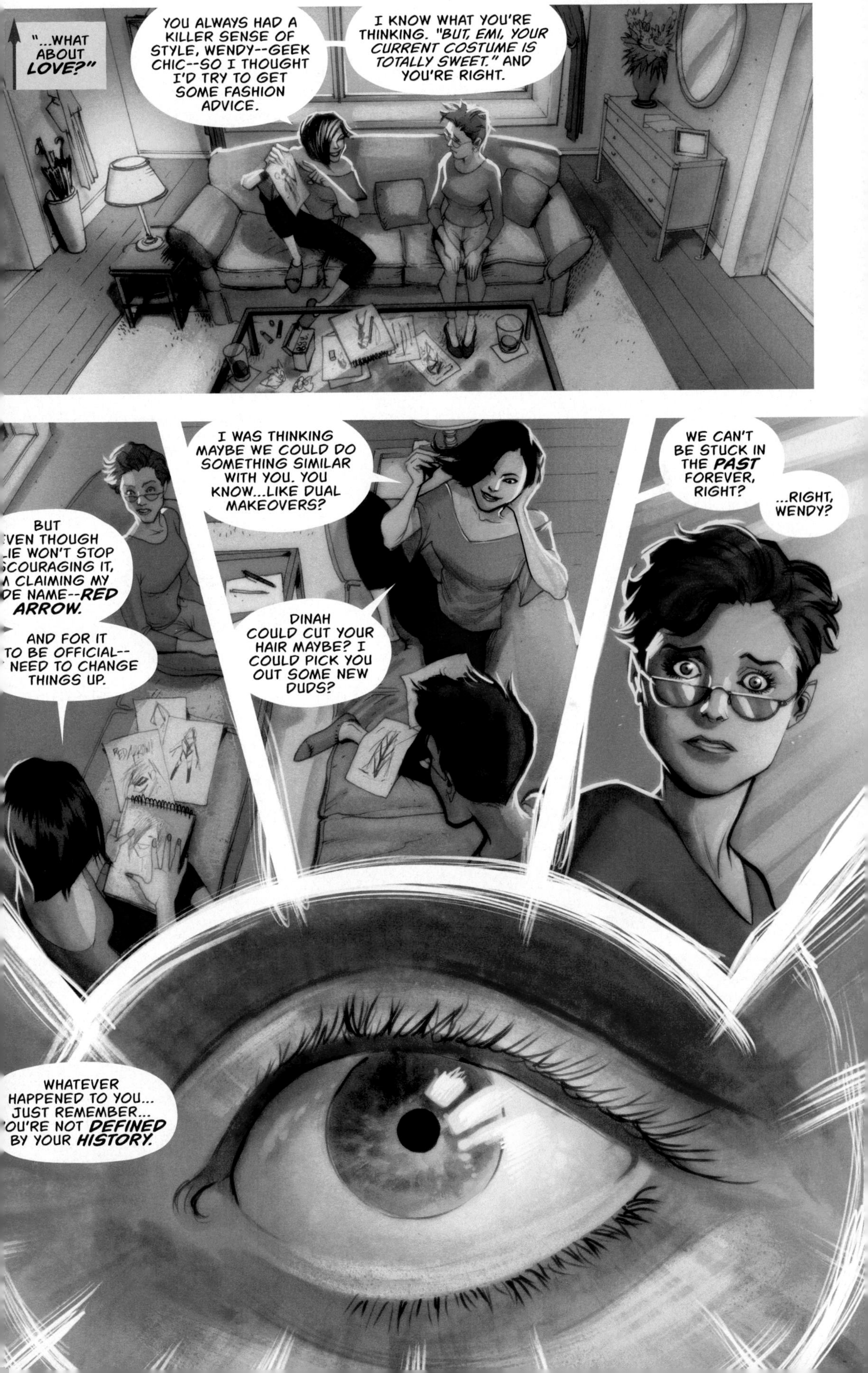
"...WHAT ABOUT LOVE?"
YOU ALWAYS HAD A KILLER SENSE OF STYLE, WENDY--GEEK CHIC--SO I THOUGHT I'D TRY TO GET SOME FASHION ADVICE.
I KNOW WHAT YOU'RE THINKING. "BUT, EMI, YOUR CURRENT COSTUME IS TOTALLY SWEET." AND YOU'RE RIGHT.
BUT VEN THOUGH IE WON'T STOP SCOURAGING IT, M CLAIMING MY DE NAME--RED ARROW.
AND FOR IT TO BE OFFICIAL-- NEED TO CHANGE THINGS UP.
I WAS THINKING MAYBE WE COULD DO SOMETHING SIMILAR WITH YOU. YOU KNOW...LIKE DUAL MAKEOVERS?
DINAH COULD CUT YOUR HAIR MAYBE? I COULD PICK YOU OUT SOME NEW DUDS?
WE CAN'T BE STUCK IN THE PAST FOREVER, RIGHT?
...RIGHT, WENDY?
WHATEVER HAPPENED TO YOU... JUST REMEMBER... OU'RE NOT DEFINED BY YOUR HISTORY.

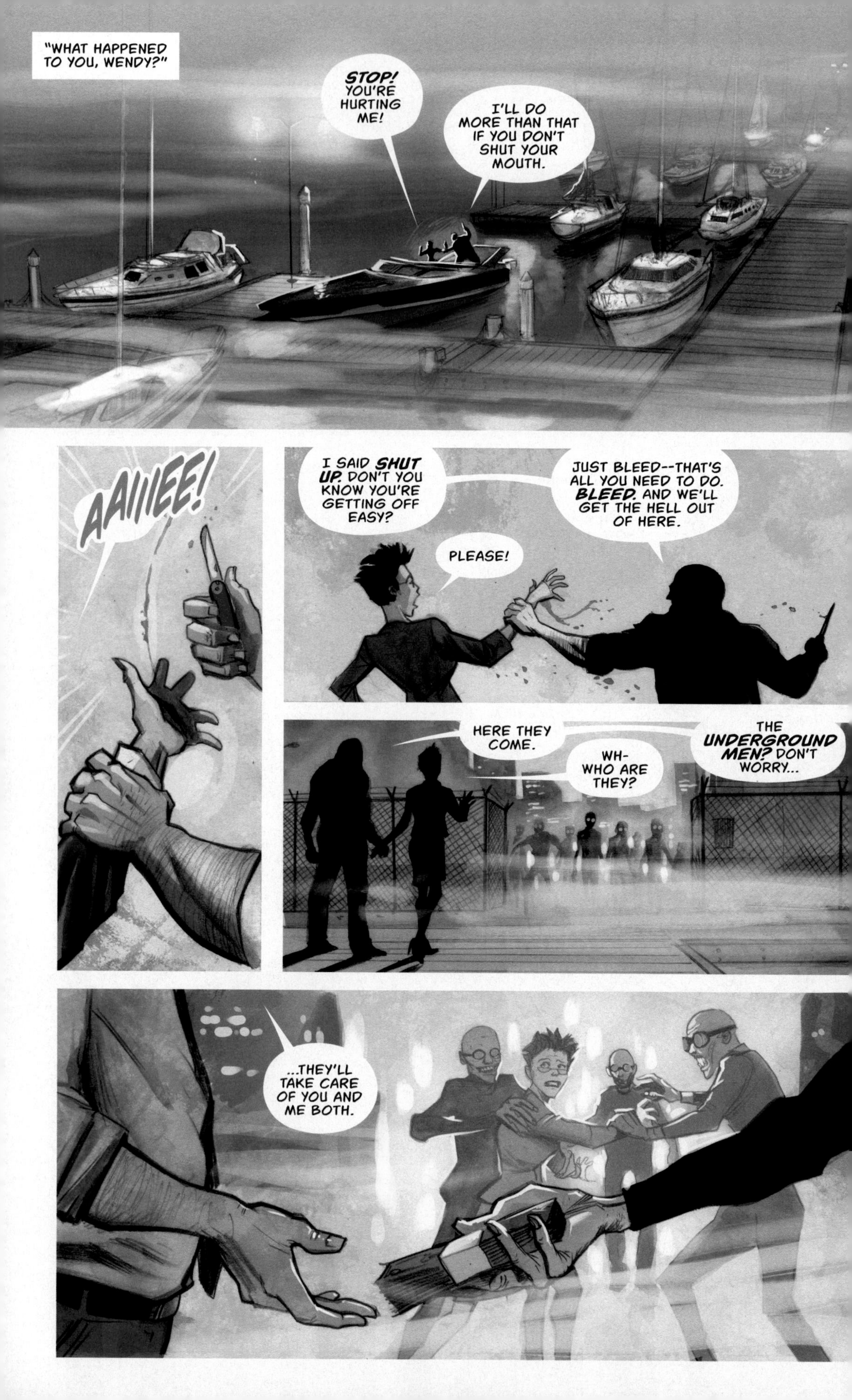
"WHAT HAPPENED TO YOU, WENDY?"
STOP! YOU'RE HURTING ME!
I'LL DO MORE THAN THAT IF YOU DON'T SHUT YOUR MOUTH.
AAIIIEE!
I SAID SHUT UP. DON'T YOU KNOW YOU'RE GETTING OFF EASY?
JUST BLEED--THAT'S ALL YOU NEED TO DO. BLEED. AND WE'LL GET THE HELL OUT OF HERE.
PLEASE!
HERE THEY COME.
WH- WHO ARE THEY?
THE UNDERGROUND MEN? DON'T WORRY...
...THEY'LL TAKE CARE OF YOU AND ME BOTH.

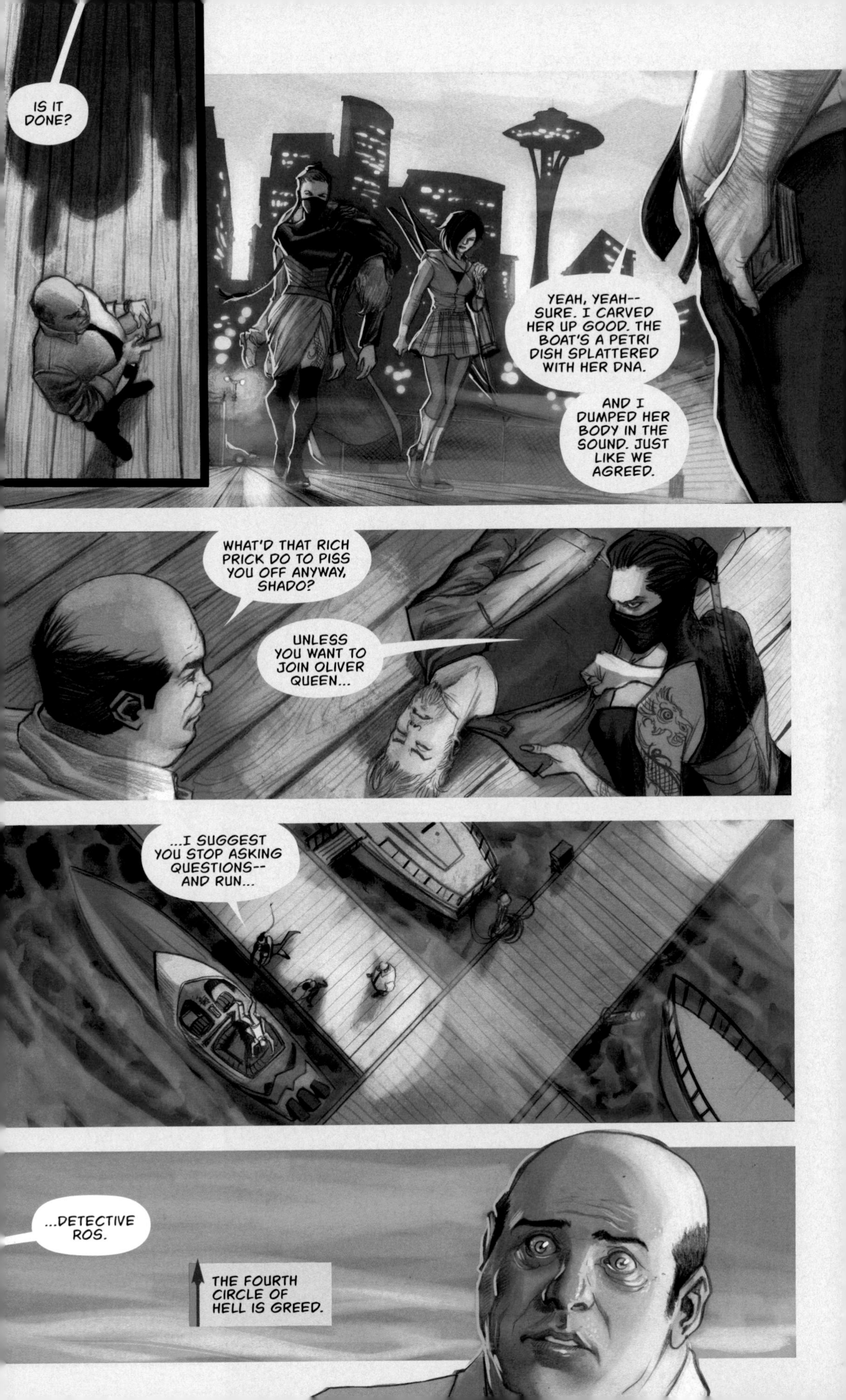
IS IT DONE?
YEAH, YEAH-- SURE. I CARVED HER UP GOOD. THE BOAT'S A PETRI DISH SPLATTERED WITH HER DNA.
AND I DUMPED HER BODY IN THE SOUND. JUST LIKE WE AGREED.
WHAT'D THAT RICH PRICK DO TO PISS YOU OFF ANYWAY, SHADO?
UNLESS YOU WANT TO JOIN OLIVER QUEEN...
...I SUGGEST YOU STOP ASKING QUESTIONS-- AND RUN...
...DETECTIVE ROS.
THE FOURTH CIRCLE OF HELL IS GREED.

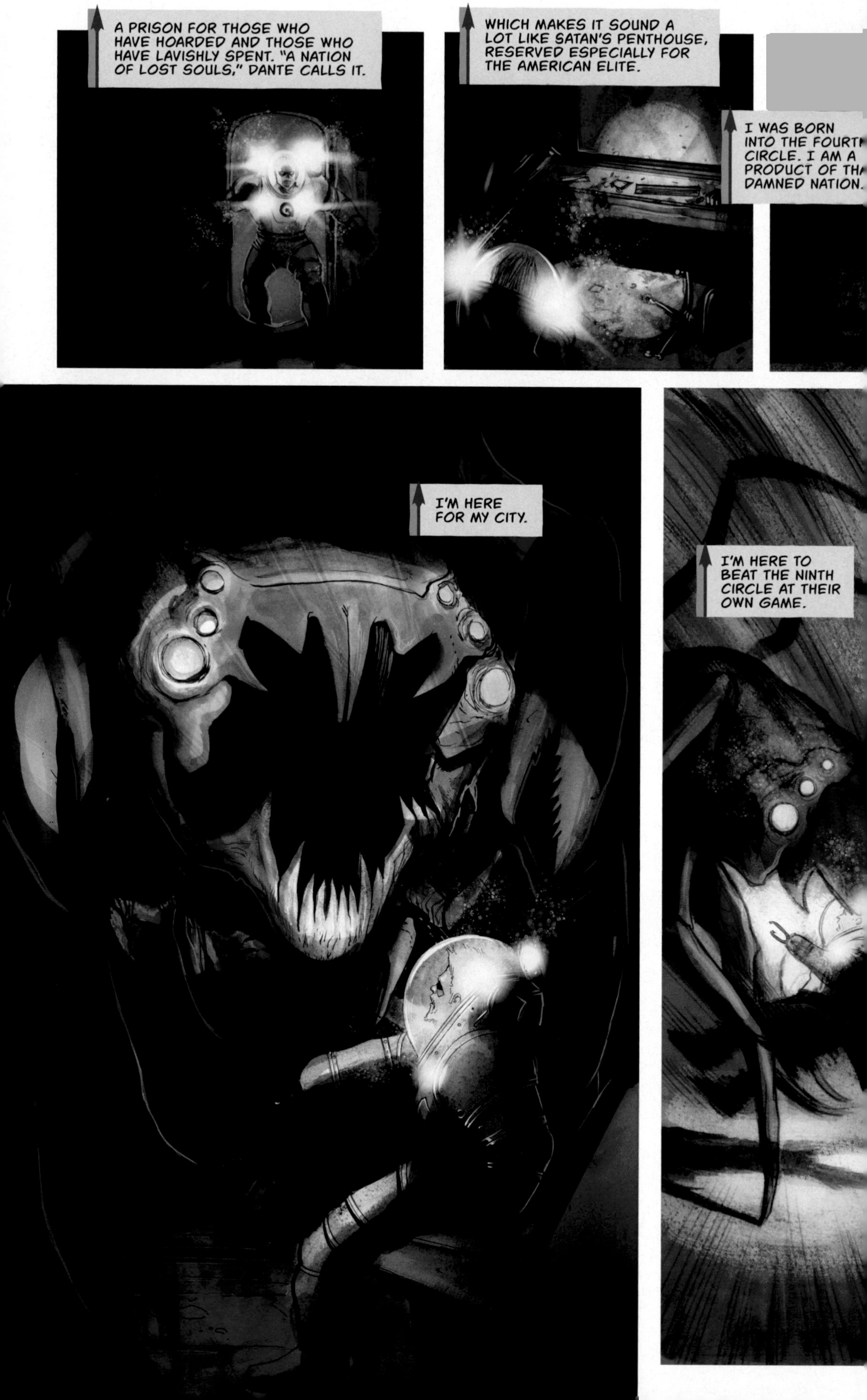
A PRISON FOR THOSE WHO HAVE HOARDED AND THOSE WHO HAVE LAVISHLY SPENT. "A NATION OF LOST SOULS," DANTE CALLS IT.
WHICH MAKES IT SOUND A LOT LIKE SATAN'S PENTHOUSE, RESERVED ESPECIALLY FOR THE AMERICAN ELITE.
I WAS BORN INTO THE FOURT CIRCLE. I AM A PRODUCT OF TH DAMNED NATION.
I'M HERE FOR MY CITY.
I'M HERE TO BEAT THE NINTH CIRCLE AT THEIR OWN GAME.

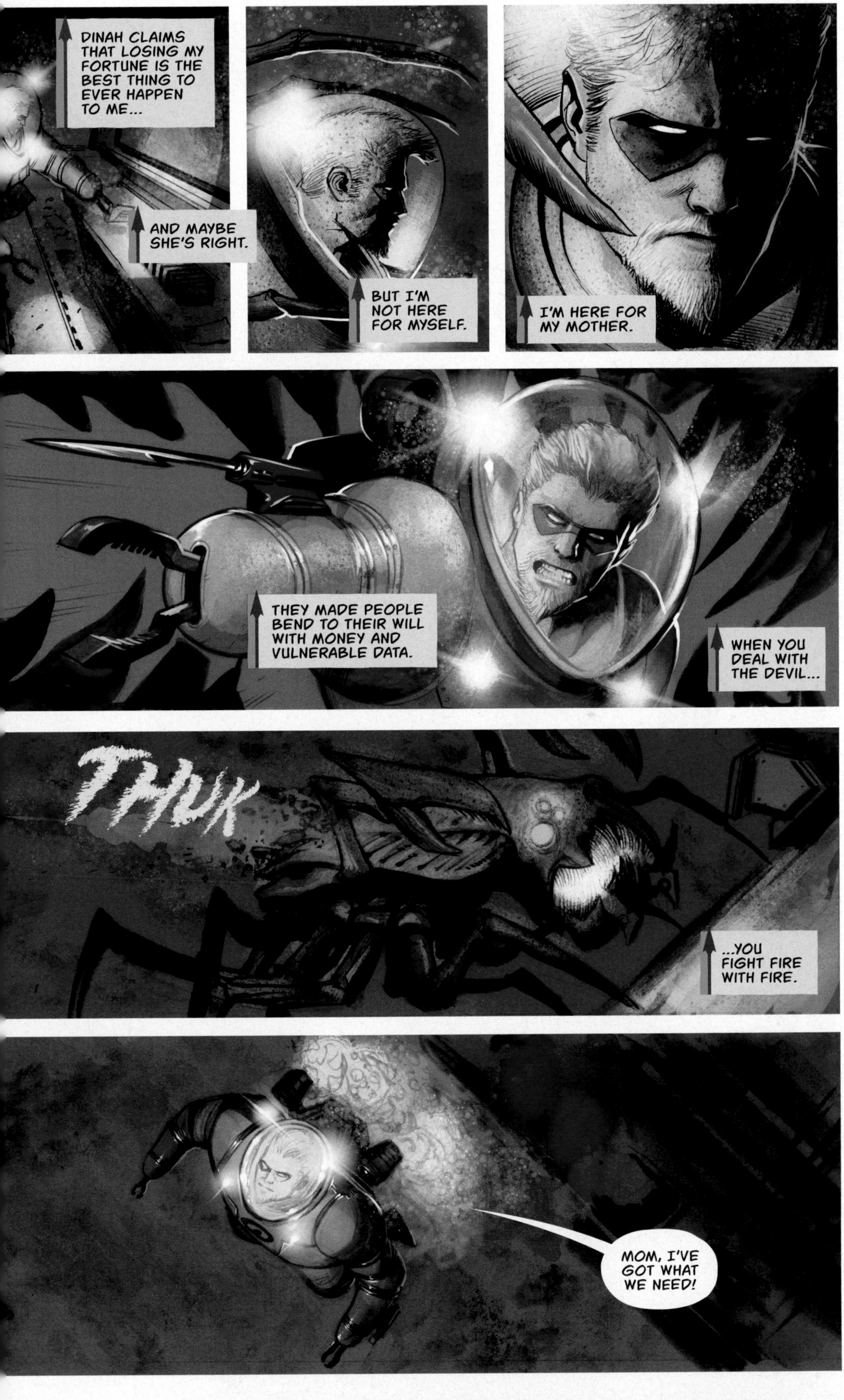
DINAH CLAIMS THAT LOSING MY FORTUNE IS THE BEST THING TO EVER HAPPEN TO ME...
AND MAYBE SHE'S RIGHT.
BUT I'M NOT HERE FOR MYSELF.
I'M HERE FOR MY MOTHER.
THEY MADE PEOPLE BEND TO THEIR WILL WITH MONEY AND VULNERABLE DATA.
WHEN YOU DEAL WITH THE DEVIL...
THUK
...YOU FIGHT FIRE WITH FIRE.
MOM, I'VE GOT WHAT WE NEED!

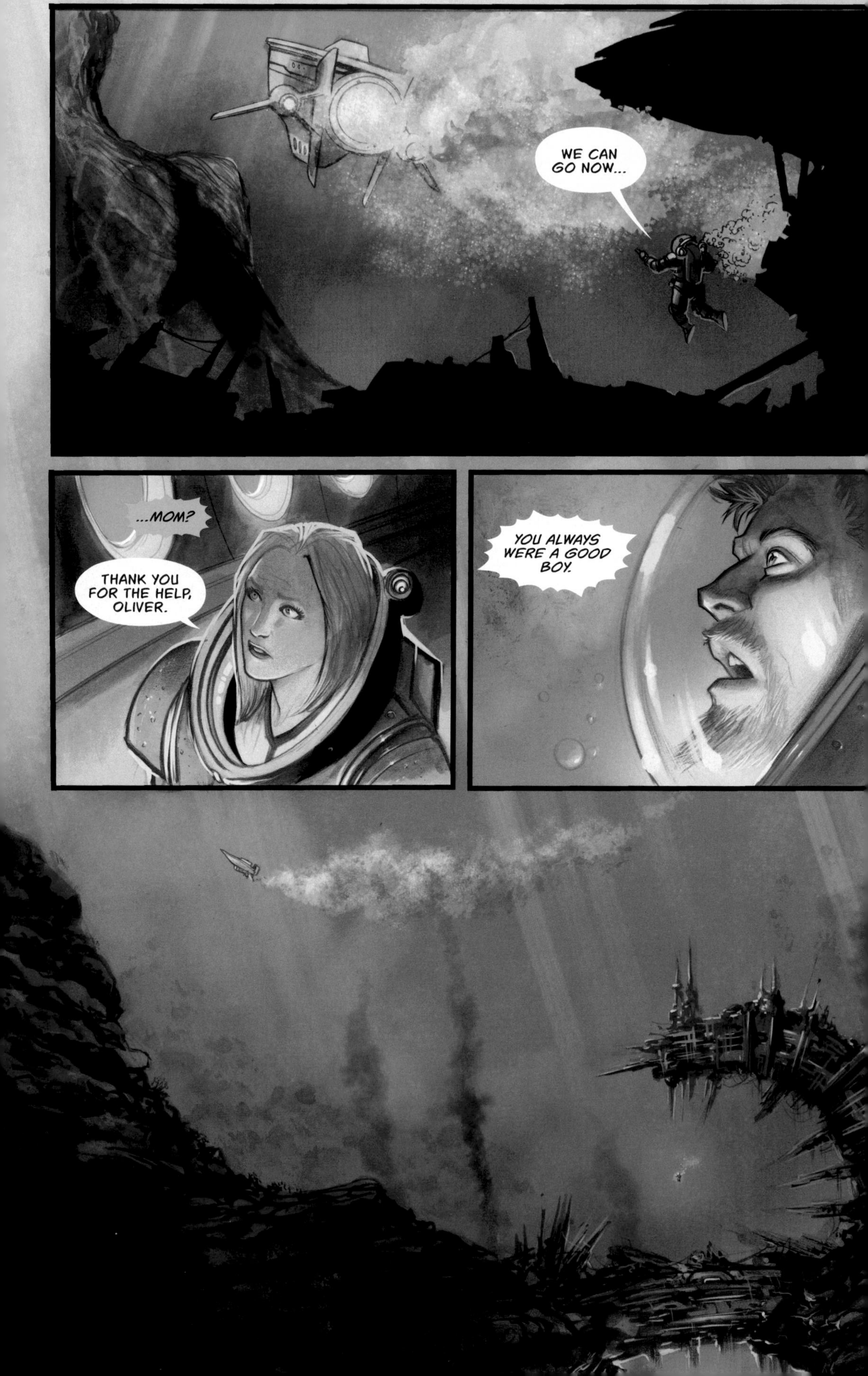

WE CAN GO NOW...
...MOM?
THANK YOU FOR THE HELP, OLIVER.
YOU ALWAYS WERE A GOOD BOY.

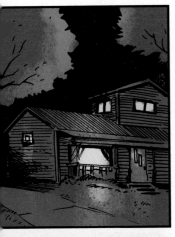

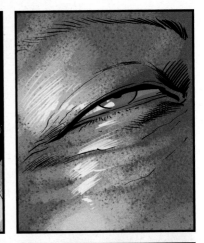

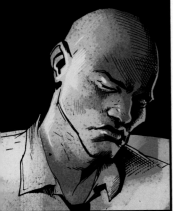

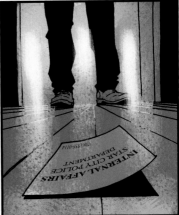

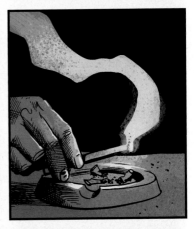

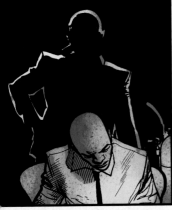

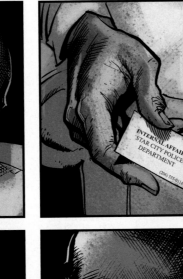

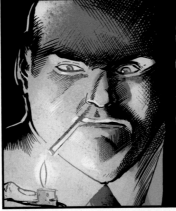

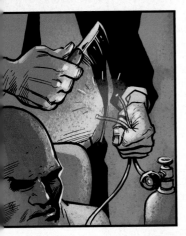

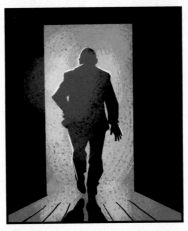

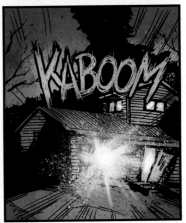

INTERNAL AFFAIRS
STAR CITY POLICE
DEPARTMENT
(206) 555-0114
INTERNAL AFFAIRS
STAR CITY POLICE
DEPARTMENT
(206) 555-0114
KABOOM

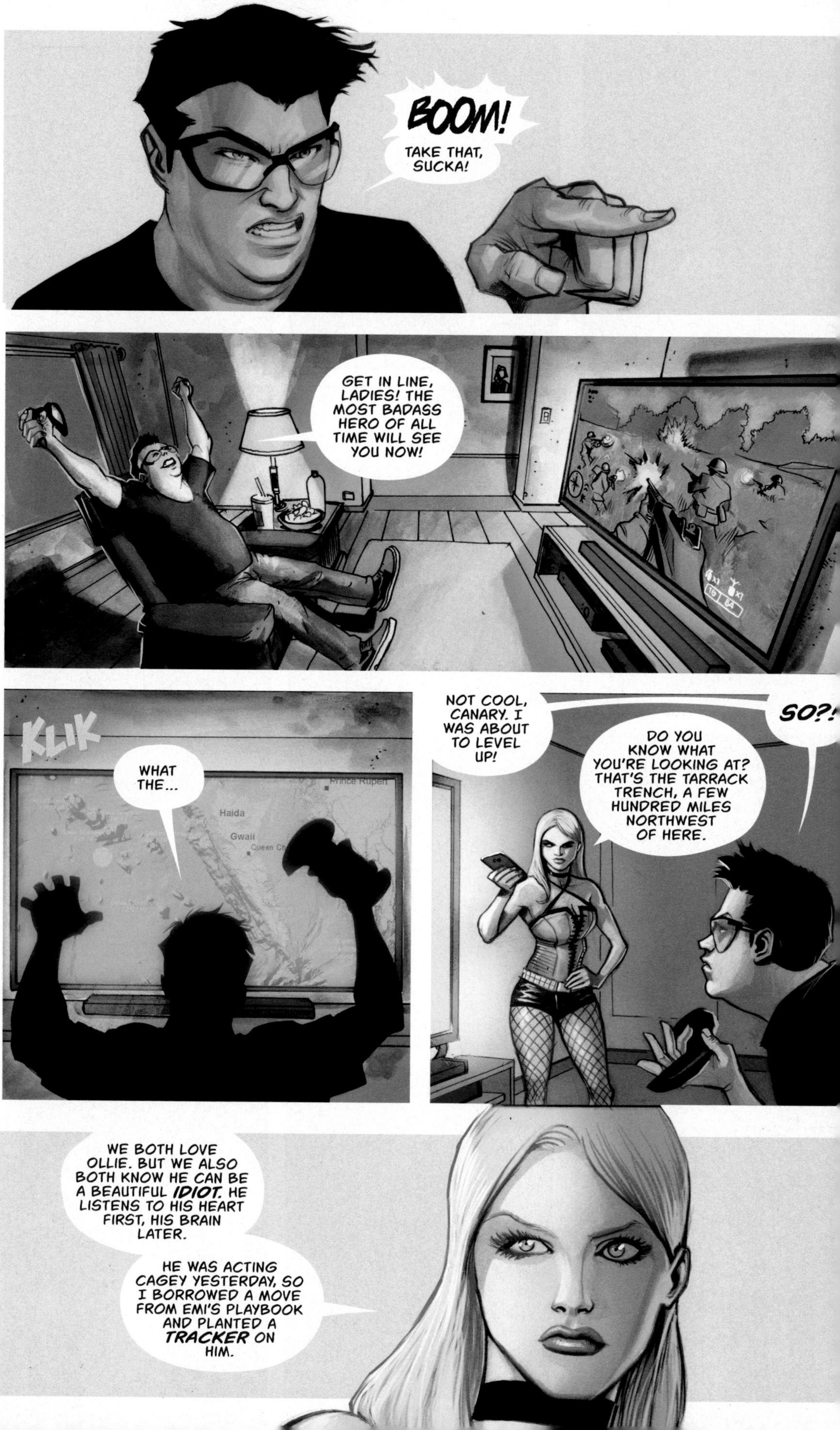
BOOM!
TAKE THAT, SUCKA!
GET IN LINE, LADIES! THE MOST BADASS HERO OF ALL TIME WILL SEE YOU NOW!
KLIK
WHAT THE...
Prince Rupert
Haida
Gwaii
NOT COOL, CANARY. I WAS ABOUT TO LEVEL UP!
SO?!
DO YOU KNOW WHAT YOU'RE LOOKING AT? THAT'S THE TARRACK TRENCH, A FEW HUNDRED MILES NORTHWEST OF HERE.
WE BOTH LOVE OLLIE. BUT WE ALSO BOTH KNOW HE CAN BE A BEAUTIFUL *IDIOT.* HE LISTENS TO HIS HEART FIRST, HIS BRAIN LATER.
HE WAS ACTING CAGEY YESTERDAY, SO I BORROWED A MOVE FROM EMI'S PLAYBOOK AND PLANTED A ***TRACKER*** ON HIM.

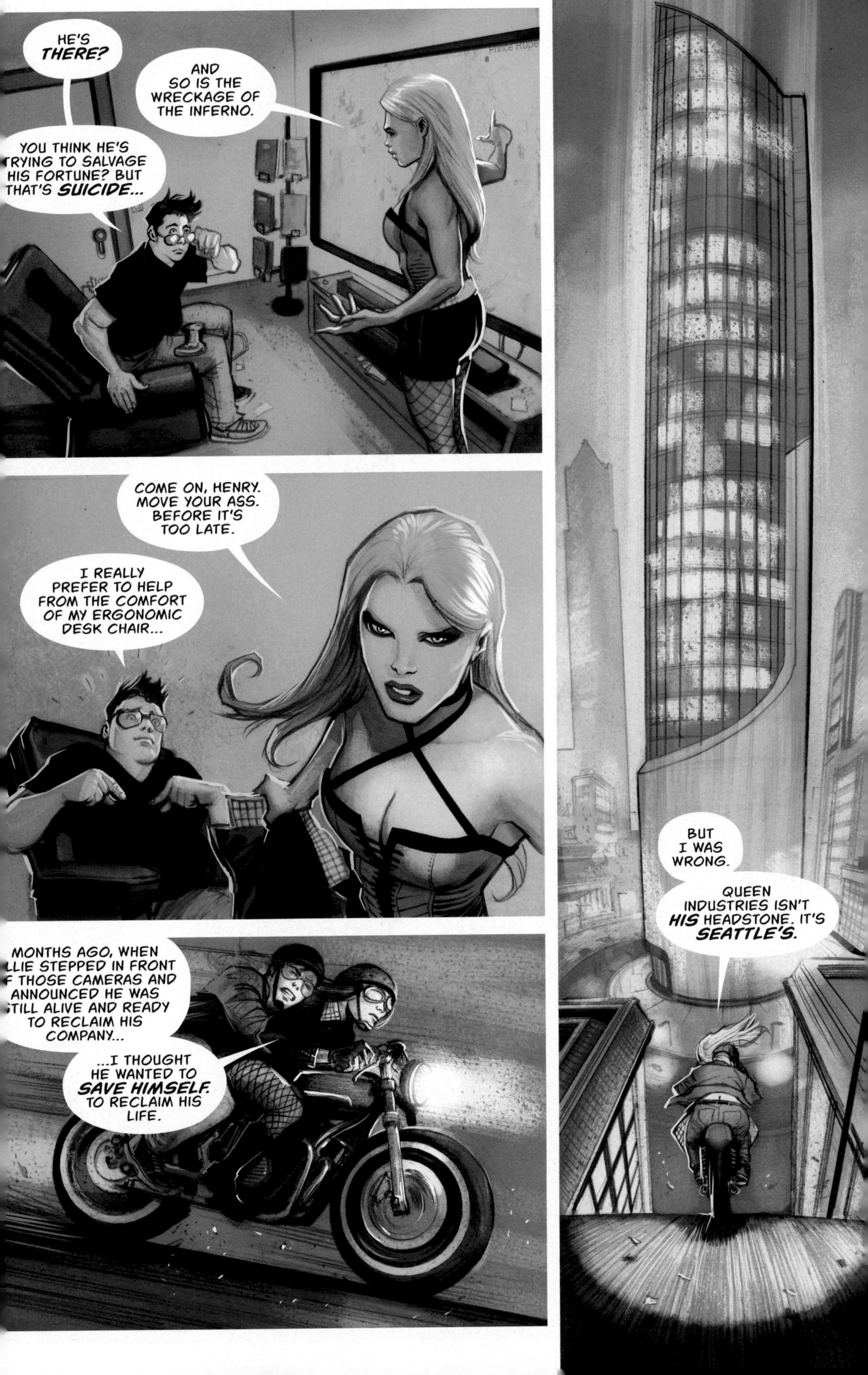
HE'S THERE?
AND SO IS THE WRECKAGE OF THE INFERNO.
YOU THINK HE'S TRYING TO SALVAGE HIS FORTUNE? BUT THAT'S SUICIDE...
COME ON, HENRY. MOVE YOUR ASS. BEFORE IT'S TOO LATE.
I REALLY PREFER TO HELP FROM THE COMFORT OF MY ERGONOMIC DESK CHAIR...
MONTHS AGO, WHEN LLIE STEPPED IN FRONT F THOSE CAMERAS AND ANNOUNCED HE WAS TILL ALIVE AND READY TO RECLAIM HIS COMPANY...
...I THOUGHT HE WANTED TO SAVE HIMSELF. TO RECLAIM HIS LIFE.
BUT I WAS WRONG.
QUEEN INDUSTRIES ISN'T HIS HEADSTONE. IT'S SEATTLE'S.

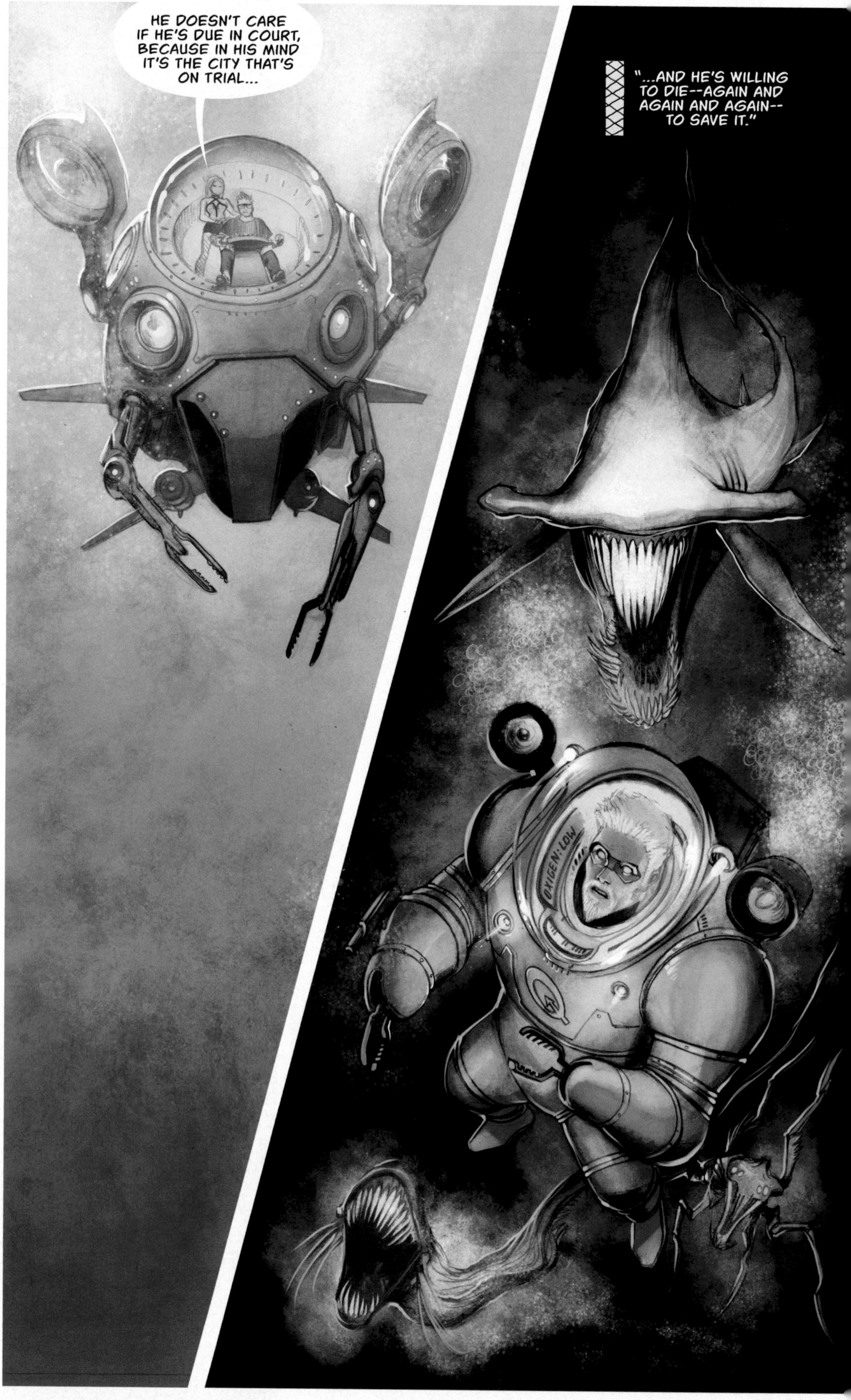
HE DOESN'T CARE IF HE'S DUE IN COURT, BECAUSE IN HIS MIND IT'S THE CITY THAT'S ON TRIAL...
"...AND HE'S WILLING TO DIE--AGAIN AND AGAIN AND AGAIN--TO SAVE IT."
OXIGEN:LOW

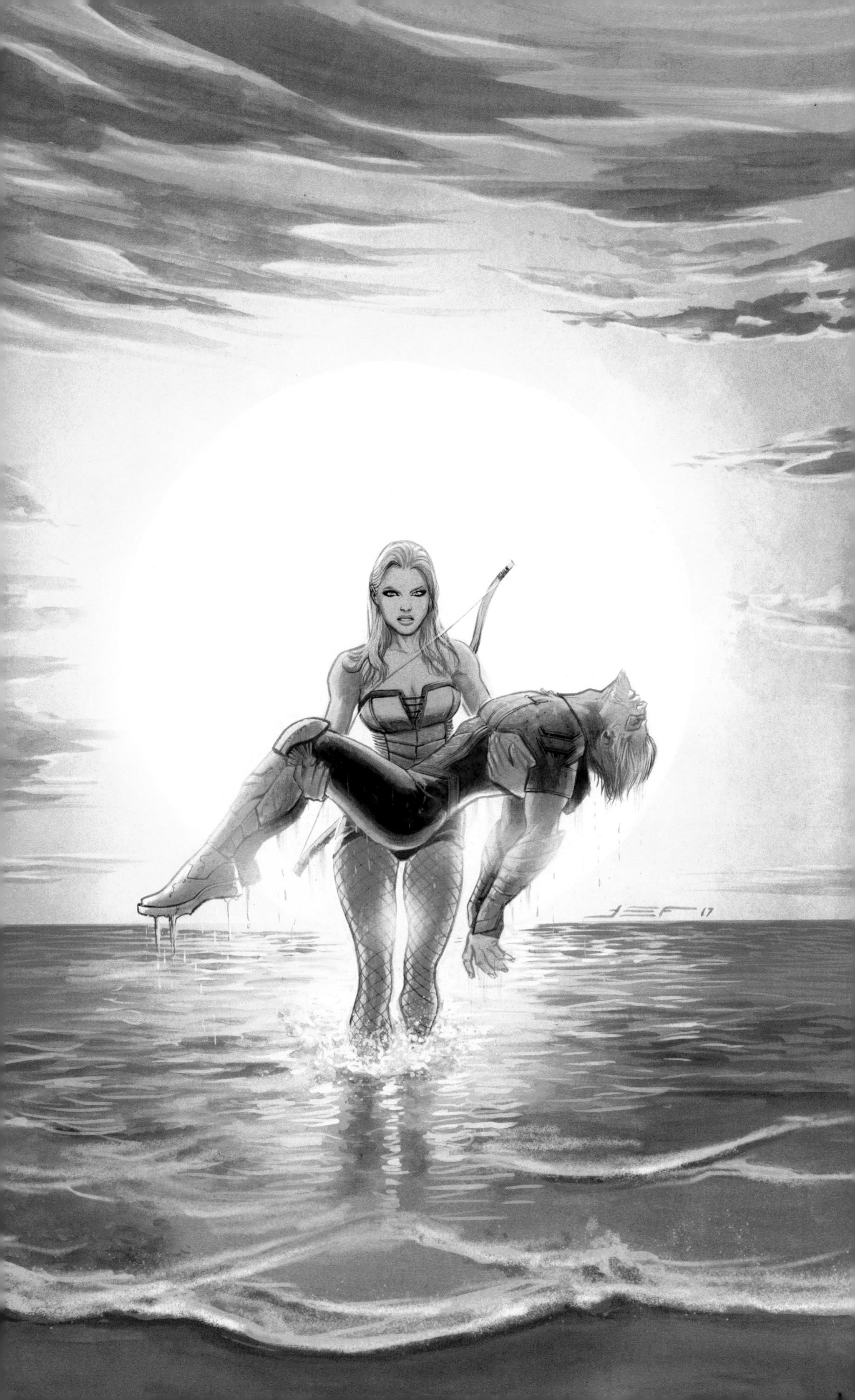

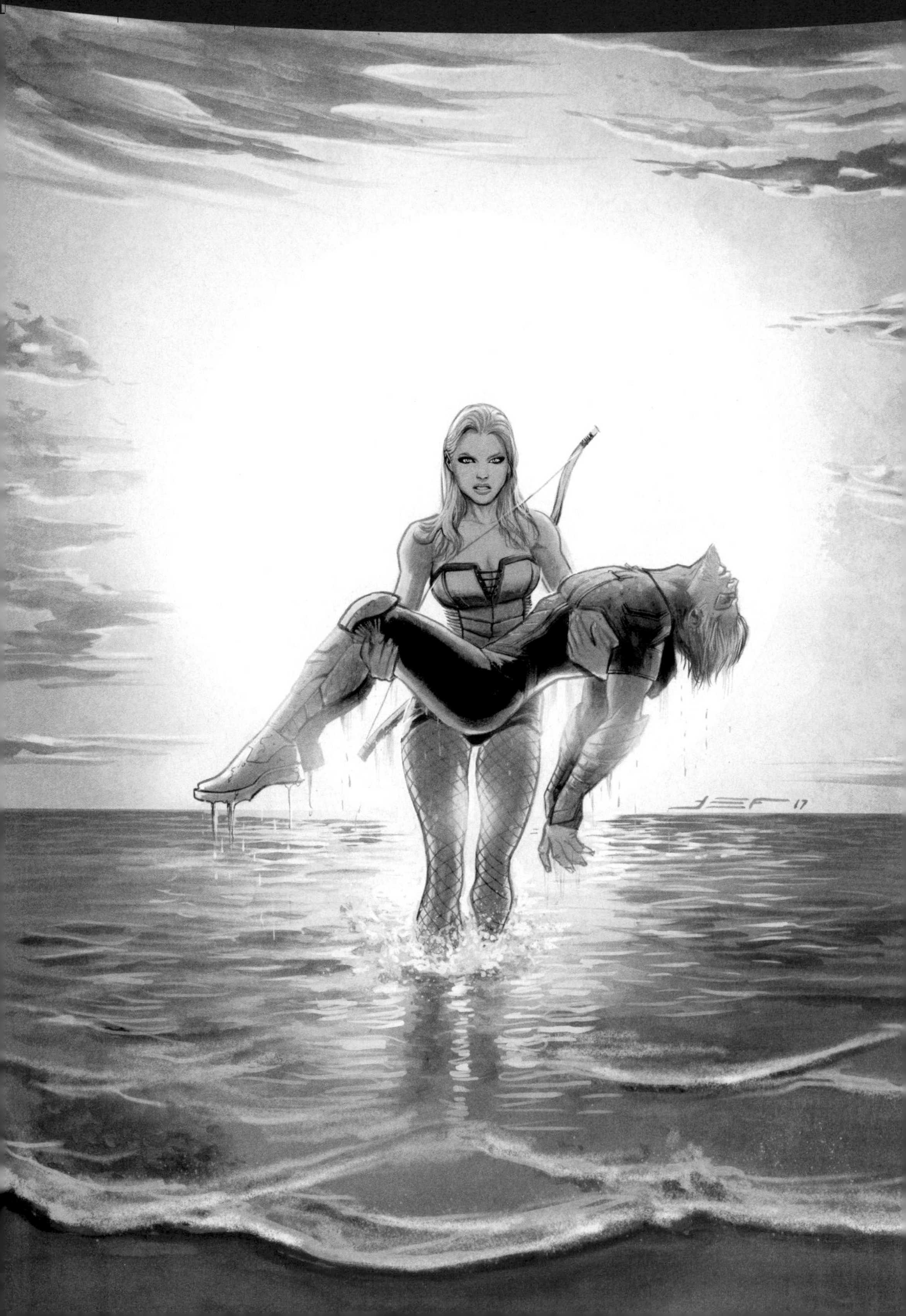

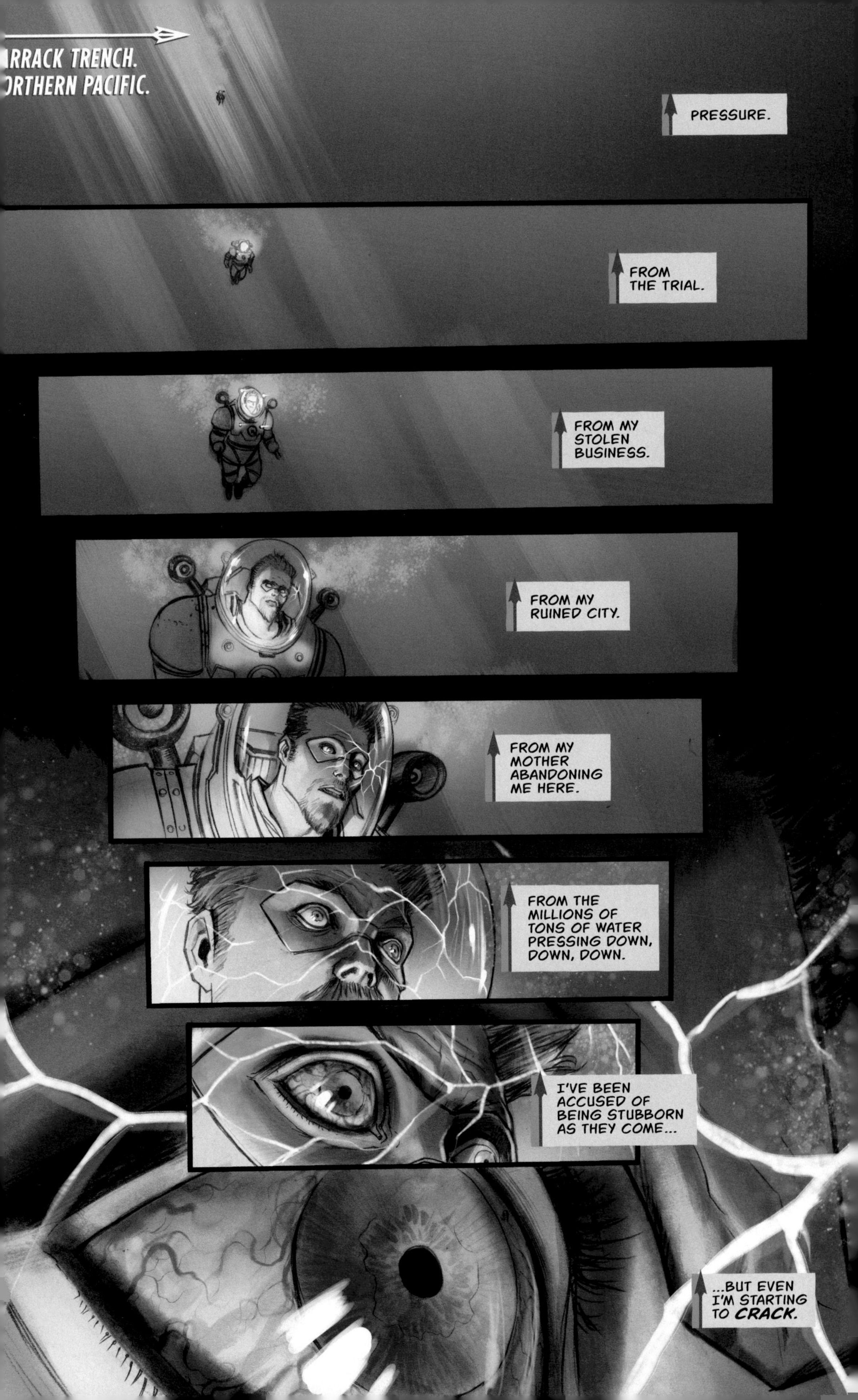

RRACK TRENCH.
ORTHERN PACIFIC.
PRESSURE.
FROM THE TRIAL.
FROM MY STOLEN BUSINESS.
FROM MY RUINED CITY.
FROM MY MOTHER ABANDONING ME HERE.
FROM THE MILLIONS OF TONS OF WATER PRESSING DOWN, DOWN, DOWN.
I'VE BEEN ACCUSED OF BEING STUBBORN AS THEY COME...
...BUT EVEN I'M STARTING TO CRACK.

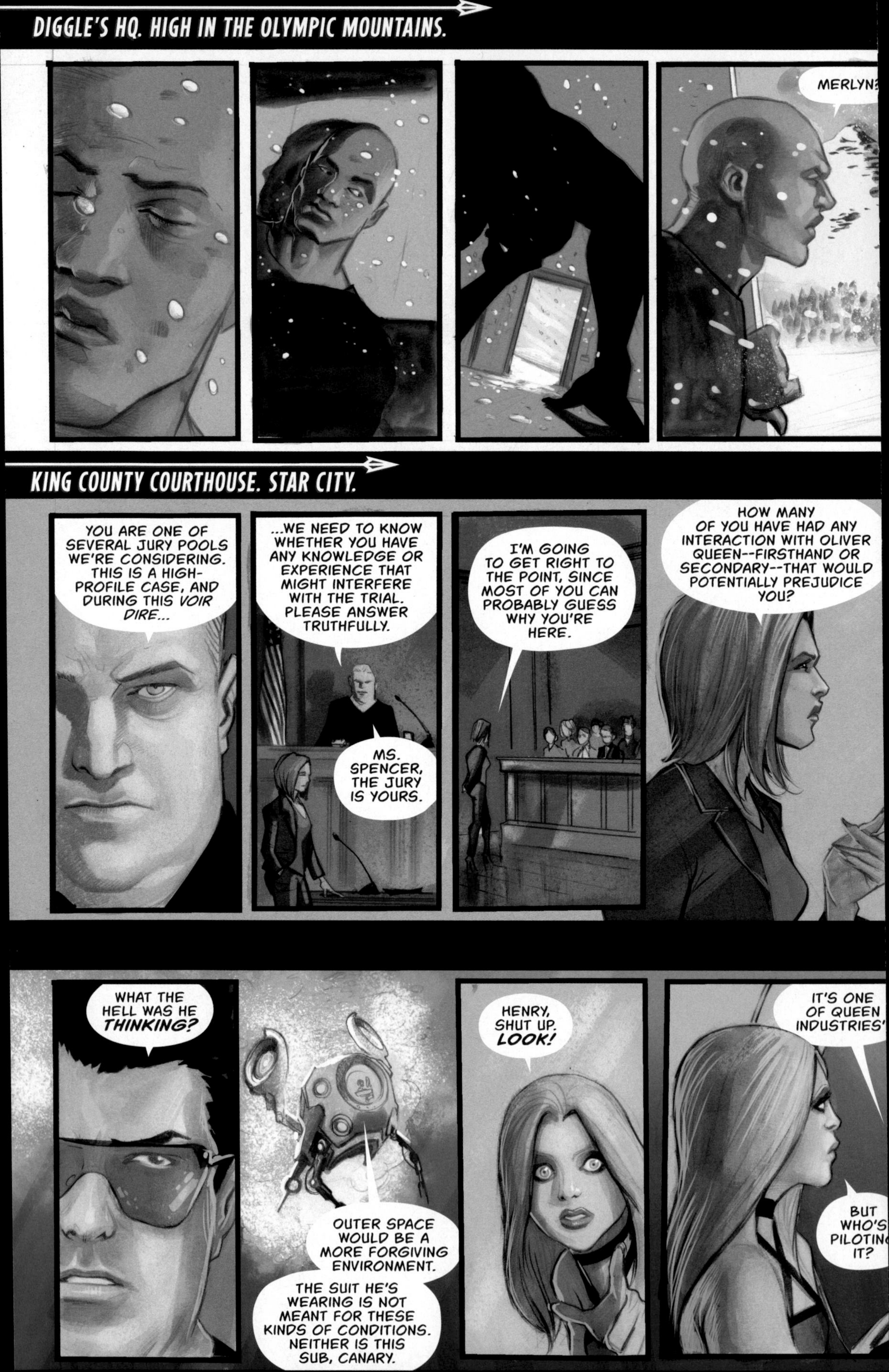
DIGGLE'S HQ. HIGH IN THE OLYMPIC MOUNTAINS.
MERLYN?
KING COUNTY COURTHOUSE. STAR CITY.
YOU ARE ONE OF SEVERAL JURY POOLS WE'RE CONSIDERING. THIS IS A HIGH-PROFILE CASE, AND DURING THIS VOIR DIRE...
...WE NEED TO KNOW WHETHER YOU HAVE ANY KNOWLEDGE OR EXPERIENCE THAT MIGHT INTERFERE WITH THE TRIAL. PLEASE ANSWER TRUTHFULLY.
MS. SPENCER, THE JURY IS YOURS.
I'M GOING TO GET RIGHT TO THE POINT, SINCE MOST OF YOU CAN PROBABLY GUESS WHY YOU'RE HERE.
HOW MANY OF YOU HAVE HAD ANY INTERACTION WITH OLIVER QUEEN--FIRSTHAND OR SECONDARY--THAT WOULD POTENTIALLY PREJUDICE YOU?
WHAT THE HELL WAS HE THINKING?
OUTER SPACE WOULD BE A MORE FORGIVING ENVIRONMENT.
THE SUIT HE'S WEARING IS NOT MEANT FOR THESE KINDS OF CONDITIONS. NEITHER IS THIS SUB, CANARY.
HENRY, SHUT UP. LOOK!
IT'S ONE OF QUEEN INDUSTRIES'
BUT WHO'S PILOTING IT?

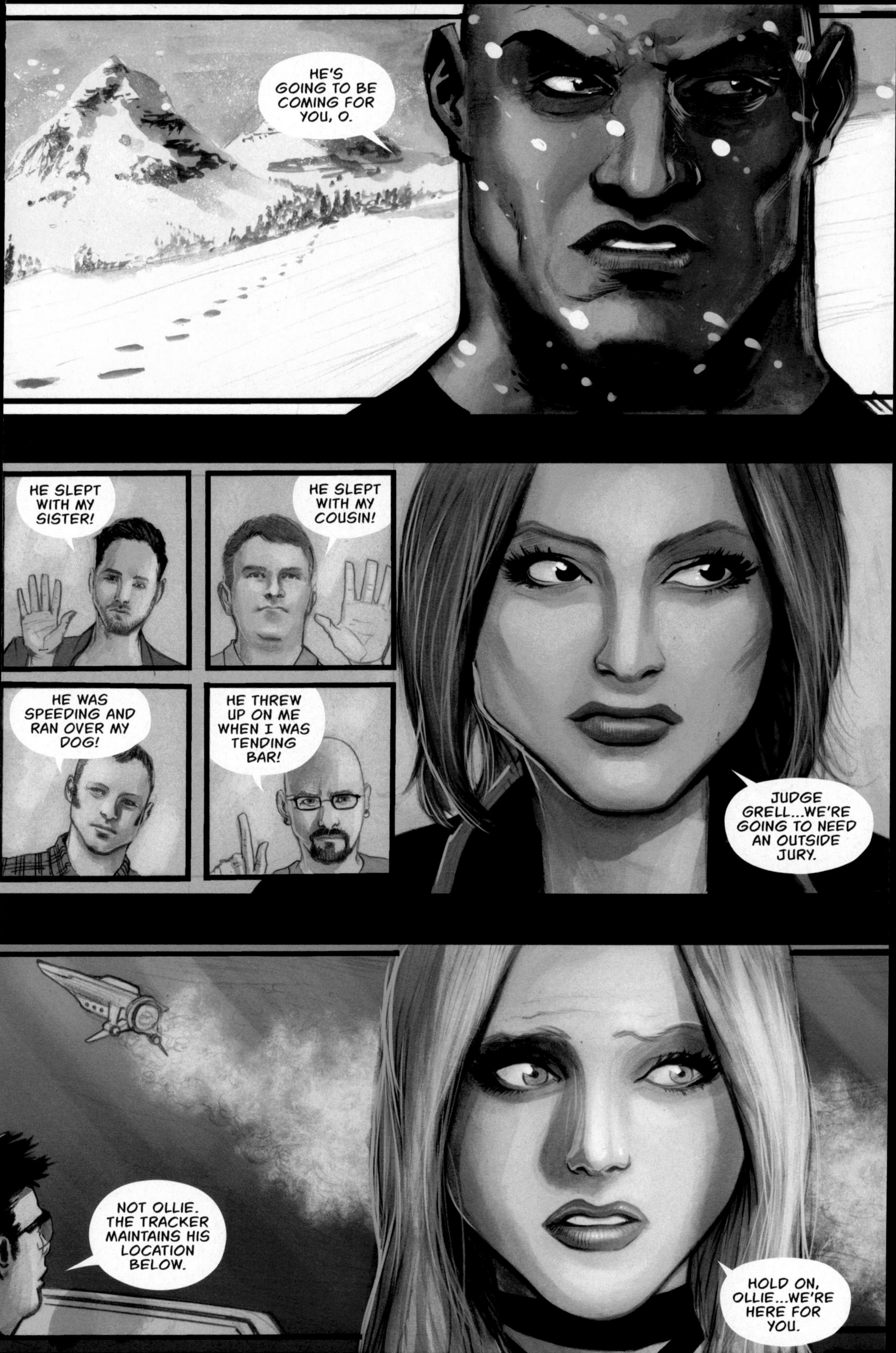
HE'S GOING TO BE COMING FOR YOU, O.
HE SLEPT WITH MY SISTER!
HE SLEPT WITH MY COUSIN!
HE WAS SPEEDING AND RAN OVER MY DOG!
HE THREW UP ON ME WHEN I WAS TENDING BAR!
JUDGE GRELL...WE'RE GOING TO NEED AN OUTSIDE JURY.
NOT OLLIE. THE TRACKER MAINTAINS HIS LOCATION BELOW.
HOLD ON, OLLIE...WE'RE HERE FOR YOU.

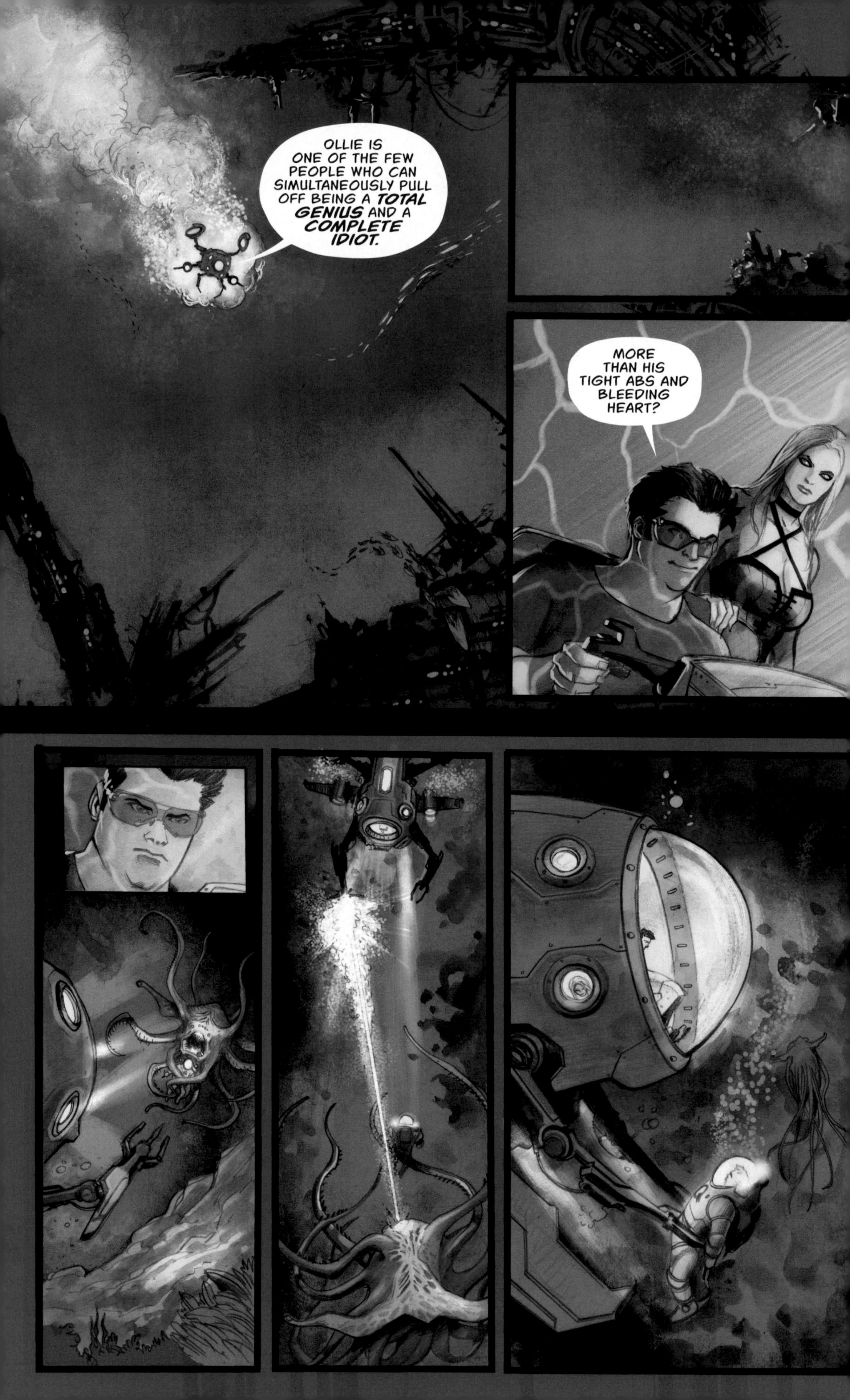
OLLIE IS ONE OF THE FEW PEOPLE WHO CAN SIMULTANEOUSLY PULL OFF BEING A **TOTAL GENIUS** AND A **COMPLETE IDIOT.**
MORE THAN HIS TIGHT ABS AND BLEEDING HEART?

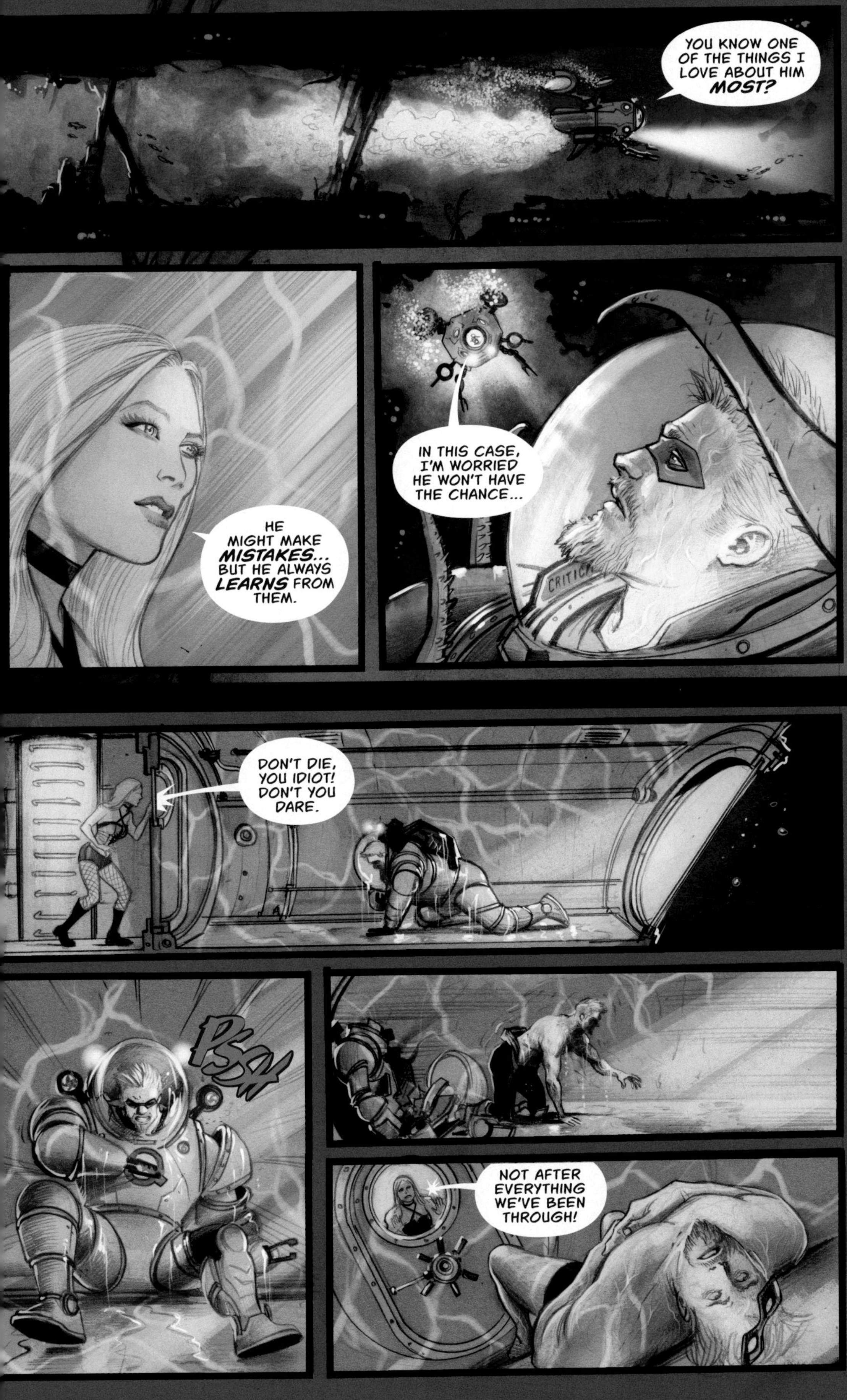
YOU KNOW ONE OF THE THINGS I LOVE ABOUT HIM MOST?
HE MIGHT MAKE MISTAKES... BUT HE ALWAYS LEARNS FROM THEM.
IN THIS CASE, I'M WORRIED HE WON'T HAVE THE CHANCE...
DON'T DIE, YOU IDIOT! DON'T YOU DARE.
PSSH
NOT AFTER EVERYTHING WE'VE BEEN THROUGH!

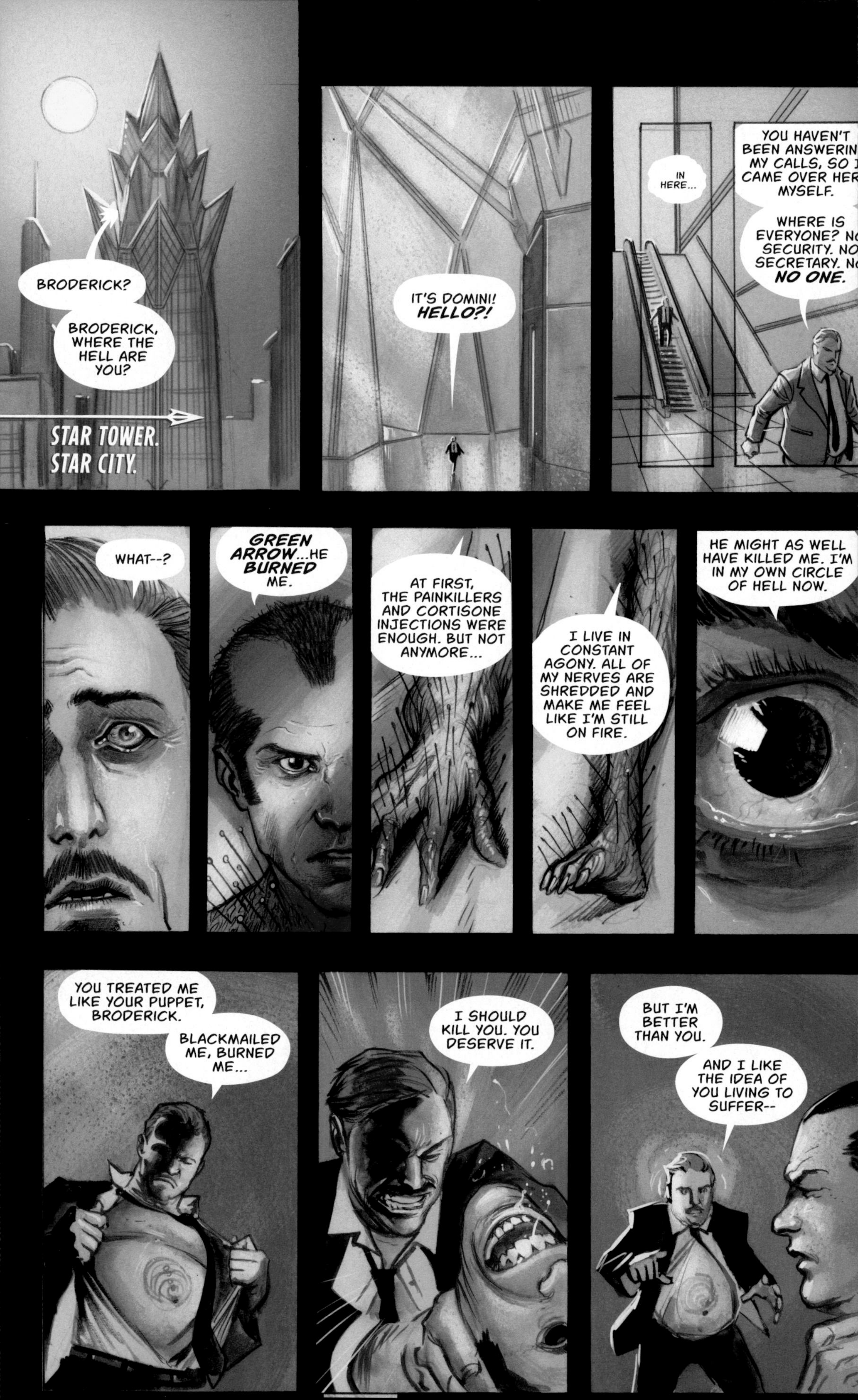
BRODERICK?
BRODERICK, WHERE THE HELL ARE YOU?
STAR TOWER. STAR CITY.
IT'S DOMINI! HELLO?!
IN HERE...
YOU HAVEN'T BEEN ANSWERIN MY CALLS, SO I CAME OVER HER MYSELF.
WHERE IS EVERYONE? N SECURITY. N SECRETARY. N NO ONE.
WHAT--?
GREEN ARROW...HE BURNED ME.
AT FIRST, THE PAINKILLERS AND CORTISONE INJECTIONS WERE ENOUGH. BUT NOT ANYMORE...
I LIVE IN CONSTANT AGONY. ALL OF MY NERVES ARE SHREDDED AND MAKE ME FEEL LIKE I'M STILL ON FIRE.
HE MIGHT AS WELL HAVE KILLED ME. I'M IN MY OWN CIRCLE OF HELL NOW.
YOU TREATED ME LIKE YOUR PUPPET, BRODERICK.
BLACKMAILED ME, BURNED ME...
I SHOULD KILL YOU. YOU DESERVE IT.
BUT I'M BETTER THAN YOU.
AND I LIKE THE IDEA OF YOU LIVING TO SUFFER--

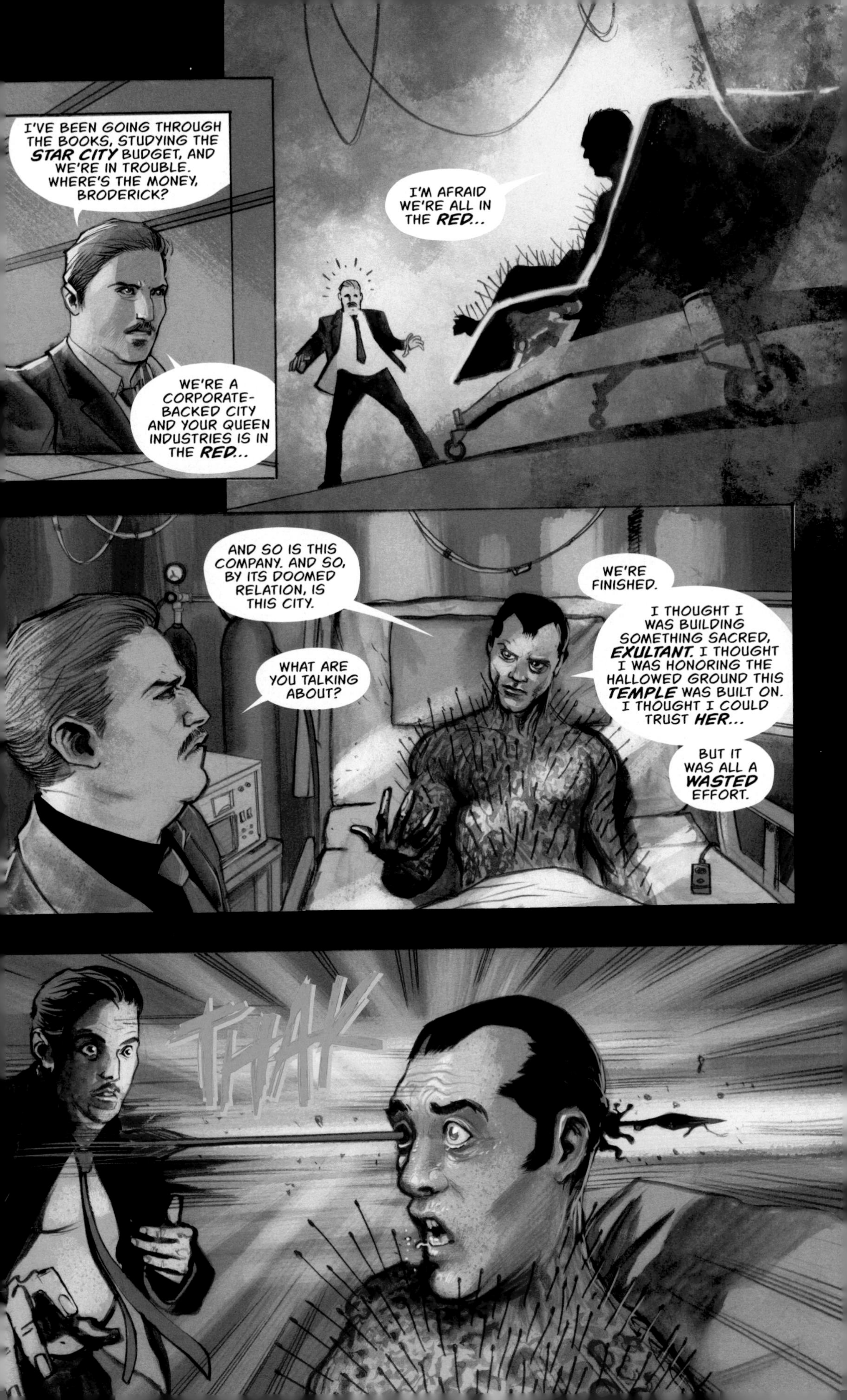
I'VE BEEN GOING THROUGH THE BOOKS, STUDYING THE STAR CITY BUDGET, AND WE'RE IN TROUBLE. WHERE'S THE MONEY, BRODERICK?
WE'RE A CORPORATE-BACKED CITY AND YOUR QUEEN INDUSTRIES IS IN THE RED...
I'M AFRAID WE'RE ALL IN THE RED...
AND SO IS THIS COMPANY. AND SO, BY ITS DOOMED RELATION, IS THIS CITY.
WHAT ARE YOU TALKING ABOUT?
WE'RE FINISHED.
I THOUGHT I WAS BUILDING SOMETHING SACRED, EXULTANT. I THOUGHT I WAS HONORING THE HALLOWED GROUND THIS TEMPLE WAS BUILT ON. I THOUGHT I COULD TRUST HER...
BUT IT WAS ALL A WASTED EFFORT.
THAK

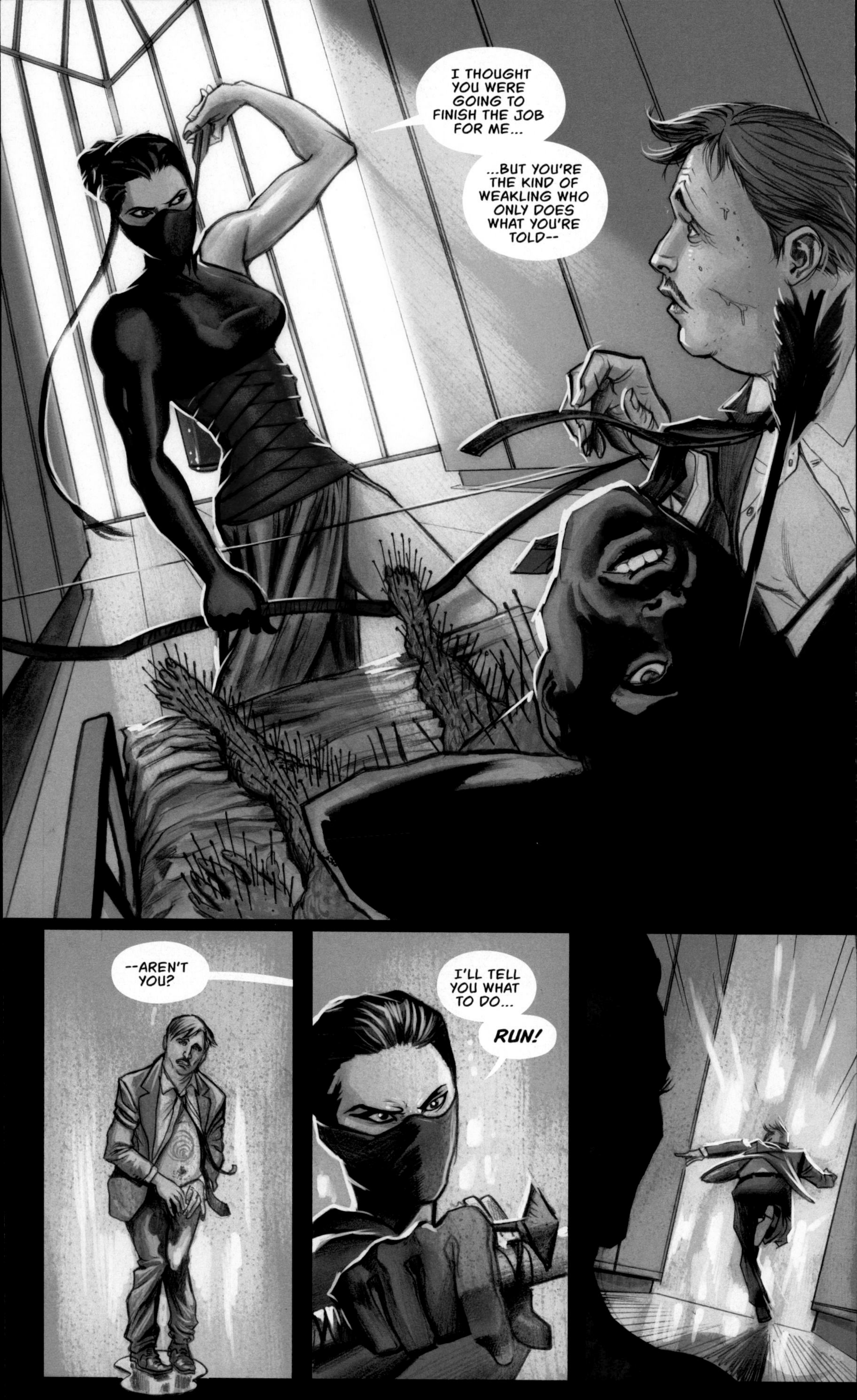
I THOUGHT YOU WERE GOING TO FINISH THE JOB FOR ME...
...BUT YOU'RE THE KIND OF WEAKLING WHO ONLY DOES WHAT YOU'RE TOLD--
--AREN'T YOU?
I'LL TELL YOU WHAT TO DO...
RUN!

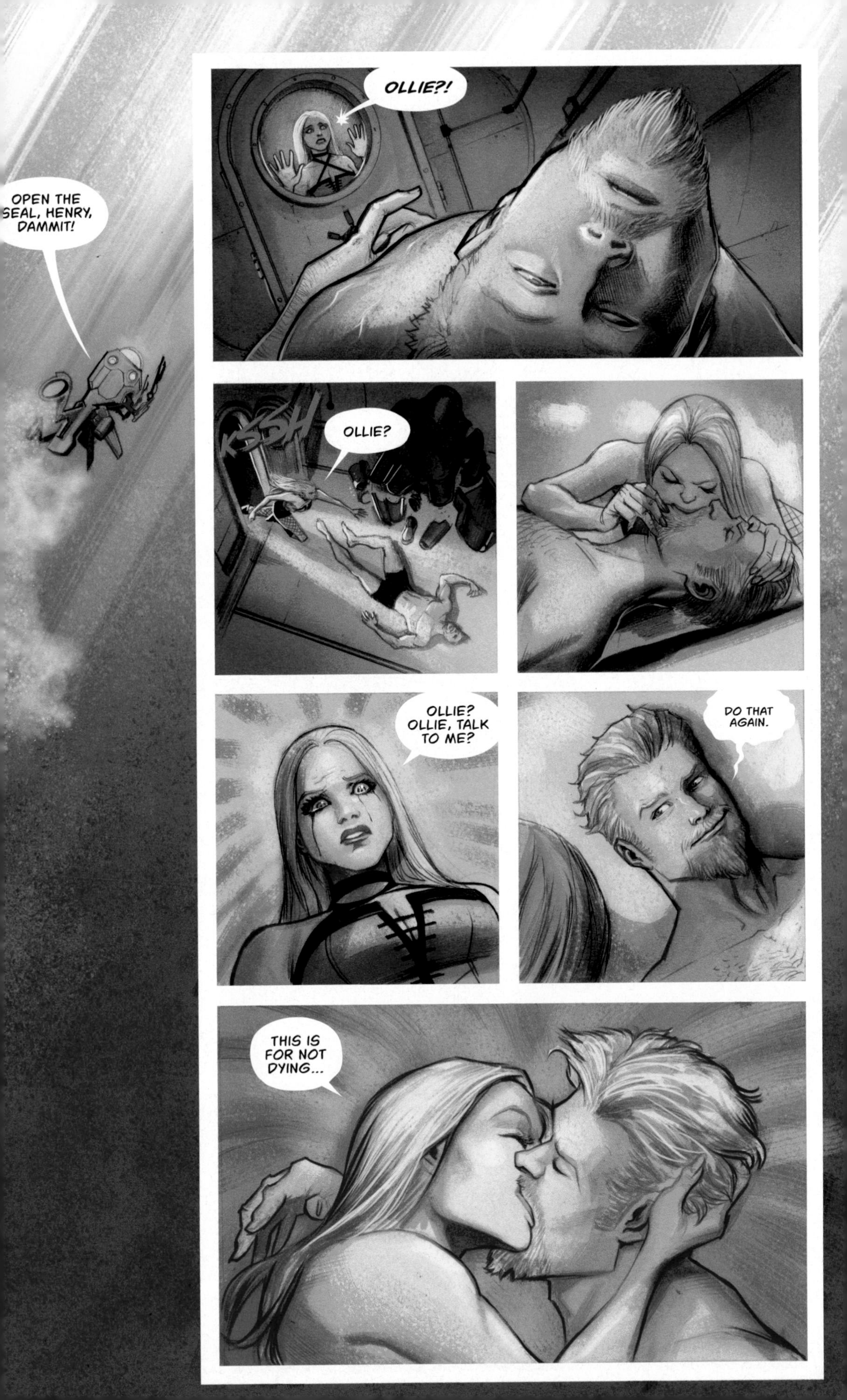
OPEN THE SEAL, HENRY, DAMMIT!
OLLIE?!
KSSH
OLLIE?
OLLIE? OLLIE, TALK TO ME?
DO THAT AGAIN.
THIS IS FOR NOT DYING...

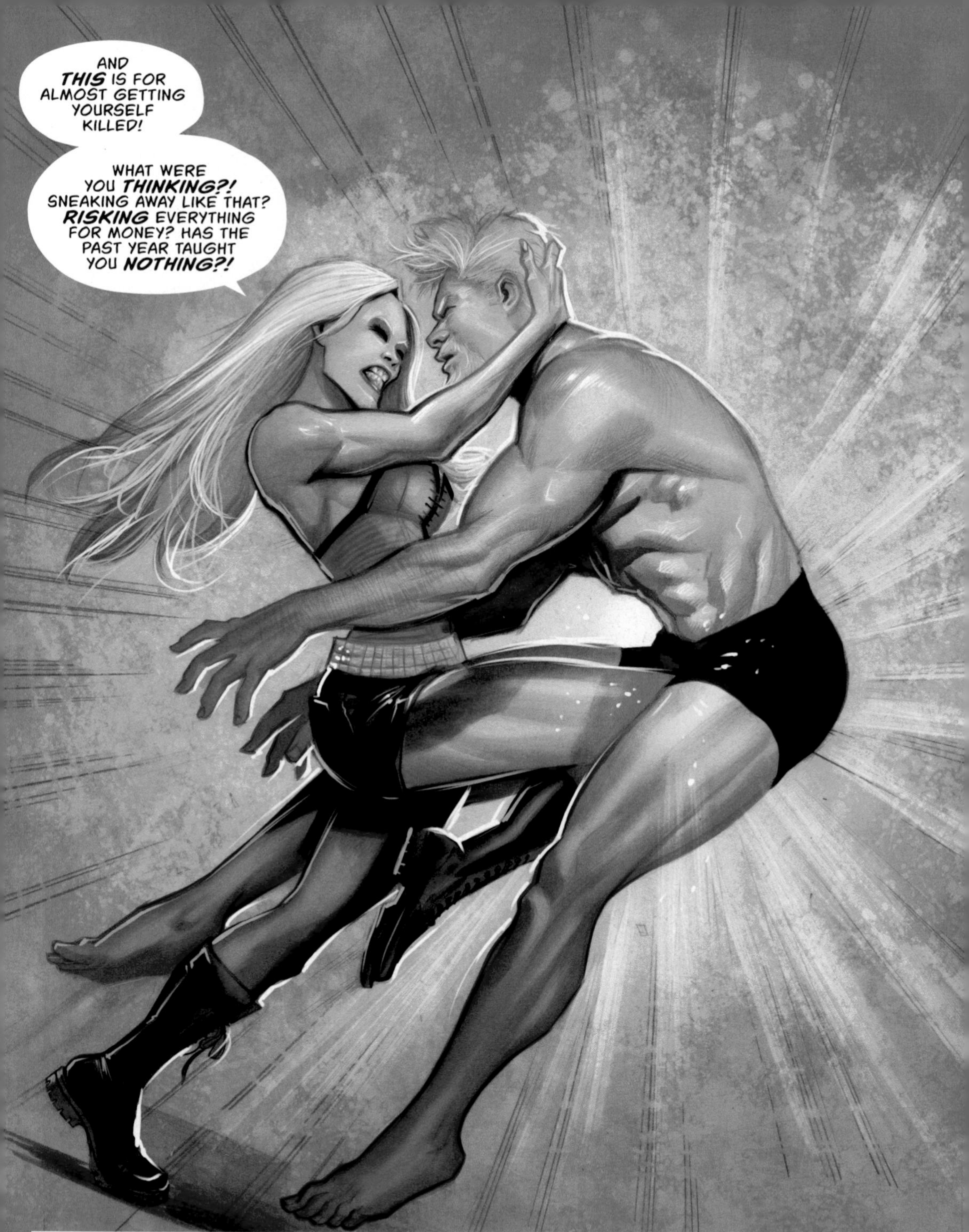
AND THIS IS FOR ALMOST GETTING YOURSELF KILLED!
WHAT WERE YOU THINKING?! SNEAKING AWAY LIKE THAT? RISKING EVERYTHING FOR MONEY? HAS THE PAST YEAR TAUGHT YOU NOTHING?!

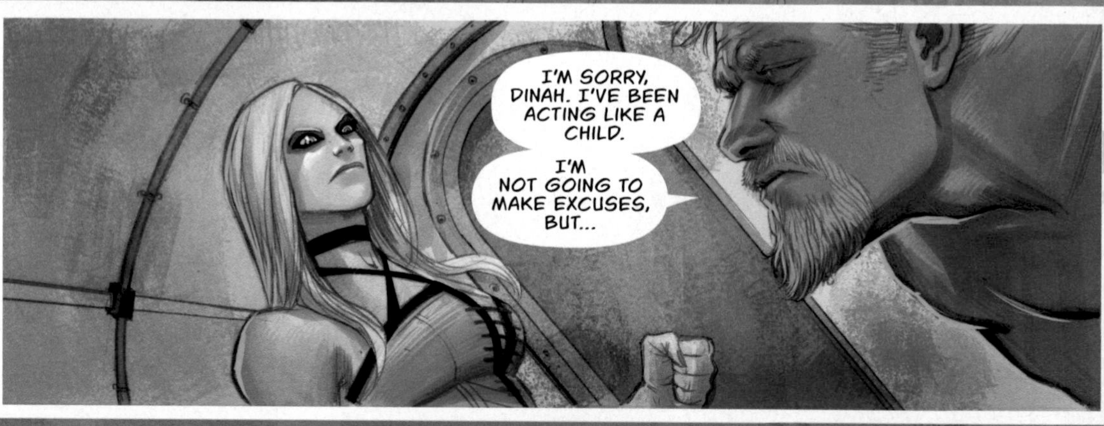
I'M SORRY, DINAH. I'VE BEEN ACTING LIKE A CHILD.
I'M NOT GOING TO MAKE EXCUSES, BUT...

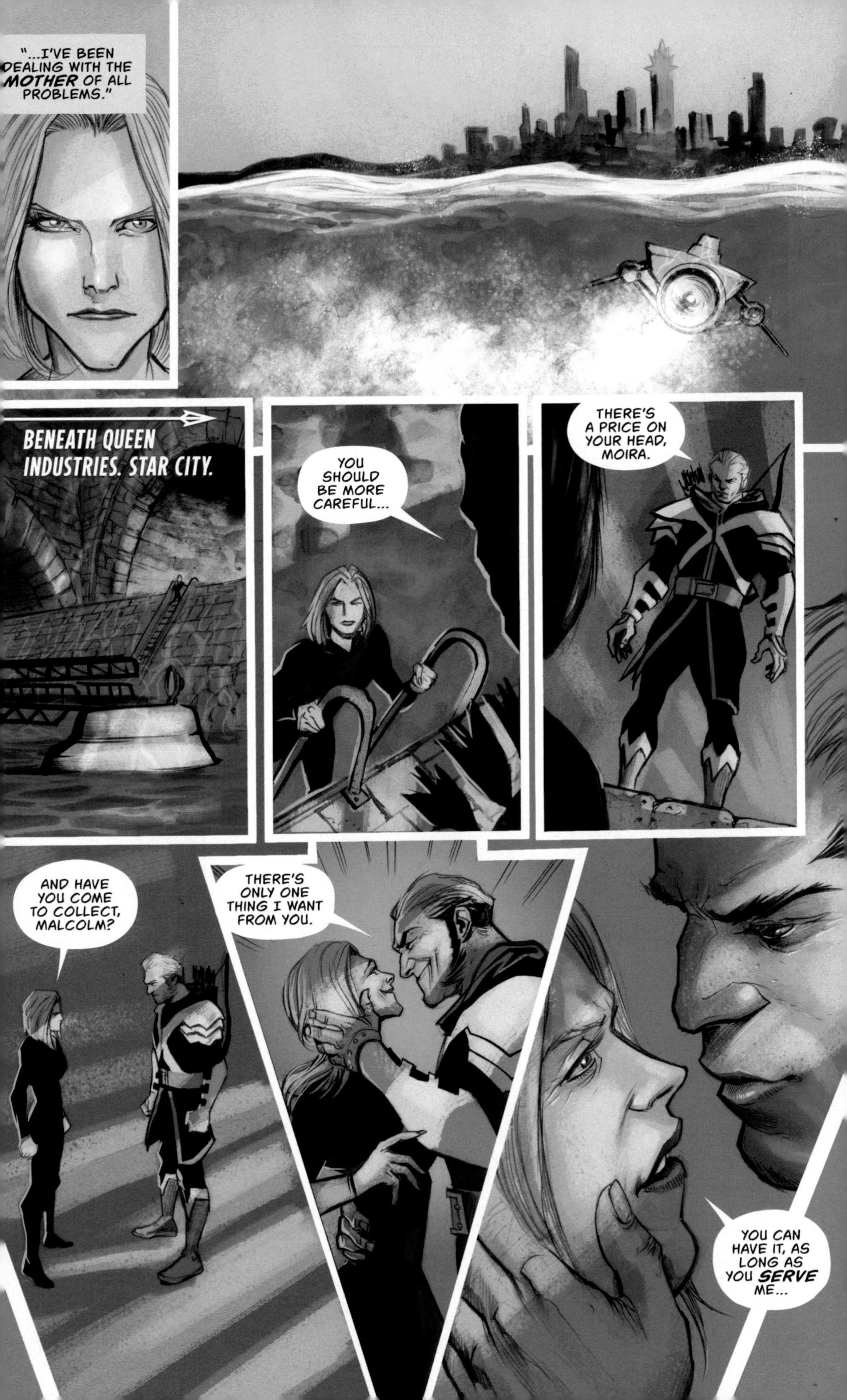
"...I'VE BEEN DEALING WITH THE MOTHER OF ALL PROBLEMS."
BENEATH QUEEN INDUSTRIES. STAR CITY.
YOU SHOULD BE MORE CAREFUL...
THERE'S A PRICE ON YOUR HEAD, MOIRA.
AND HAVE YOU COME TO COLLECT, MALCOLM?
THERE'S ONLY ONE THING I WANT FROM YOU.
YOU CAN HAVE IT, AS LONG AS YOU SERVE ME...

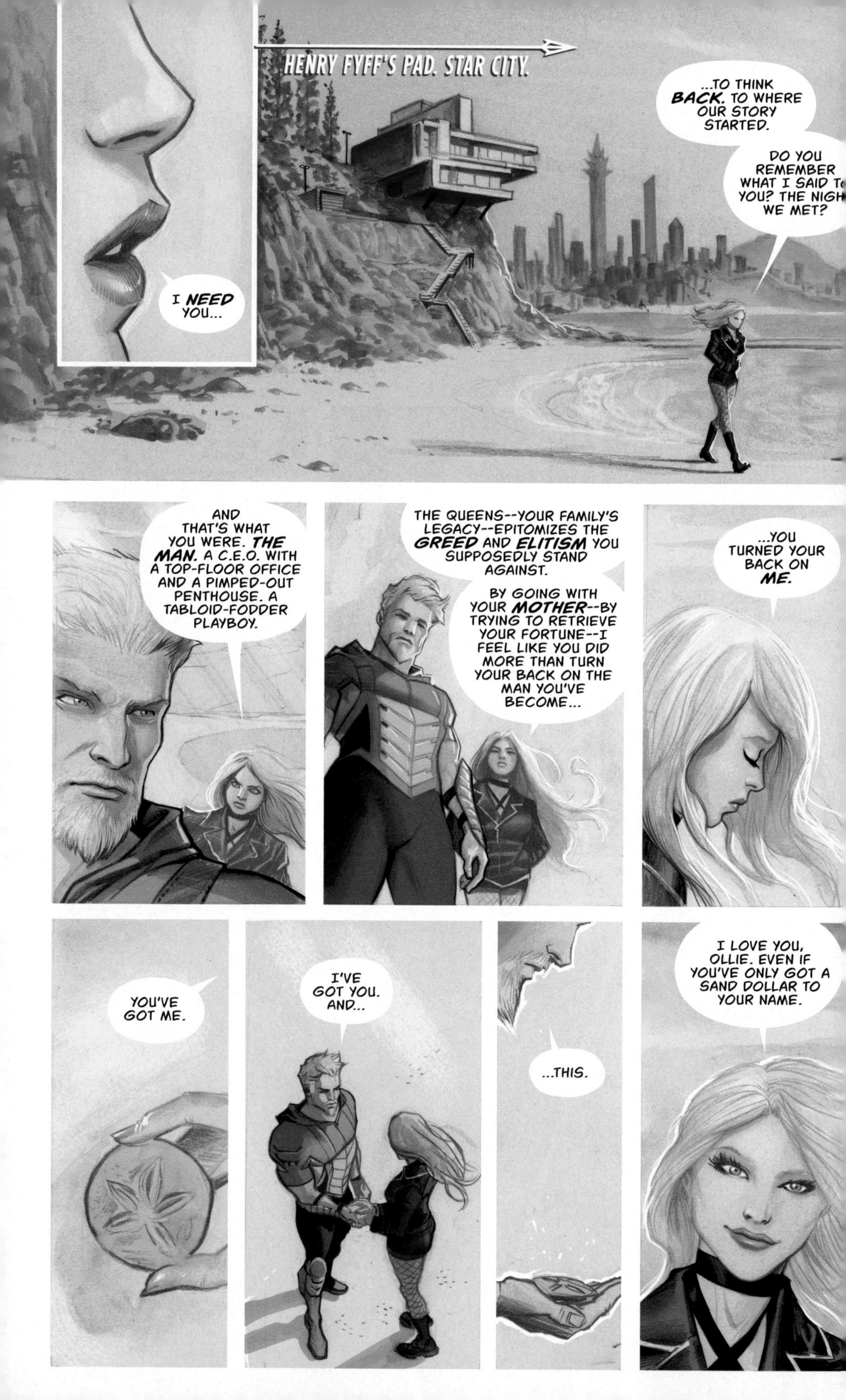
I NEED YOU...
HENRY FYFF'S PAD. STAR CITY.
...TO THINK BACK. TO WHERE OUR STORY STARTED.
DO YOU REMEMBER WHAT I SAID T YOU? THE NIGH WE MET?
AND THAT'S WHAT YOU WERE. THE MAN. A C.E.O. WITH A TOP-FLOOR OFFICE AND A PIMPED-OUT PENTHOUSE. A TABLOID-FODDER PLAYBOY.
THE QUEENS--YOUR FAMILY'S LEGACY--EPITOMIZES THE GREED AND ELITISM YOU SUPPOSEDLY STAND AGAINST.
BY GOING WITH YOUR MOTHER--BY TRYING TO RETRIEVE YOUR FORTUNE--I FEEL LIKE YOU DID MORE THAN TURN YOUR BACK ON THE MAN YOU'VE BECOME...
...YOU TURNED YOUR BACK ON ME.
YOU'VE GOT ME.
I'VE GOT YOU. AND...
...THIS.
I LOVE YOU, OLLIE. EVEN IF YOU'VE ONLY GOT A SAND DOLLAR TO YOUR NAME.

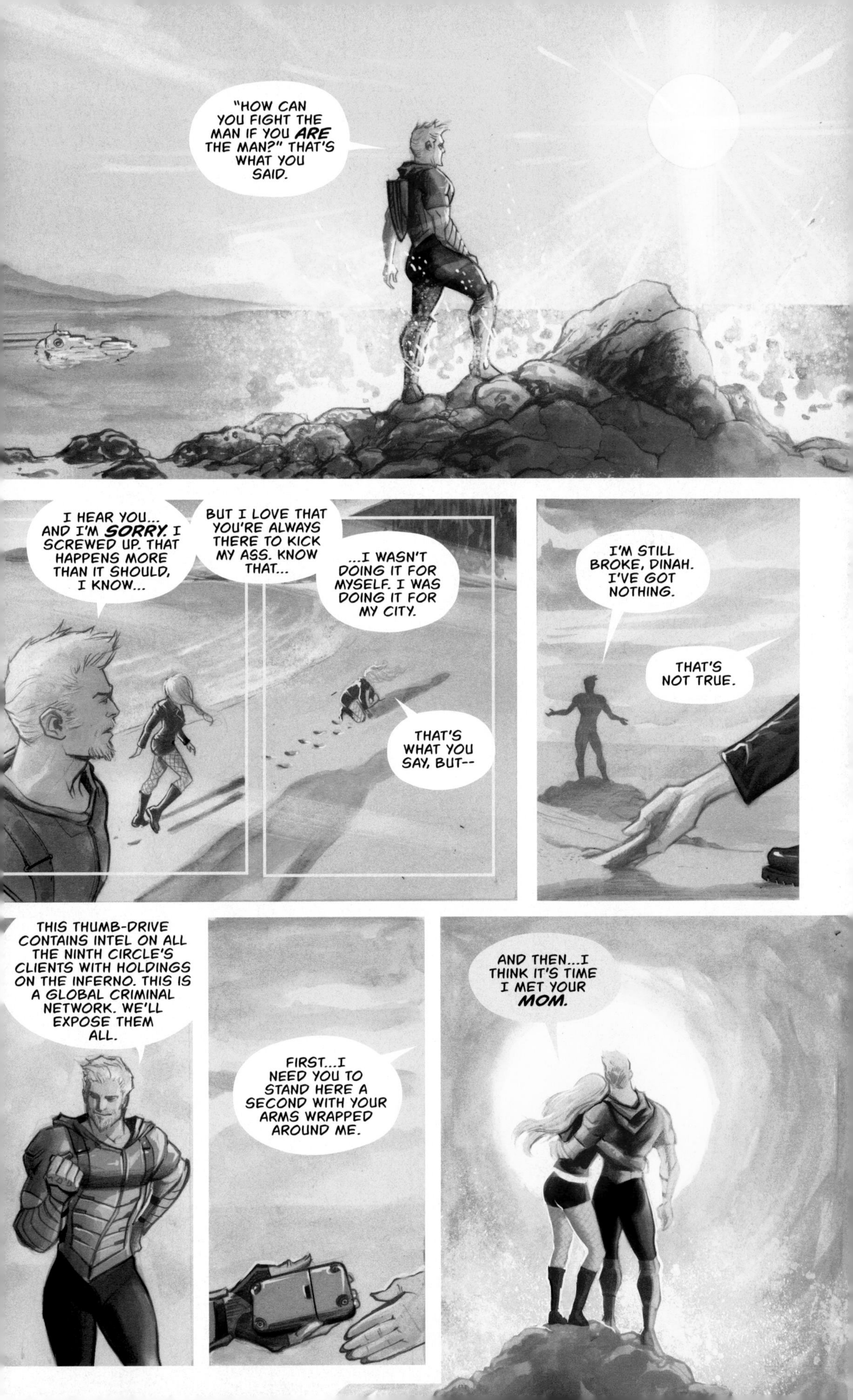
"HOW CAN YOU FIGHT THE MAN IF YOU ARE THE MAN?" THAT'S WHAT YOU SAID.
I HEAR YOU... AND I'M SORRY. I SCREWED UP. THAT HAPPENS MORE THAN IT SHOULD, I KNOW...
BUT I LOVE THAT YOU'RE ALWAYS THERE TO KICK MY ASS. KNOW THAT...
...I WASN'T DOING IT FOR MYSELF. I WAS DOING IT FOR MY CITY.
THAT'S WHAT YOU SAY, BUT--
I'M STILL BROKE, DINAH. I'VE GOT NOTHING.
THAT'S NOT TRUE.
THIS THUMB-DRIVE CONTAINS INTEL ON ALL THE NINTH CIRCLE'S CLIENTS WITH HOLDINGS ON THE INFERNO. THIS IS A GLOBAL CRIMINAL NETWORK. WE'LL EXPOSE THEM ALL.
FIRST...I NEED YOU TO STAND HERE A SECOND WITH YOUR ARMS WRAPPED AROUND ME.
AND THEN...I THINK IT'S TIME I MET YOUR MOM.

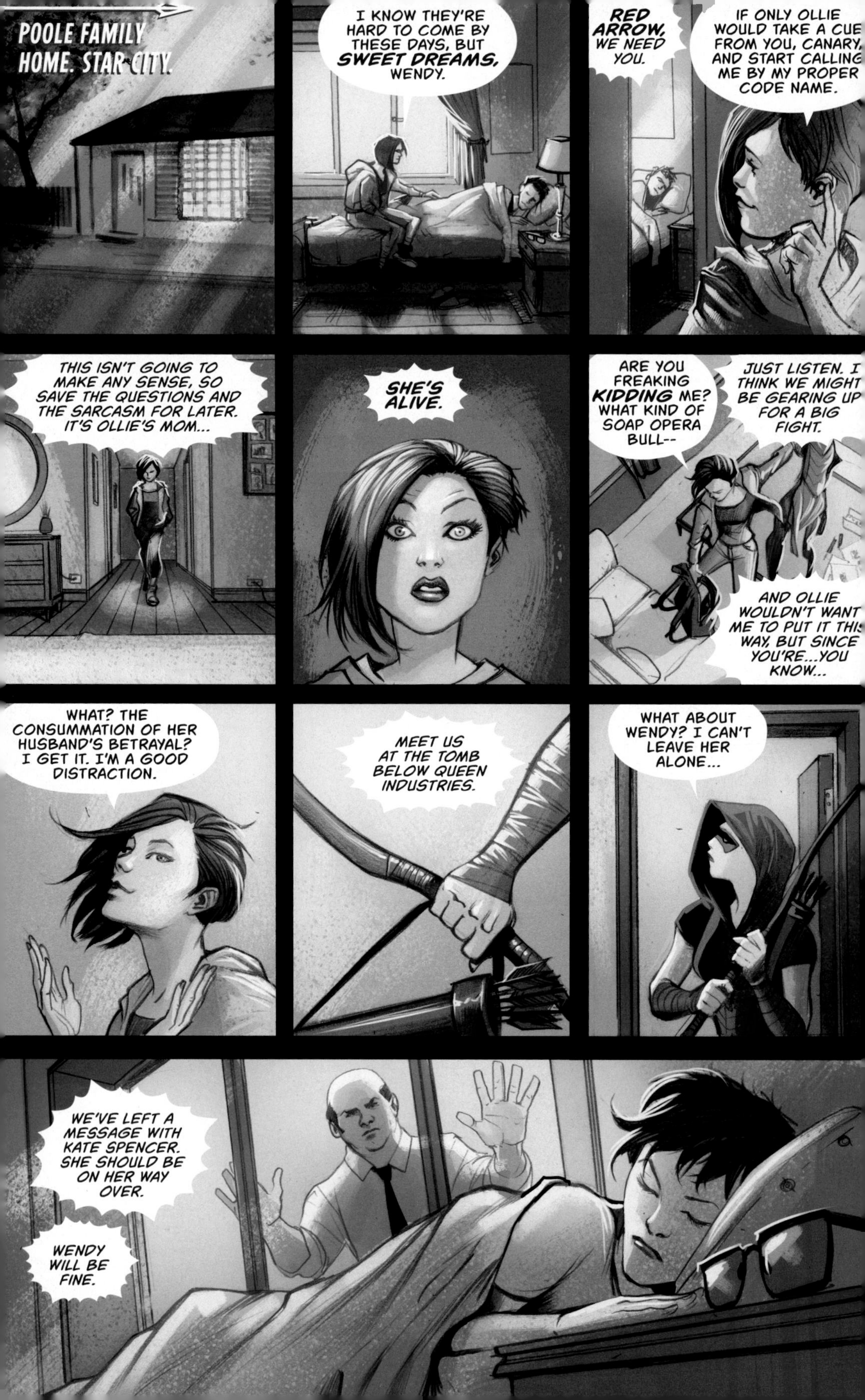
POOLE FAMILY HOME. STAR CITY.
I KNOW THEY'RE HARD TO COME BY THESE DAYS, BUT SWEET DREAMS, WENDY.
RED ARROW, WE NEED YOU.
IF ONLY OLLIE WOULD TAKE A CUE FROM YOU, CANARY, AND START CALLING ME BY MY PROPER CODE NAME.
THIS ISN'T GOING TO MAKE ANY SENSE, SO SAVE THE QUESTIONS AND THE SARCASM FOR LATER. IT'S OLLIE'S MOM...
SHE'S ALIVE.
ARE YOU FREAKING KIDDING ME? WHAT KIND OF SOAP OPERA BULL--
JUST LISTEN. I THINK WE MIGHT BE GEARING UP FOR A BIG FIGHT.
AND OLLIE WOULDN'T WANT ME TO PUT IT THIS WAY, BUT SINCE YOU'RE...YOU KNOW...
WHAT? THE CONSUMMATION OF HER HUSBAND'S BETRAYAL? I GET IT. I'M A GOOD DISTRACTION.
MEET US AT THE TOMB BELOW QUEEN INDUSTRIES.
WHAT ABOUT WENDY? I CAN'T LEAVE HER ALONE...
WE'VE LEFT A MESSAGE WITH KATE SPENCER. SHE SHOULD BE ON HER WAY OVER.
WENDY WILL BE FINE.

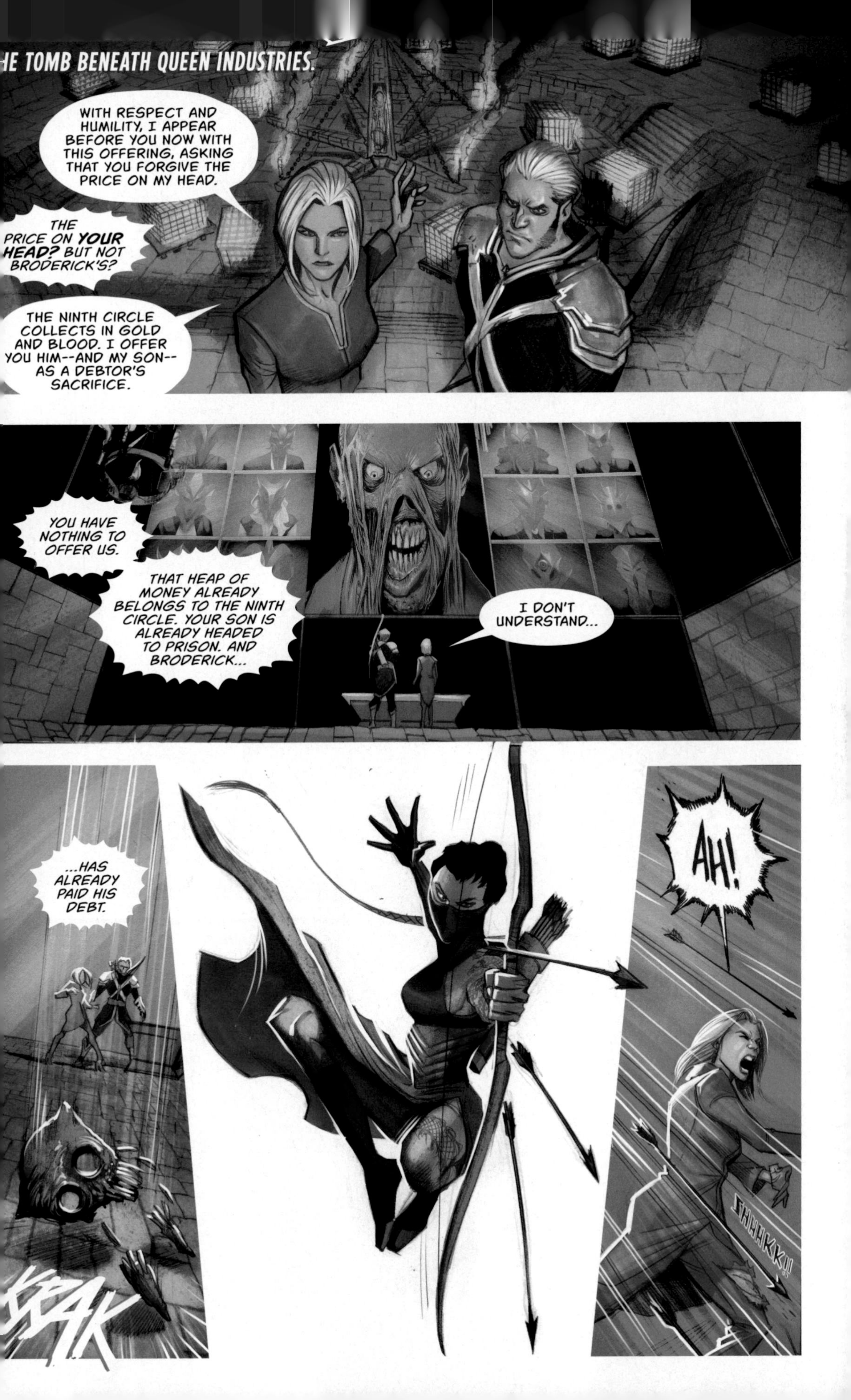
HE TOMB BENEATH QUEEN INDUSTRIES.
WITH RESPECT AND HUMILITY, I APPEAR BEFORE YOU NOW WITH THIS OFFERING, ASKING THAT YOU FORGIVE THE PRICE ON MY HEAD.
THE PRICE ON YOUR HEAD? BUT NOT BRODERICK'S?
THE NINTH CIRCLE COLLECTS IN GOLD AND BLOOD. I OFFER YOU HIM--AND MY SON--AS A DEBTOR'S SACRIFICE.
YOU HAVE NOTHING TO OFFER US.
THAT HEAP OF MONEY ALREADY BELONGS TO THE NINTH CIRCLE. YOUR SON IS ALREADY HEADED TO PRISON. AND BRODERICK...
I DON'T UNDERSTAND...
...HAS ALREADY PAID HIS DEBT.
KRAK
AH!
SHHHKK!!

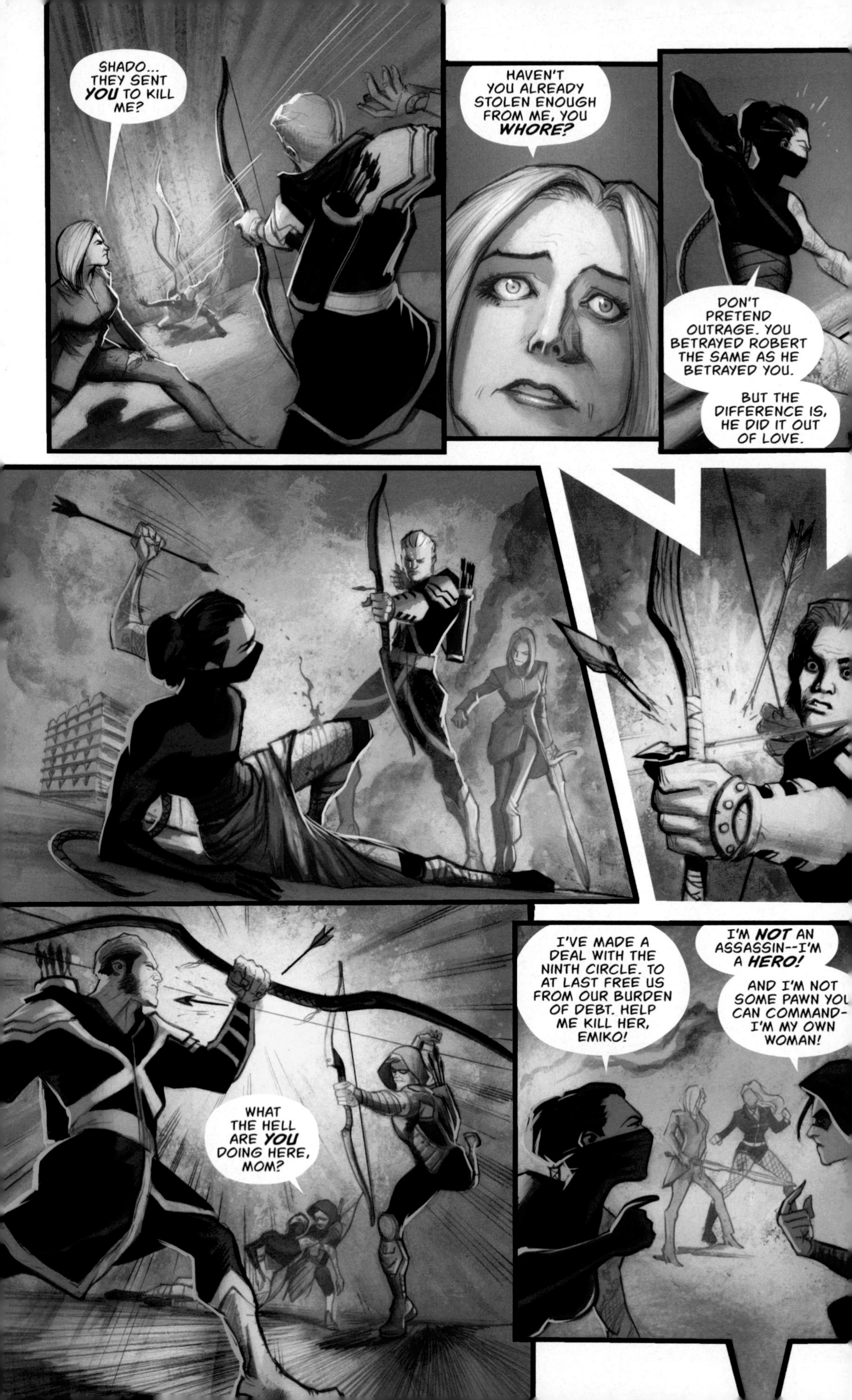
SHADO... THEY SENT YOU TO KILL ME?
HAVEN'T YOU ALREADY STOLEN ENOUGH FROM ME, YOU WHORE?
DON'T PRETEND OUTRAGE. YOU BETRAYED ROBERT THE SAME AS HE BETRAYED YOU.
BUT THE DIFFERENCE IS, HE DID IT OUT OF LOVE.
WHAT THE HELL ARE YOU DOING HERE, MOM?
I'VE MADE A DEAL WITH THE NINTH CIRCLE. TO AT LAST FREE US FROM OUR BURDEN OF DEBT. HELP ME KILL HER, EMIKO!
I'M NOT AN ASSASSIN--I'M A HERO!
AND I'M NOT SOME PAWN YOU CAN COMMAND-I'M MY OWN WOMAN!

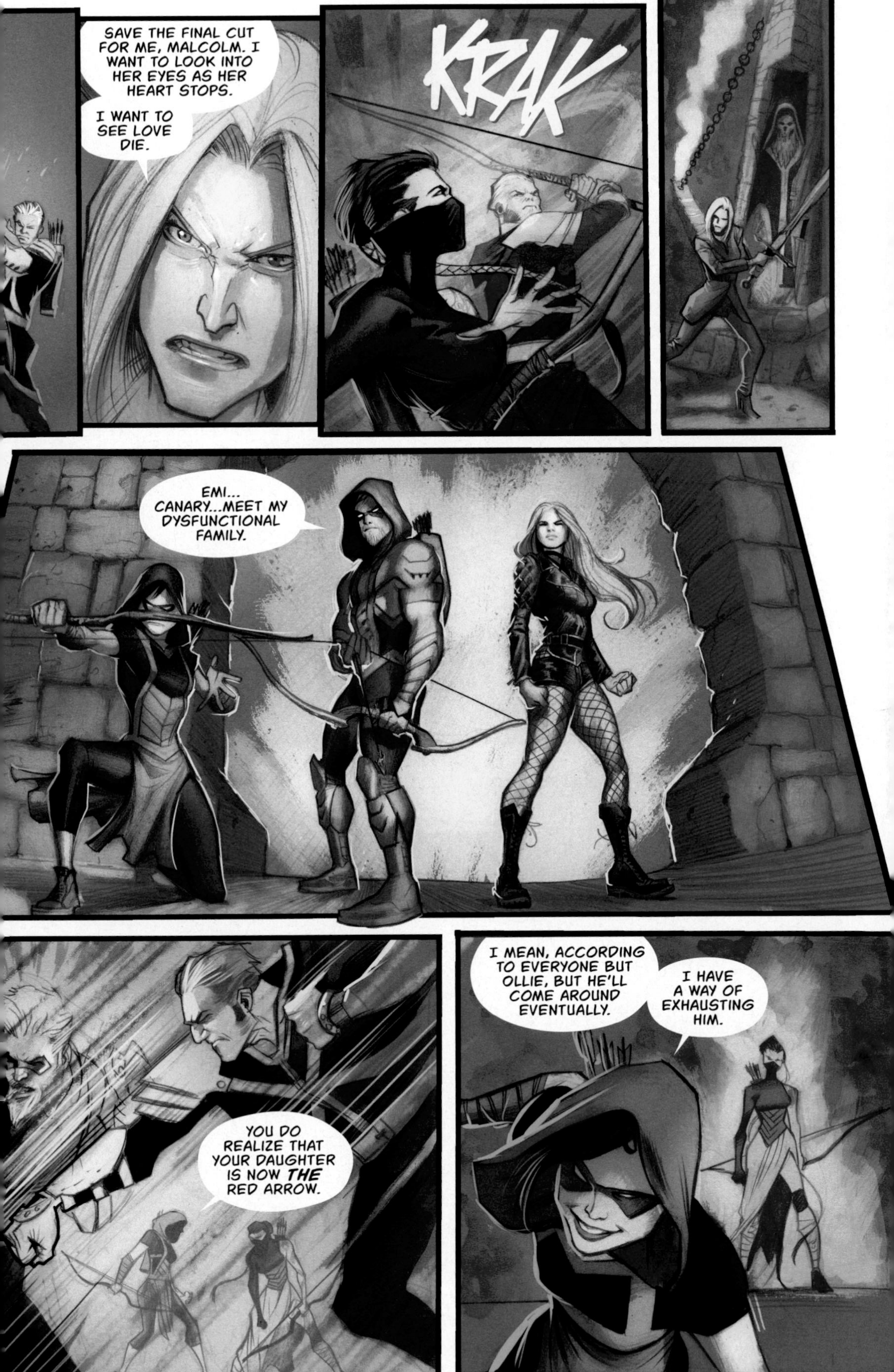

SAVE THE FINAL CUT FOR ME, MALCOLM. I WANT TO LOOK INTO HER EYES AS HER HEART STOPS.
I WANT TO SEE LOVE DIE.
KRAK
EMI... CANARY...MEET MY DYSFUNCTIONAL FAMILY.
YOU DO REALIZE THAT YOUR DAUGHTER IS NOW *THE* RED ARROW.
I MEAN, ACCORDING TO EVERYONE BUT OLLIE, BUT HE'LL COME AROUND EVENTUALLY.
I HAVE A WAY OF EXHAUSTING HIM.

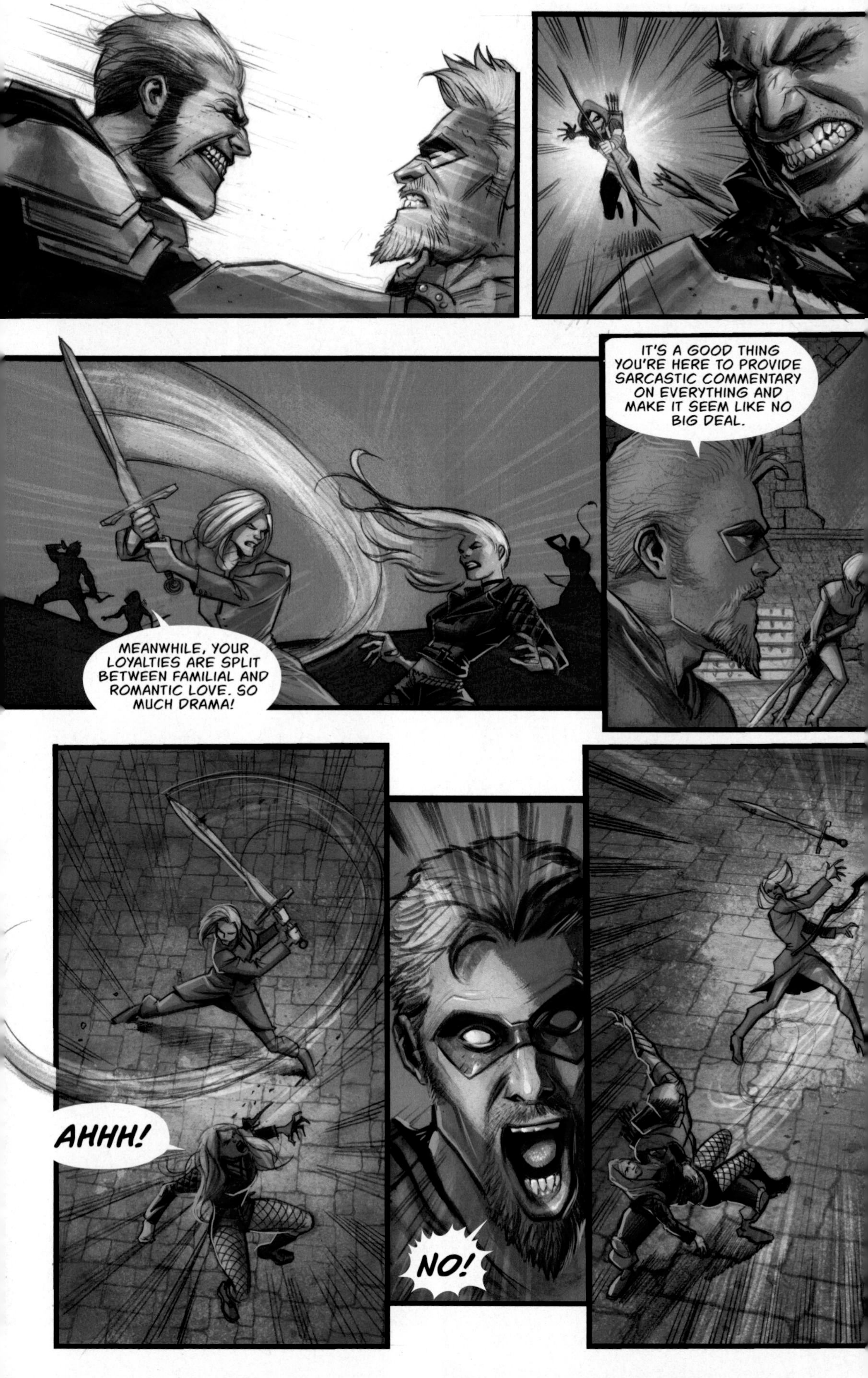
IT'S A GOOD THING YOU'RE HERE TO PROVIDE SARCASTIC COMMENTARY ON EVERYTHING AND MAKE IT SEEM LIKE NO BIG DEAL.
MEANWHILE, YOUR LOYALTIES ARE SPLIT BETWEEN FAMILIAL AND ROMANTIC LOVE. SO MUCH DRAMA!
AHHH!
NO!

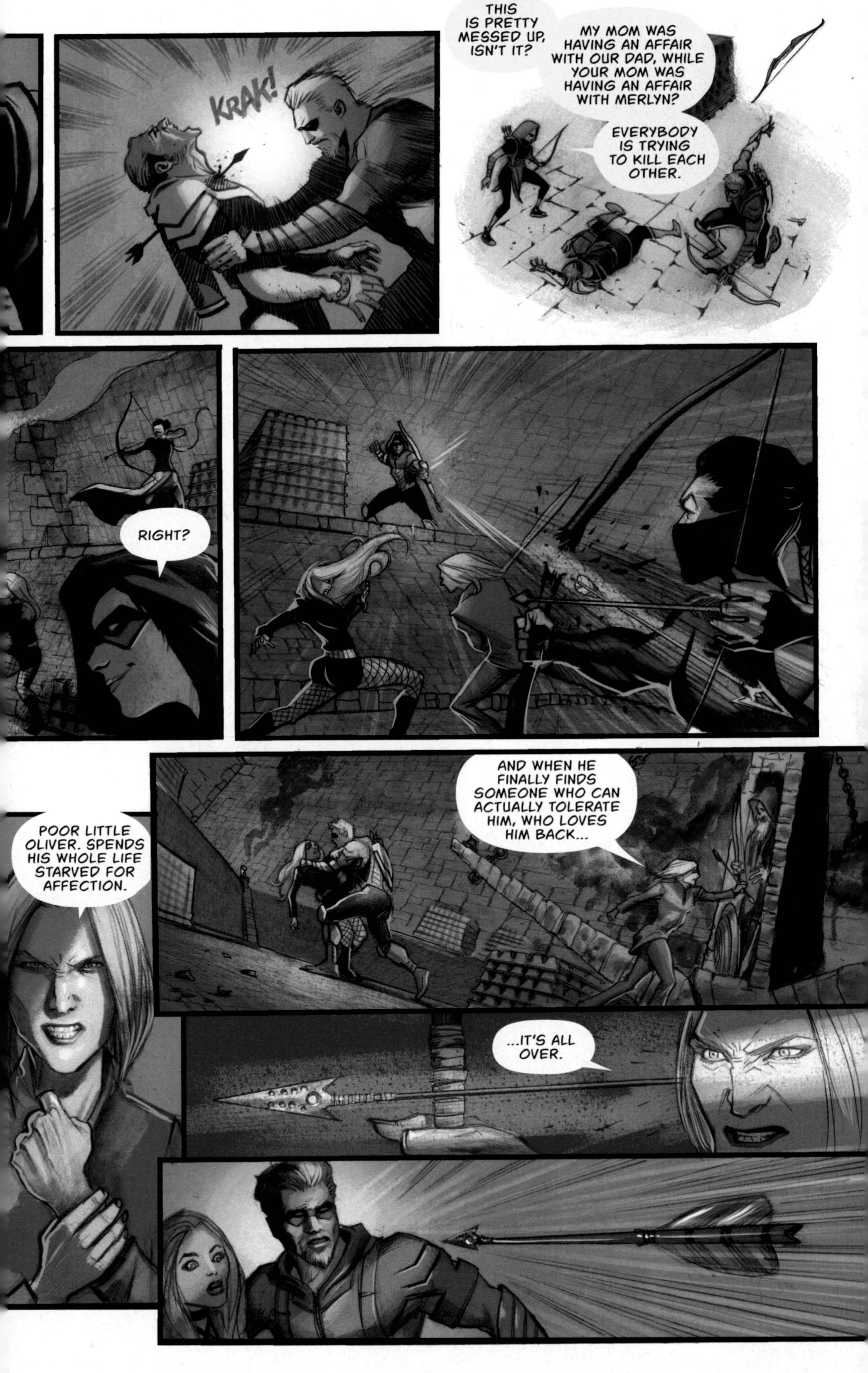
KRAK!
THIS IS PRETTY MESSED UP, ISN'T IT?
MY MOM WAS HAVING AN AFFAIR WITH OUR DAD, WHILE YOUR MOM WAS HAVING AN AFFAIR WITH MERLYN?
EVERYBODY IS TRYING TO KILL EACH OTHER.
RIGHT?
POOR LITTLE OLIVER. SPENDS HIS WHOLE LIFE STARVED FOR AFFECTION.
AND WHEN HE FINALLY FINDS SOMEONE WHO CAN ACTUALLY TOLERATE HIM, WHO LOVES HIM BACK...
...IT'S ALL OVER.

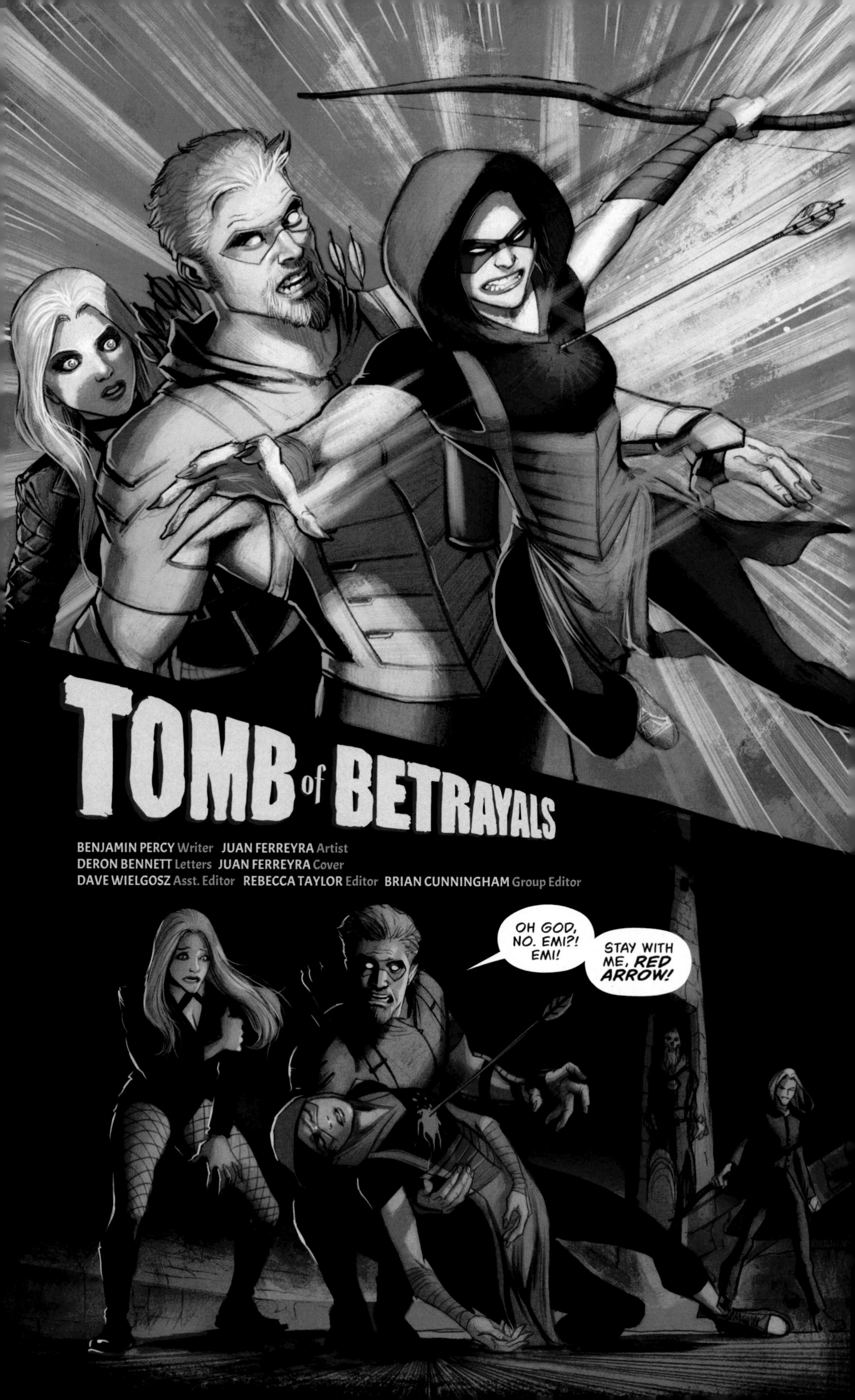
TOMB of BETRAYALS
BENJAMIN PERCY Writer JUAN FERREYRA Artist
DERON BENNETT Letters JUAN FERREYRA Cover
DAVE WIELGOSZ Asst. Editor REBECCA TAYLOR Editor BRIAN CUNNINGHAM Group Editor
OH GOD, NO. EMI?! EMI!
STAY WITH ME, RED ARROW!

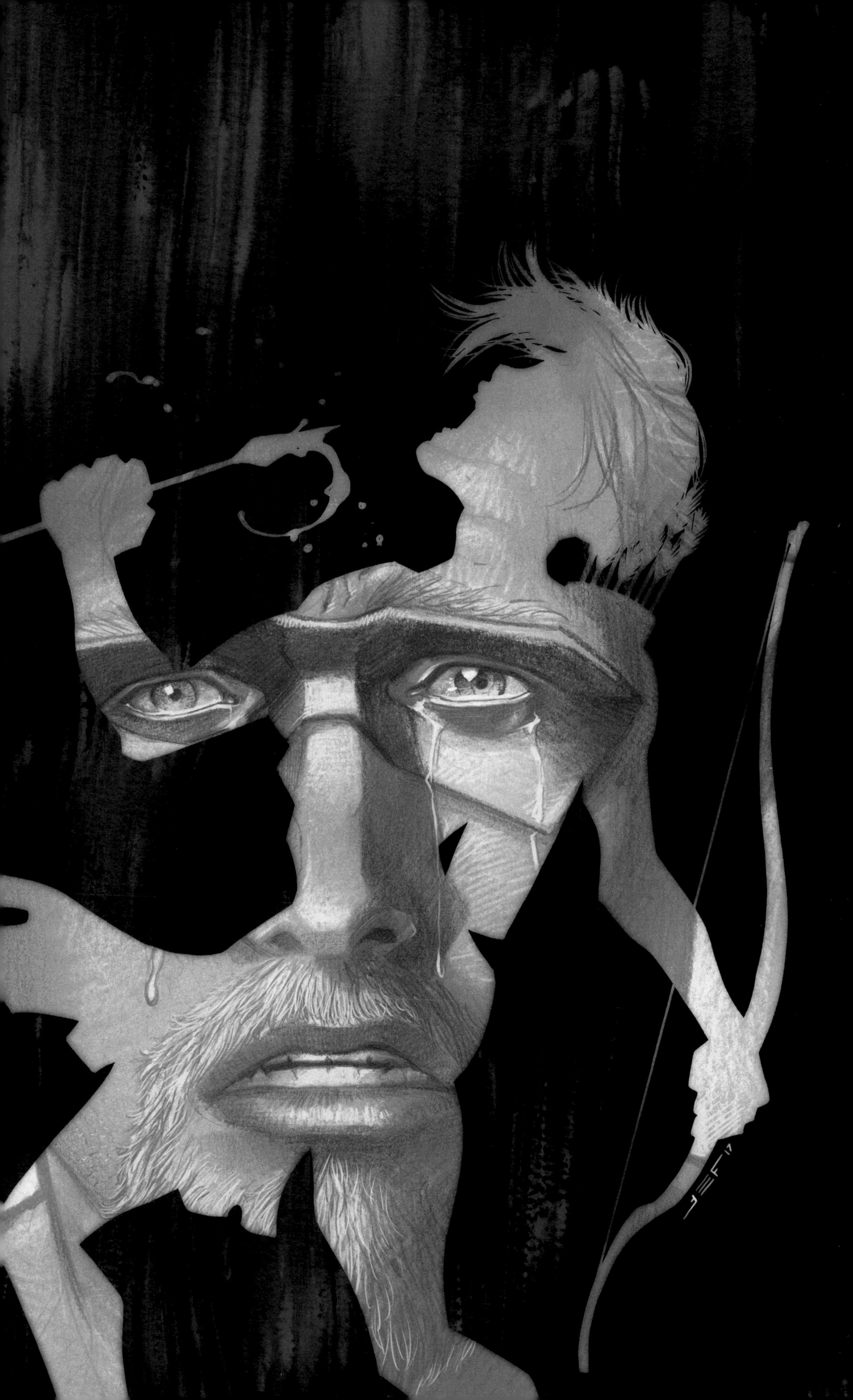

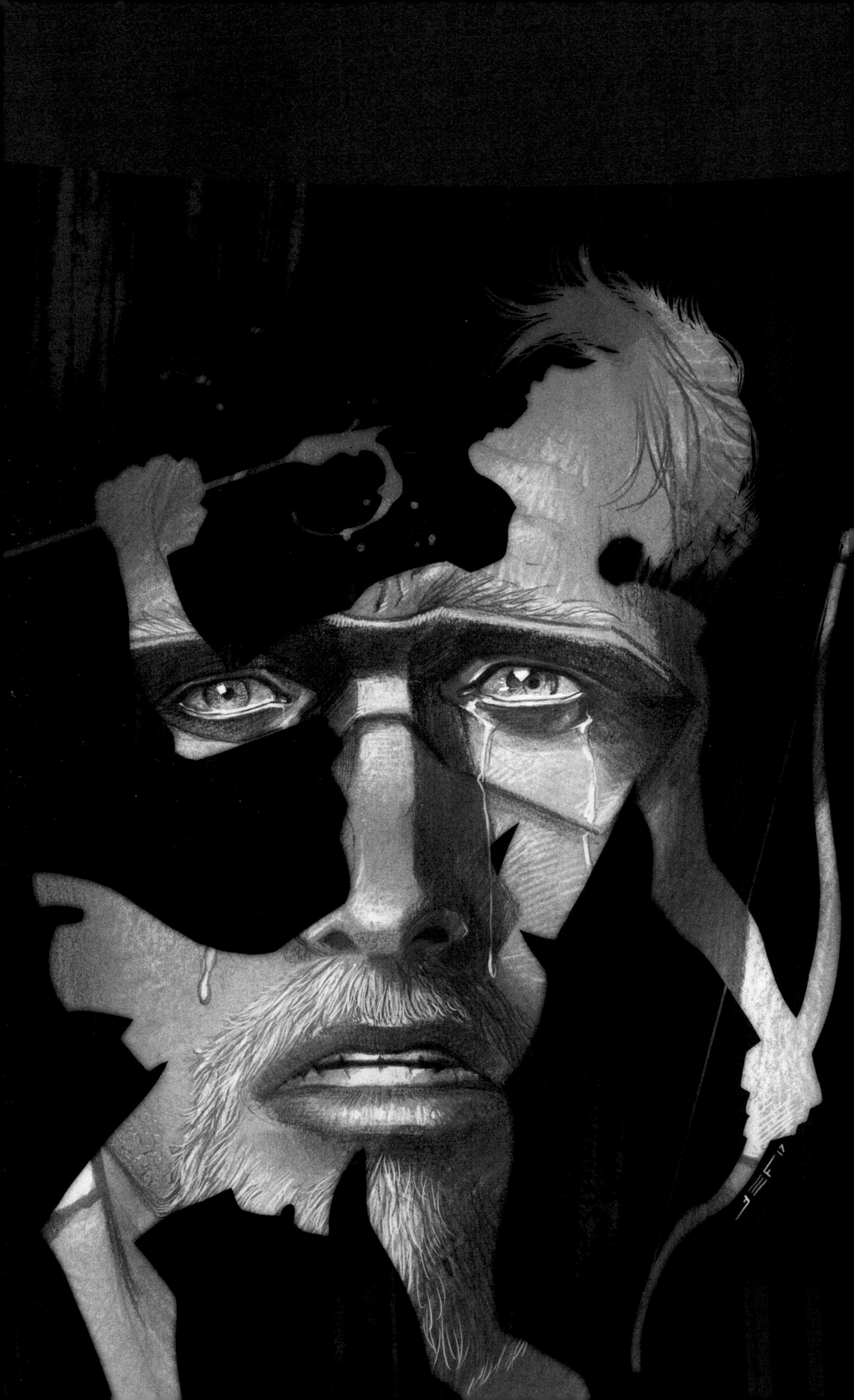

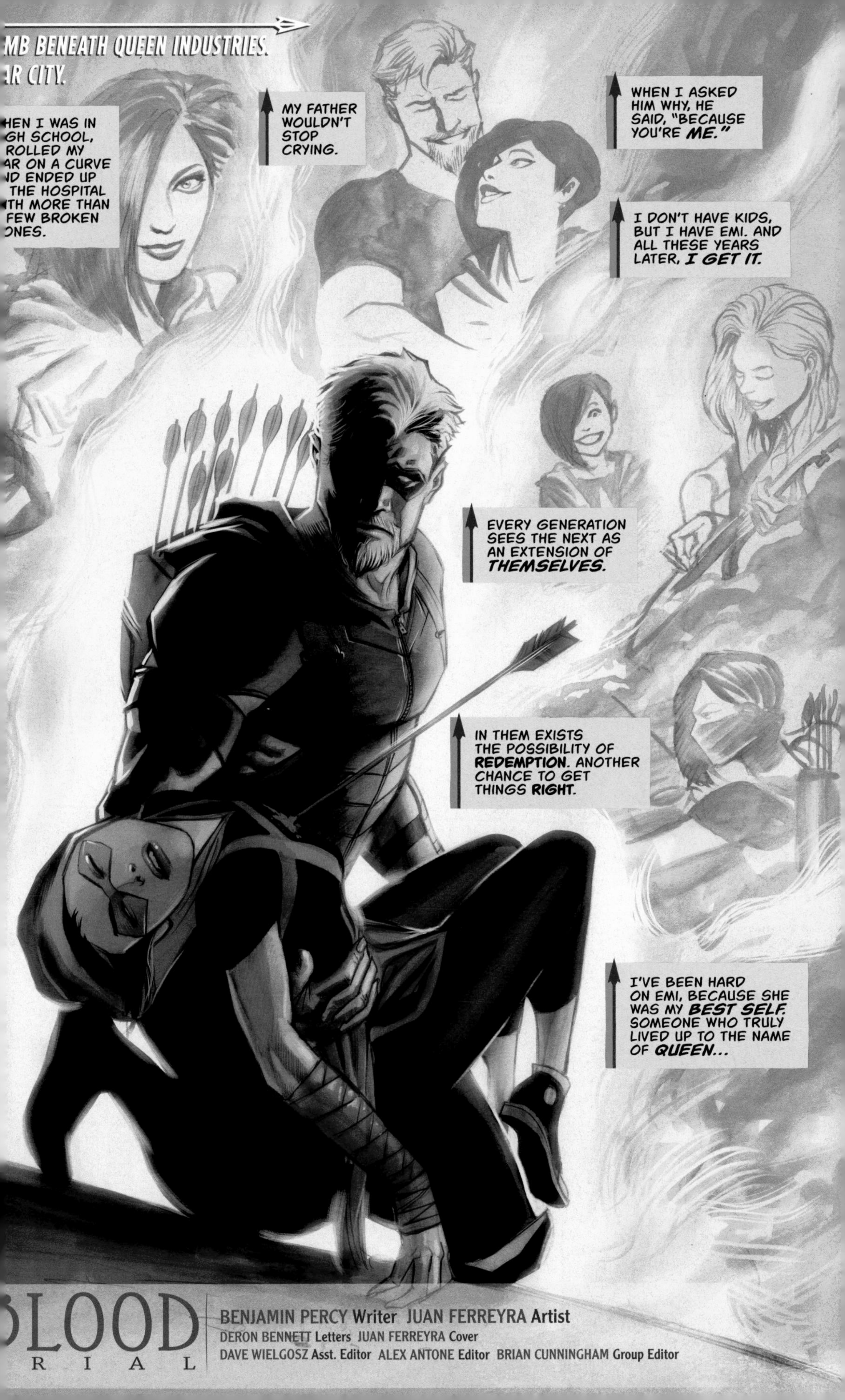

MB BENEATH QUEEN INDUSTRIES.
IR CITY.
HEN I WAS IN GH SCHOOL, ROLLED MY AR ON A CURVE ND ENDED UP THE HOSPITAL TH MORE THAN FEW BROKEN ONES.
MY FATHER WOULDN'T STOP CRYING.
WHEN I ASKED HIM WHY, HE SAID, "BECAUSE YOU'RE ME."
I DON'T HAVE KIDS, BUT I HAVE EMI. AND ALL THESE YEARS LATER, I GET IT.
EVERY GENERATION SEES THE NEXT AS AN EXTENSION OF THEMSELVES.
IN THEM EXISTS THE POSSIBILITY OF REDEMPTION. ANOTHER CHANCE TO GET THINGS RIGHT.
I'VE BEEN HARD ON EMI, BECAUSE SHE WAS MY BEST SELF. SOMEONE WHO TRULY LIVED UP TO THE NAME OF QUEEN...
BLOOD
RIAL
BENJAMIN PERCY Writer JUAN FERREYRA Artist
DERON BENNETT Letters JUAN FERREYRA Cover
DAVE WIELGOSZ Asst. Editor ALEX ANTONE Editor BRIAN CUNNINGHAM Group Editor

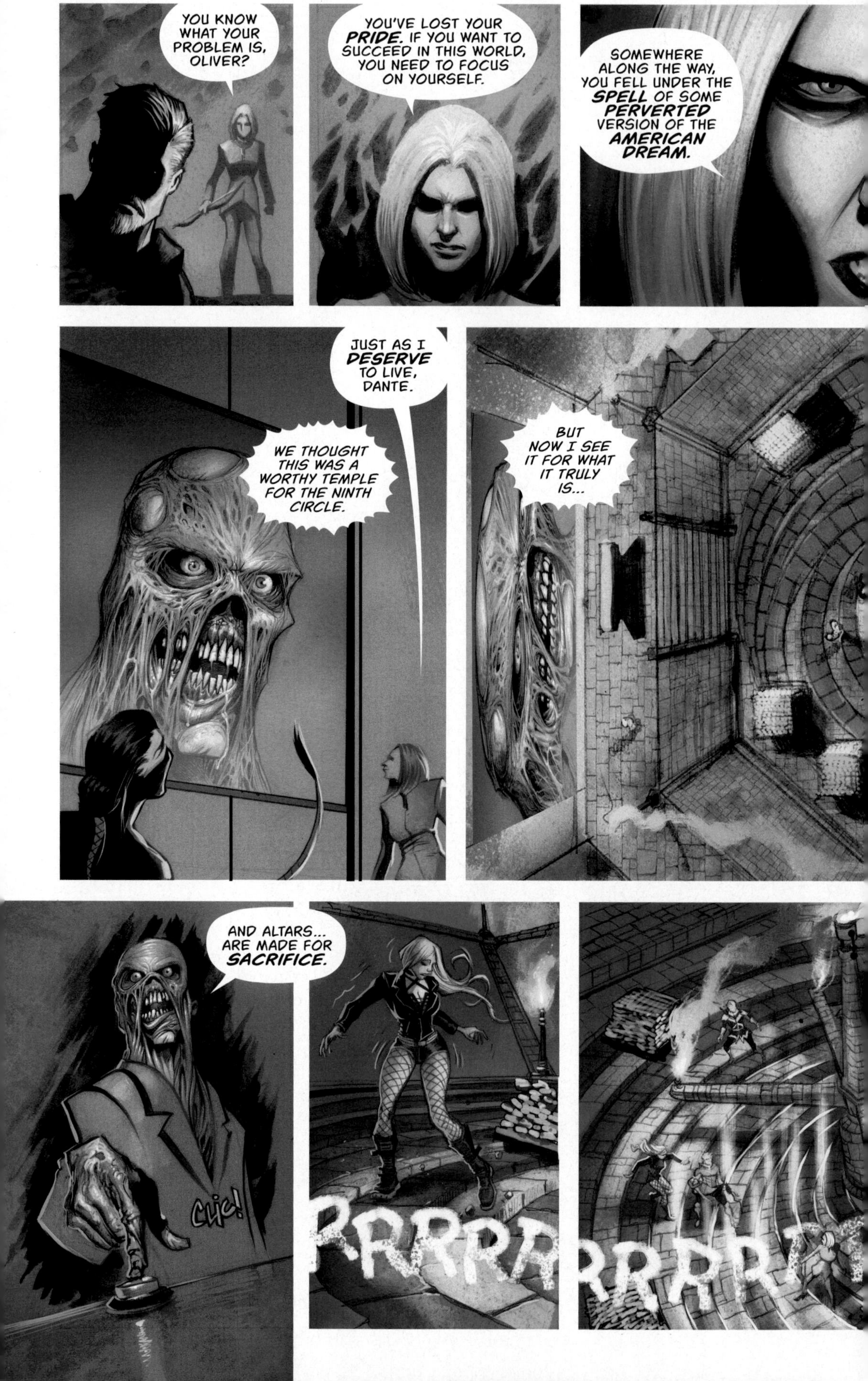
YOU KNOW WHAT YOUR PROBLEM IS, OLIVER?
YOU'VE LOST YOUR **PRIDE.** IF YOU WANT TO SUCCEED IN THIS WORLD, YOU NEED TO FOCUS ON YOURSELF.
SOMEWHERE ALONG THE WAY, YOU FELL UNDER THE **SPELL** OF SOME **PERVERTED** VERSION OF THE **AMERICAN DREAM.**
JUST AS I **DESERVE** TO LIVE, DANTE.
WE THOUGHT THIS WAS A WORTHY TEMPLE FOR THE NINTH CIRCLE.
BUT NOW I SEE IT FOR WHAT IT TRULY IS...
AND ALTARS... ARE MADE FOR **SACRIFICE.**
CLIC!
RRRRR
RRRRRT

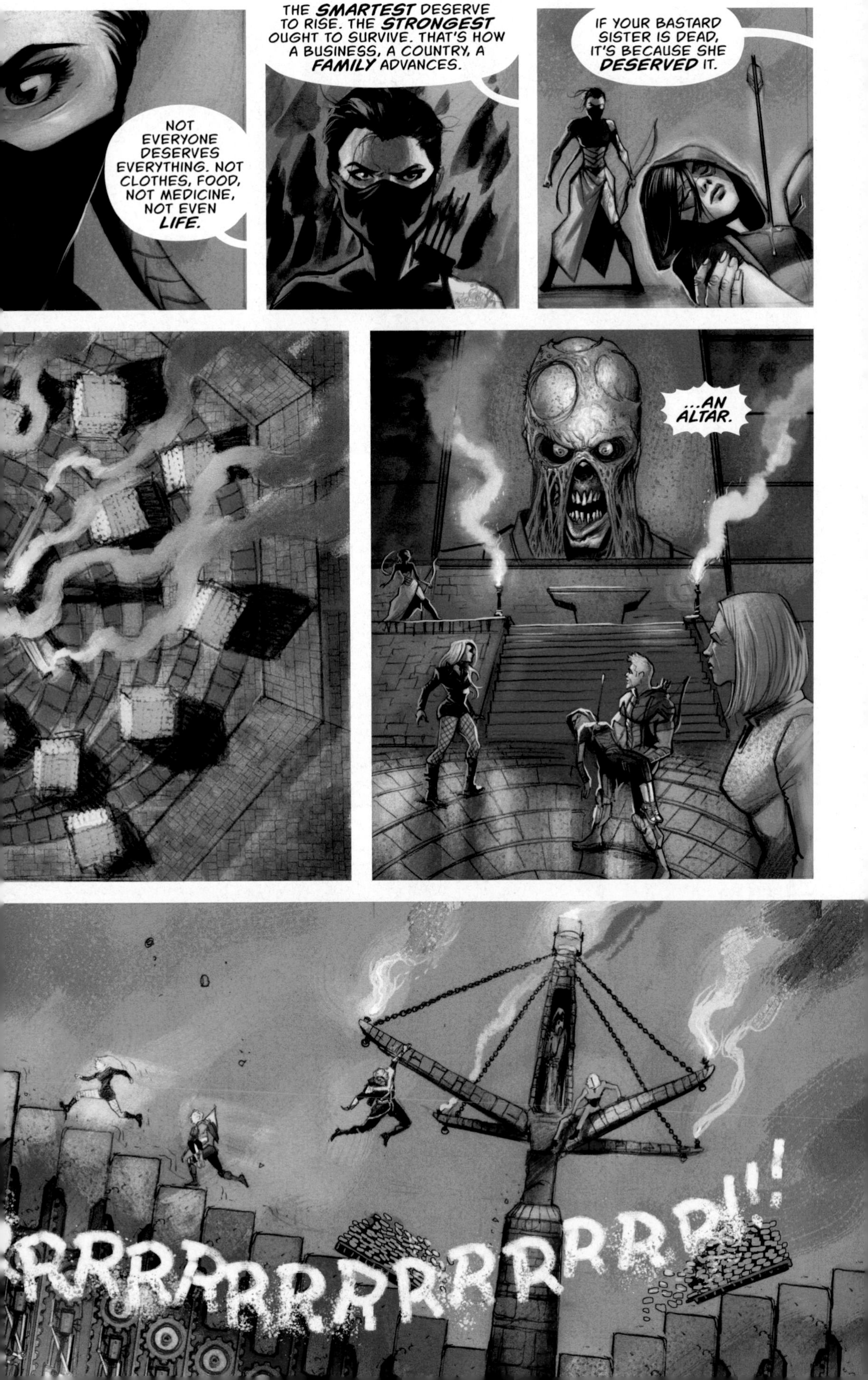
NOT EVERYONE DESERVES EVERYTHING. NOT CLOTHES, FOOD, NOT MEDICINE, NOT EVEN LIFE.
THE SMARTEST DESERVE TO RISE. THE STRONGEST OUGHT TO SURVIVE. THAT'S HOW A BUSINESS, A COUNTRY, A FAMILY ADVANCES.
IF YOUR BASTARD SISTER IS DEAD, IT'S BECAUSE SHE DESERVED IT.
...AN ALTAR.
RRRRRRRRRRRRRB!!

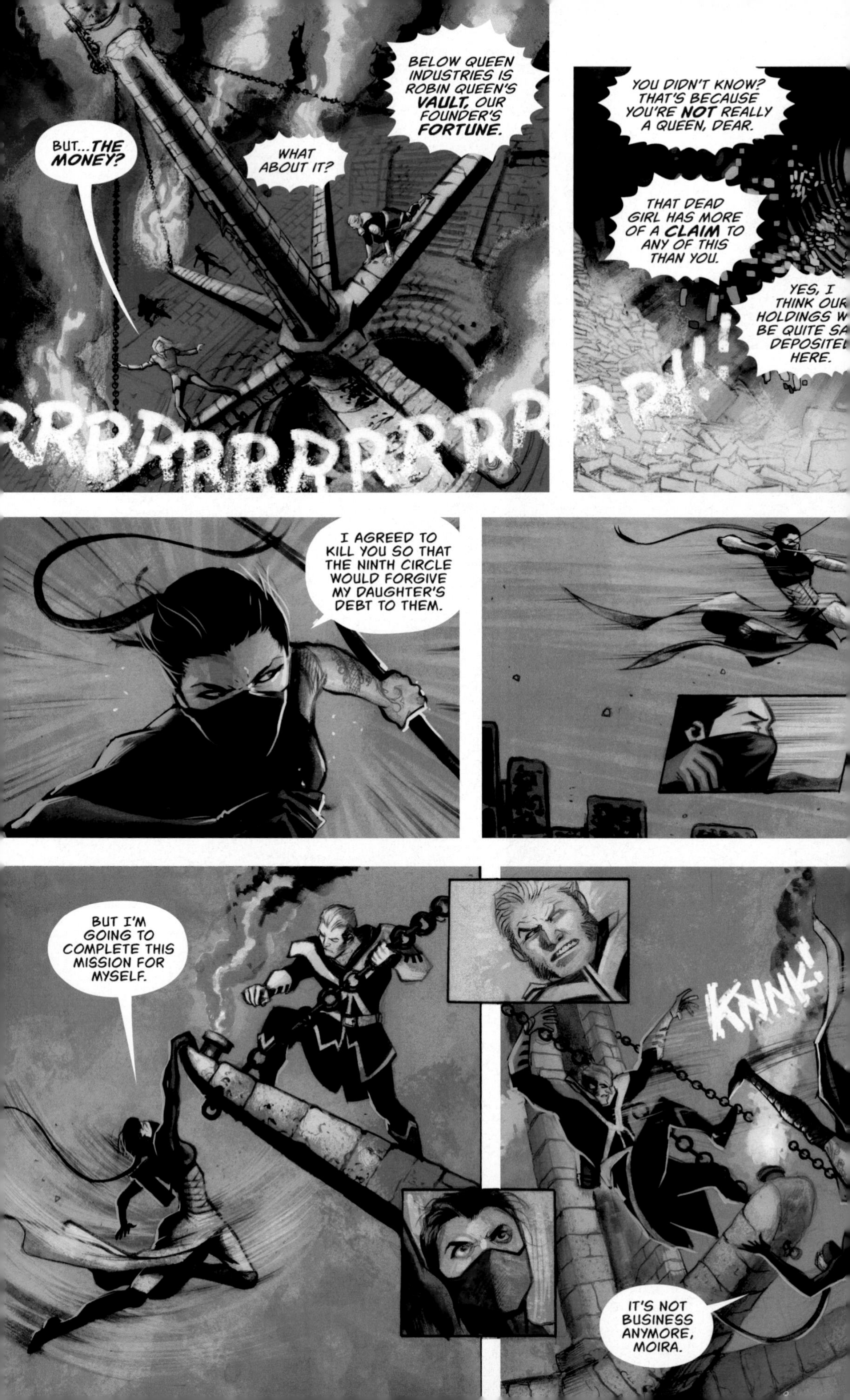
BUT...THE MONEY?
WHAT ABOUT IT?
BELOW QUEEN INDUSTRIES IS ROBIN QUEEN'S VAULT, OUR FOUNDER'S FORTUNE.
YOU DIDN'T KNOW? THAT'S BECAUSE YOU'RE NOT REALLY A QUEEN, DEAR.
THAT DEAD GIRL HAS MORE OF A CLAIM TO ANY OF THIS THAN YOU.
YES, I THINK OUR HOLDINGS W BE QUITE SA DEPOSITE HERE.
I AGREED TO KILL YOU SO THAT THE NINTH CIRCLE WOULD FORGIVE MY DAUGHTER'S DEBT TO THEM.
BUT I'M GOING TO COMPLETE THIS MISSION FOR MYSELF.
KNNK!
IT'S NOT BUSINESS ANYMORE, MOIRA.

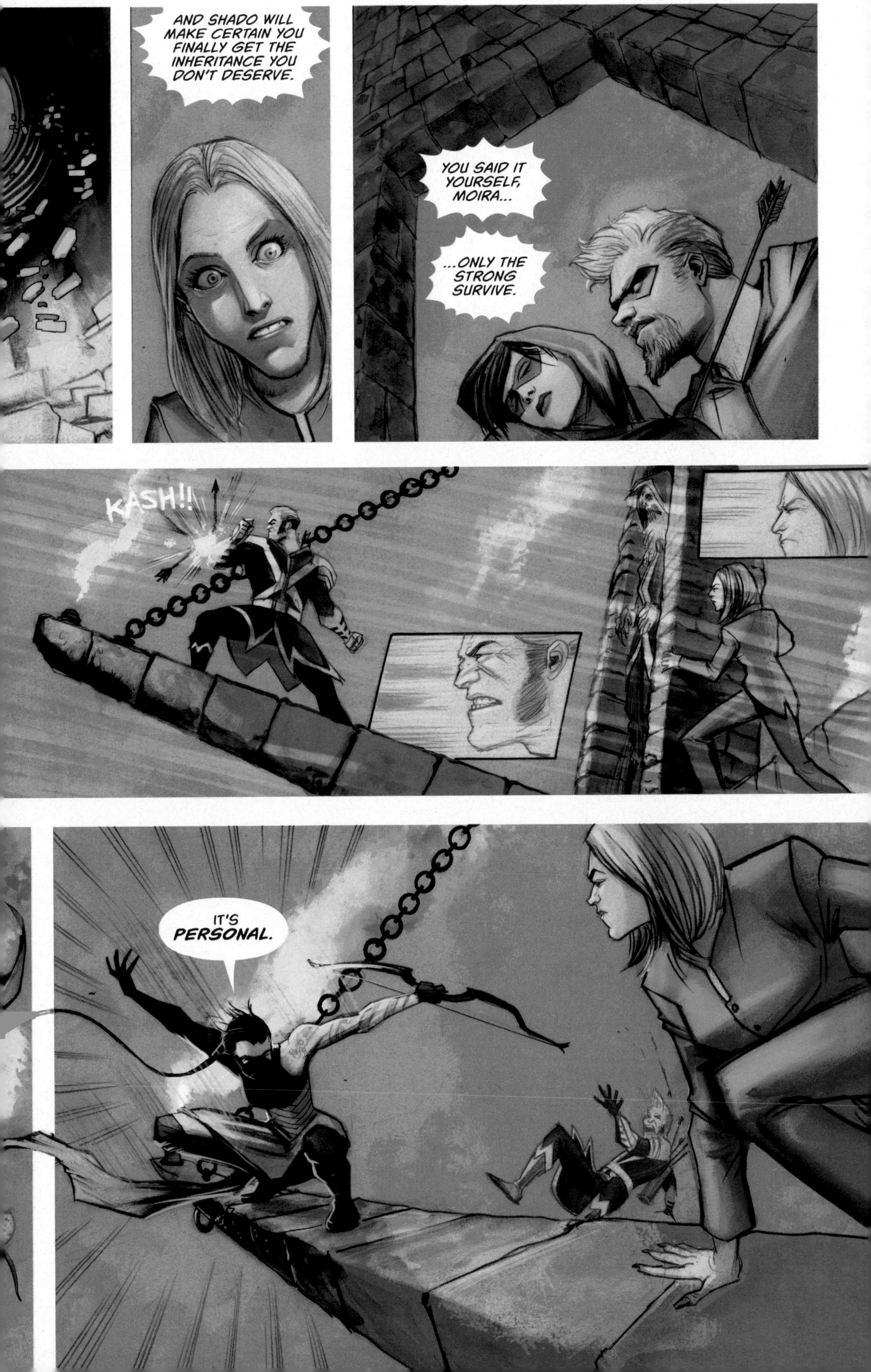
AND SHADO WILL MAKE CERTAIN YOU FINALLY GET THE INHERITANCE YOU DON'T DESERVE.
YOU SAID IT YOURSELF, MOIRA...
...ONLY THE STRONG SURVIVE.
KASH!!
IT'S PERSONAL.

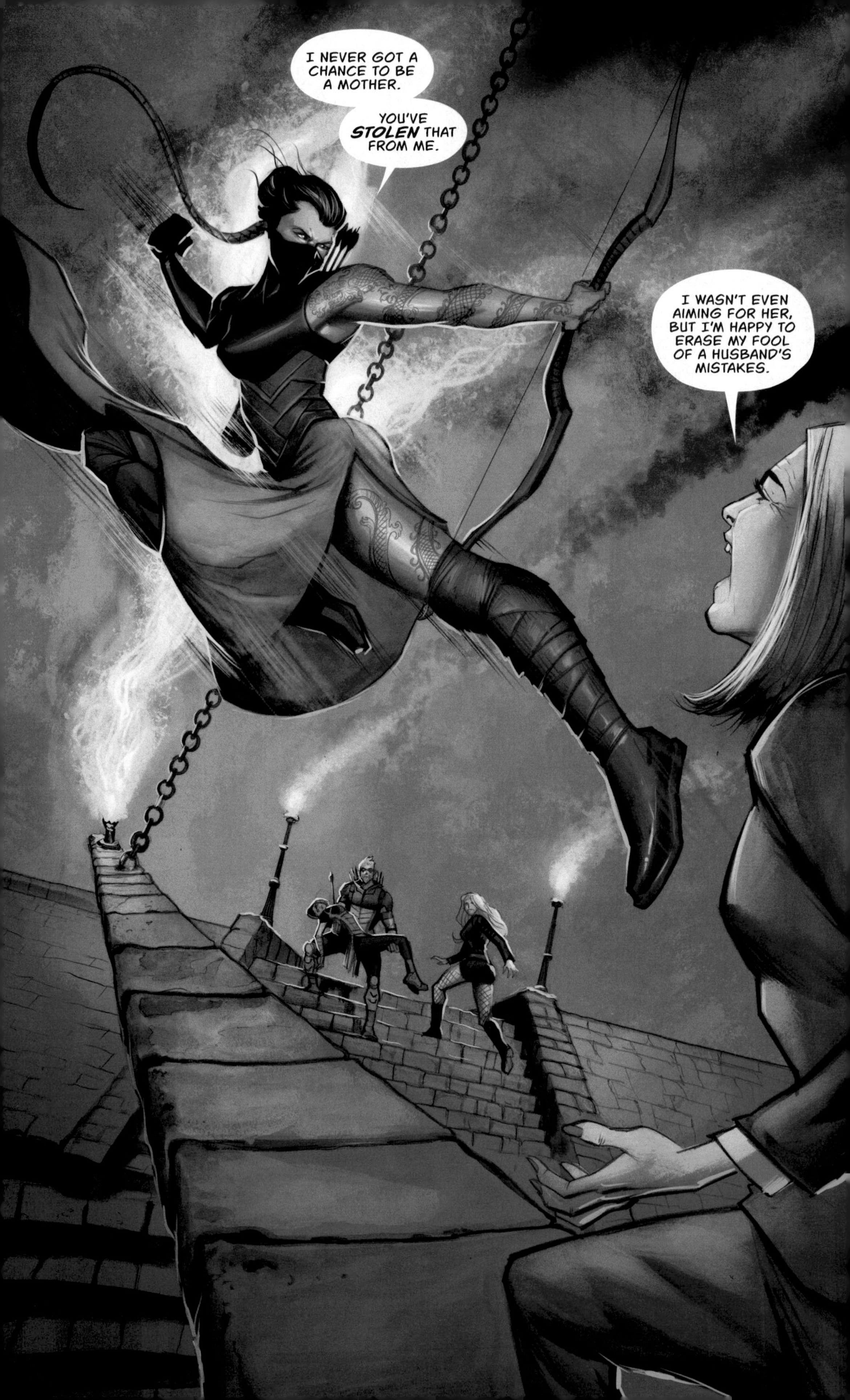
I NEVER GOT A CHANCE TO BE A MOTHER.
YOU'VE STOLEN THAT FROM ME.
I WASN'T EVEN AIMING FOR HER, BUT I'M HAPPY TO ERASE MY FOOL OF A HUSBAND'S MISTAKES.

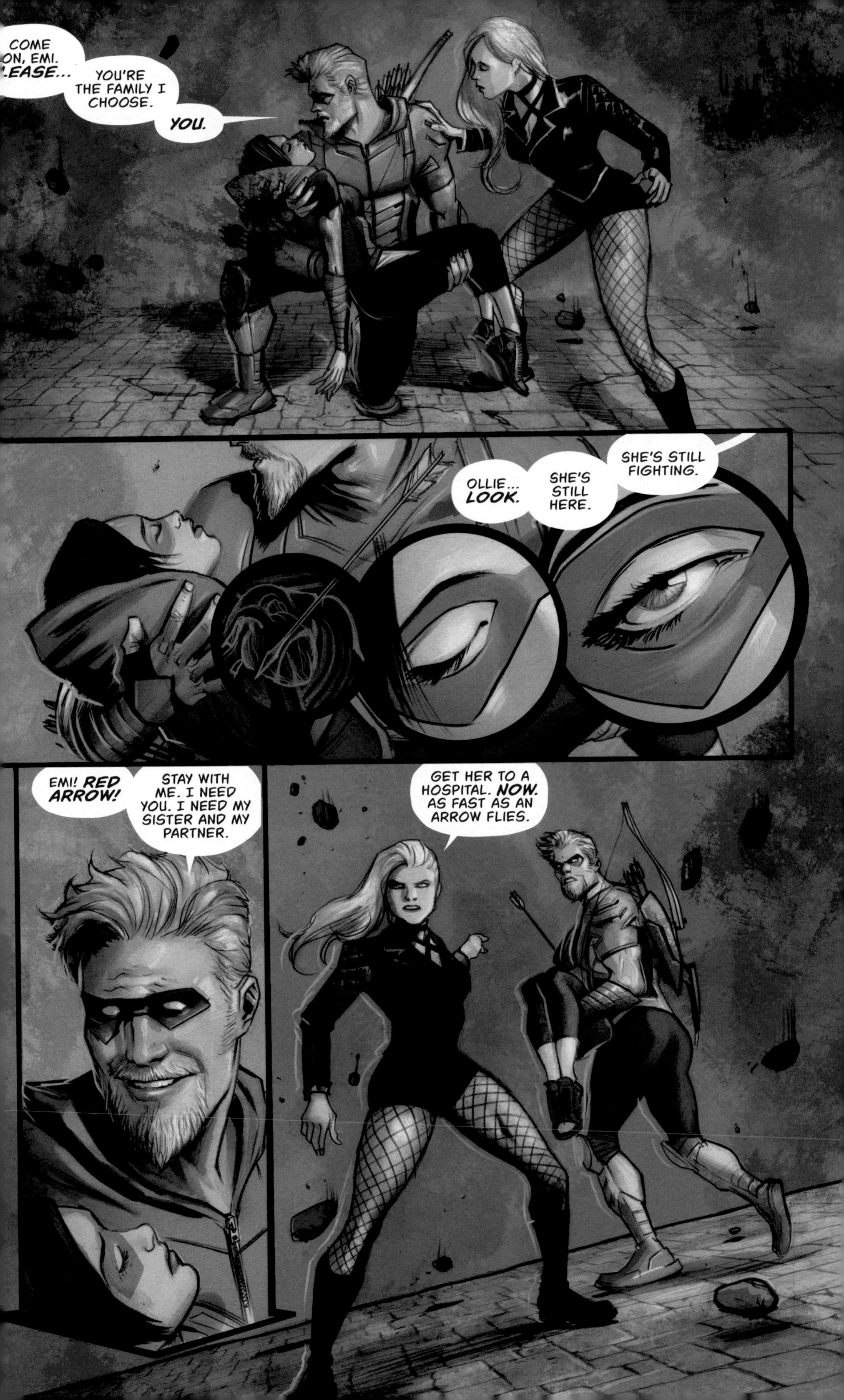
COME ON, EMI. PLEASE...
YOU'RE THE FAMILY I CHOOSE.
YOU.
OLLIE... **LOOK.**
SHE'S STILL HERE.
SHE'S STILL FIGHTING.
EMI! **RED ARROW!**
STAY WITH ME. I NEED YOU. I NEED MY SISTER AND MY PARTNER.
GET HER TO A HOSPITAL. **NOW.** AS FAST AS AN ARROW FLIES.

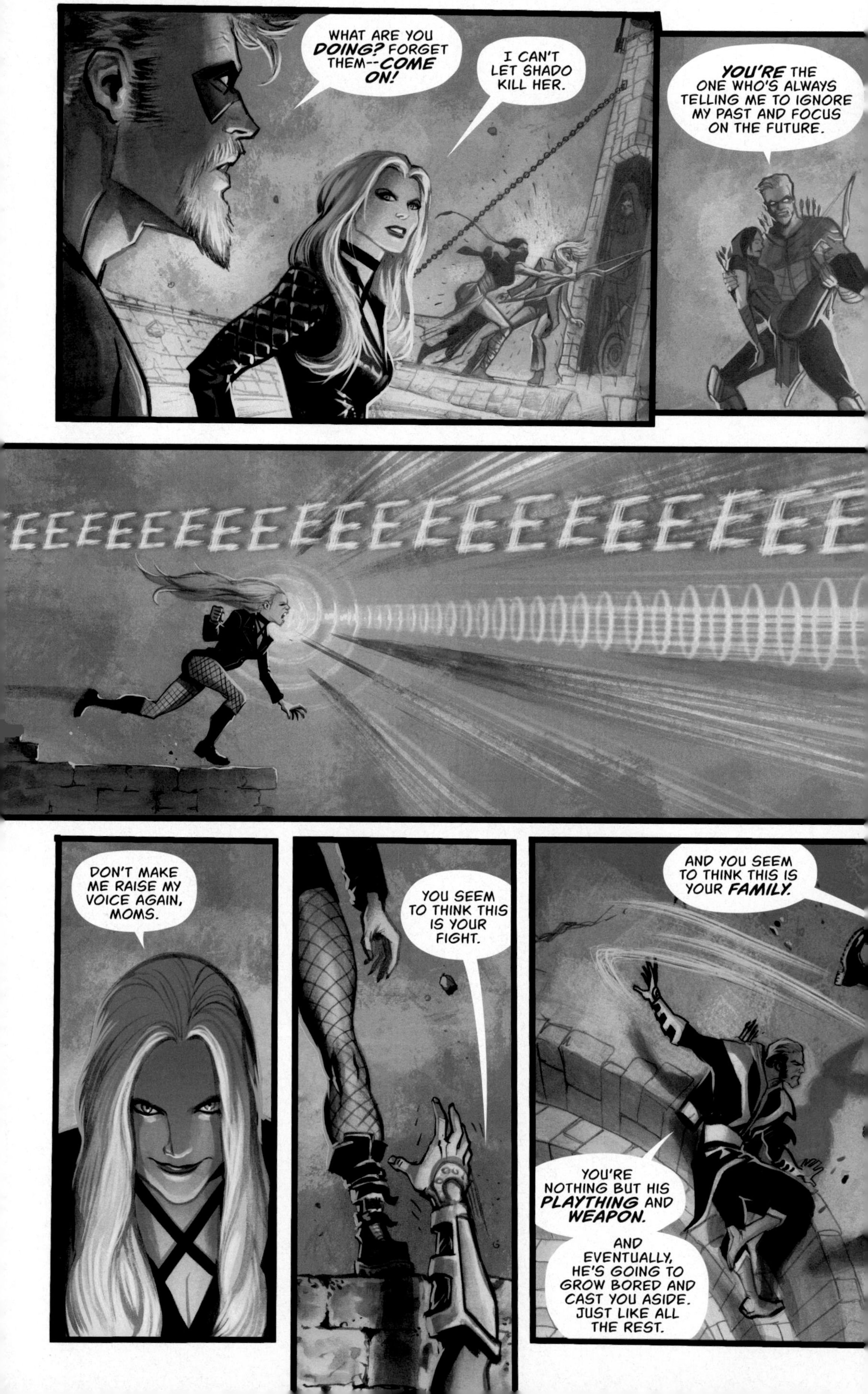
WHAT ARE YOU *DOING?* FORGET THEM--*COME ON!*
I CAN'T LET SHADO KILL HER.
YOU'RE THE ONE WHO'S ALWAYS TELLING ME TO IGNORE MY PAST AND FOCUS ON THE FUTURE.
EEEEEEEEEEEEEEEEEEEEEEEE
DON'T MAKE ME RAISE MY VOICE AGAIN, MOMS.
YOU SEEM TO THINK THIS IS YOUR FIGHT.
AND YOU SEEM TO THINK THIS IS YOUR *FAMILY.*
YOU'RE NOTHING BUT HIS *PLAYTHING* AND *WEAPON.*
AND EVENTUALLY, HE'S GOING TO GROW BORED AND CAST YOU ASIDE. JUST LIKE ALL THE REST.

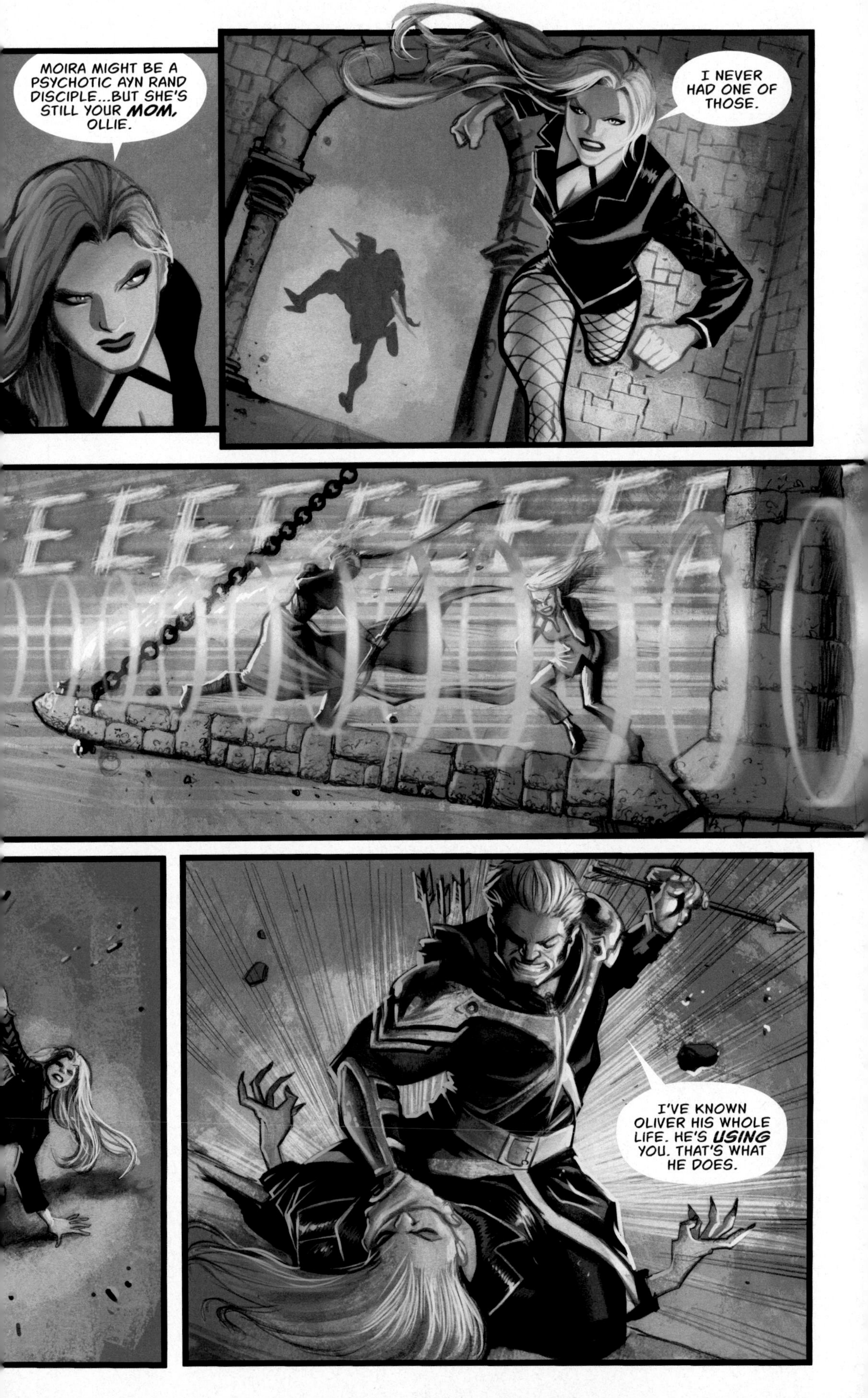
MOIRA MIGHT BE A PSYCHOTIC AYN RAND DISCIPLE...BUT SHE'S STILL YOUR MOM, OLLIE.
I NEVER HAD ONE OF THOSE.
I'VE KNOWN OLIVER HIS WHOLE LIFE. HE'S USING YOU. THAT'S WHAT HE DOES.

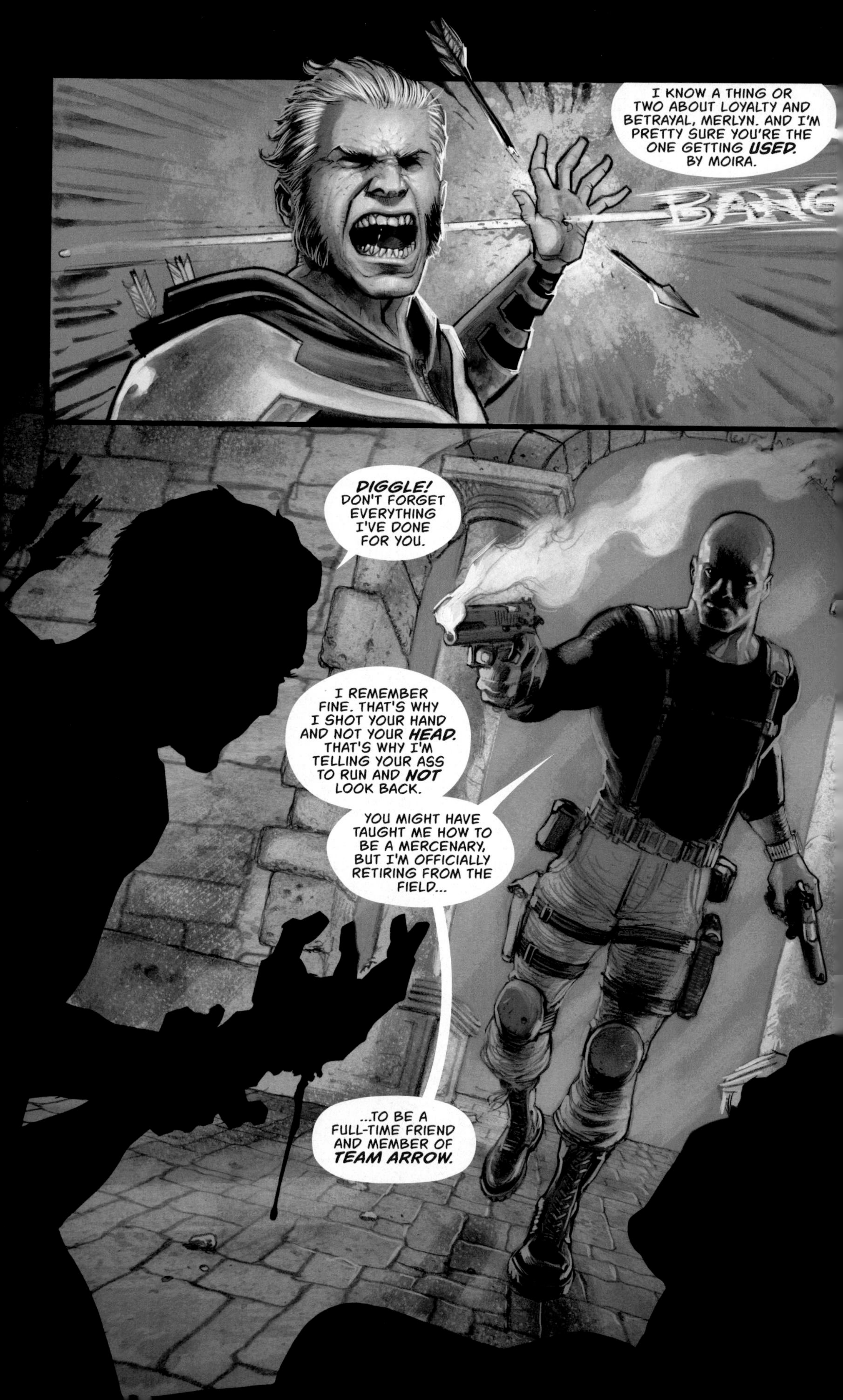

I KNOW A THING OR TWO ABOUT LOYALTY AND BETRAYAL, MERLYN. AND I'M PRETTY SURE YOU'RE THE ONE GETTING **USED.** BY MOIRA.
BANG
DIGGLE! DON'T FORGET EVERYTHING I'VE DONE FOR YOU.
I REMEMBER FINE. THAT'S WHY I SHOT YOUR HAND AND NOT YOUR **HEAD.** THAT'S WHY I'M TELLING YOUR ASS TO RUN AND **NOT** LOOK BACK.
YOU MIGHT HAVE TAUGHT ME HOW TO BE A MERCENARY, BUT I'M OFFICIALLY RETIRING FROM THE FIELD...
...TO BE A FULL-TIME FRIEND AND MEMBER OF **TEAM ARROW.**

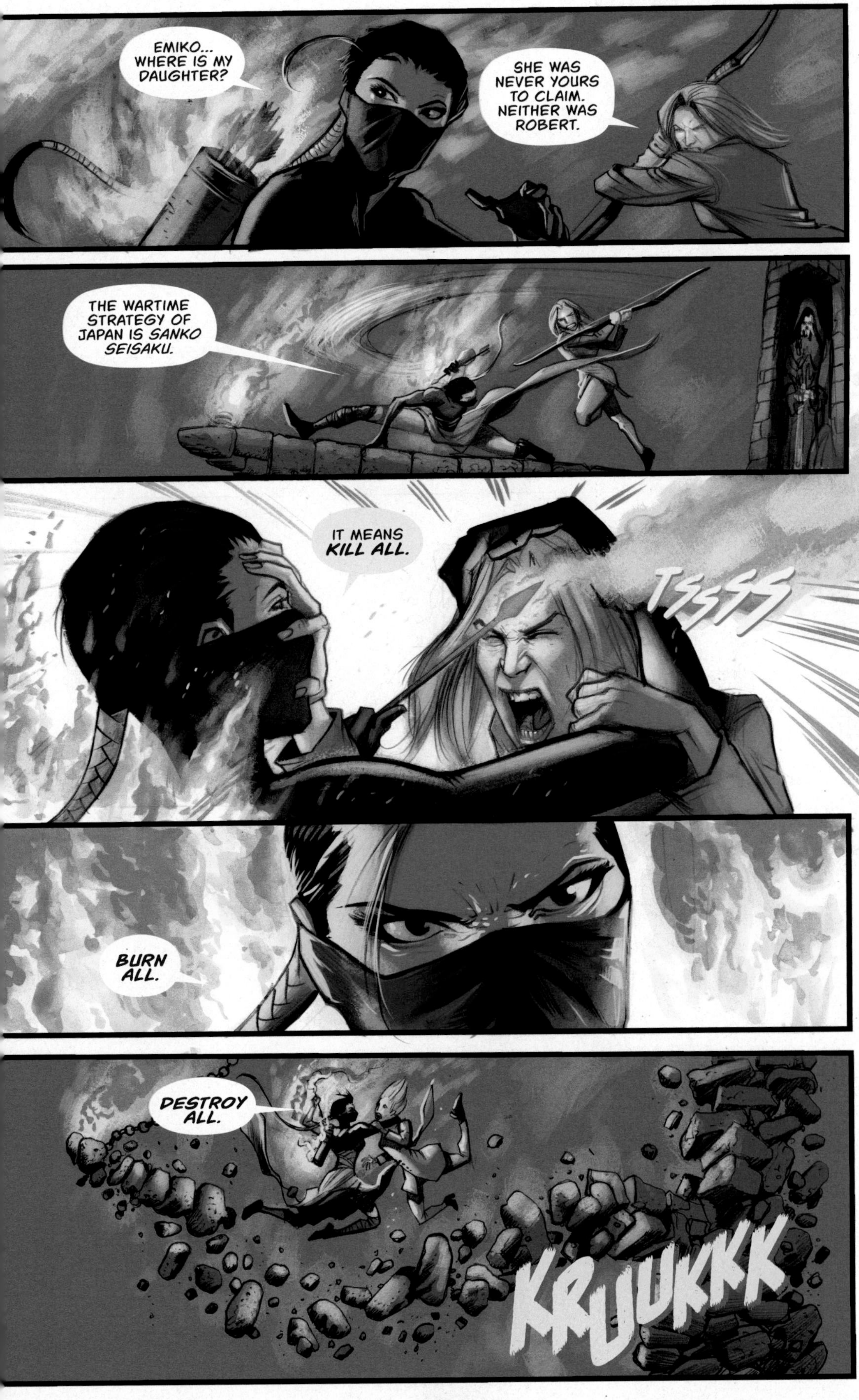
EMIKO... WHERE IS MY DAUGHTER?
SHE WAS NEVER YOURS TO CLAIM. NEITHER WAS ROBERT.
THE WARTIME STRATEGY OF JAPAN IS SANKO SEISAKU.
IT MEANS KILL ALL.
TSSSS
BURN ALL.
DESTROY ALL.
KRUUKKK

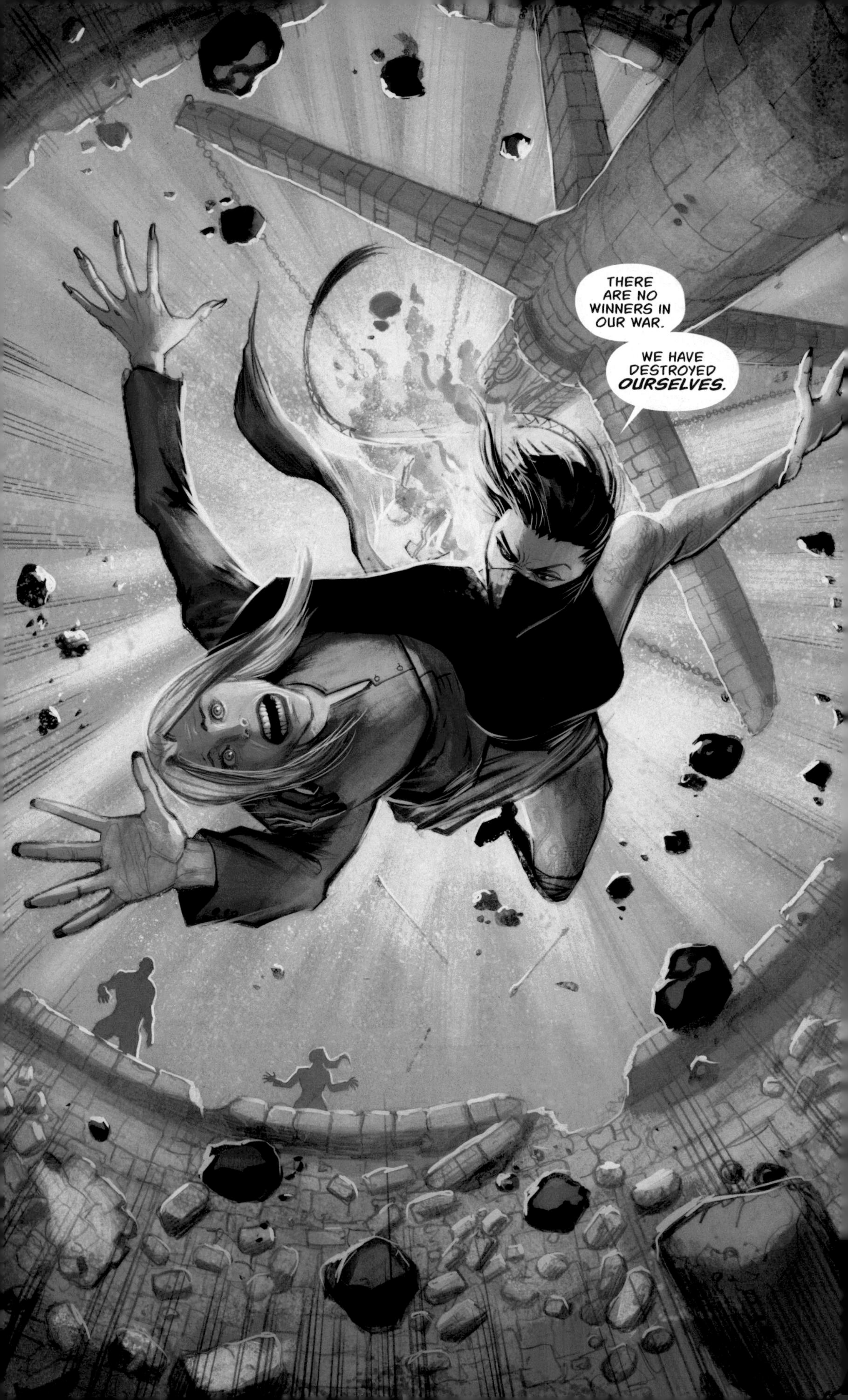
THERE ARE NO WINNERS IN OUR WAR.
WE HAVE DESTROYED OURSELVES.

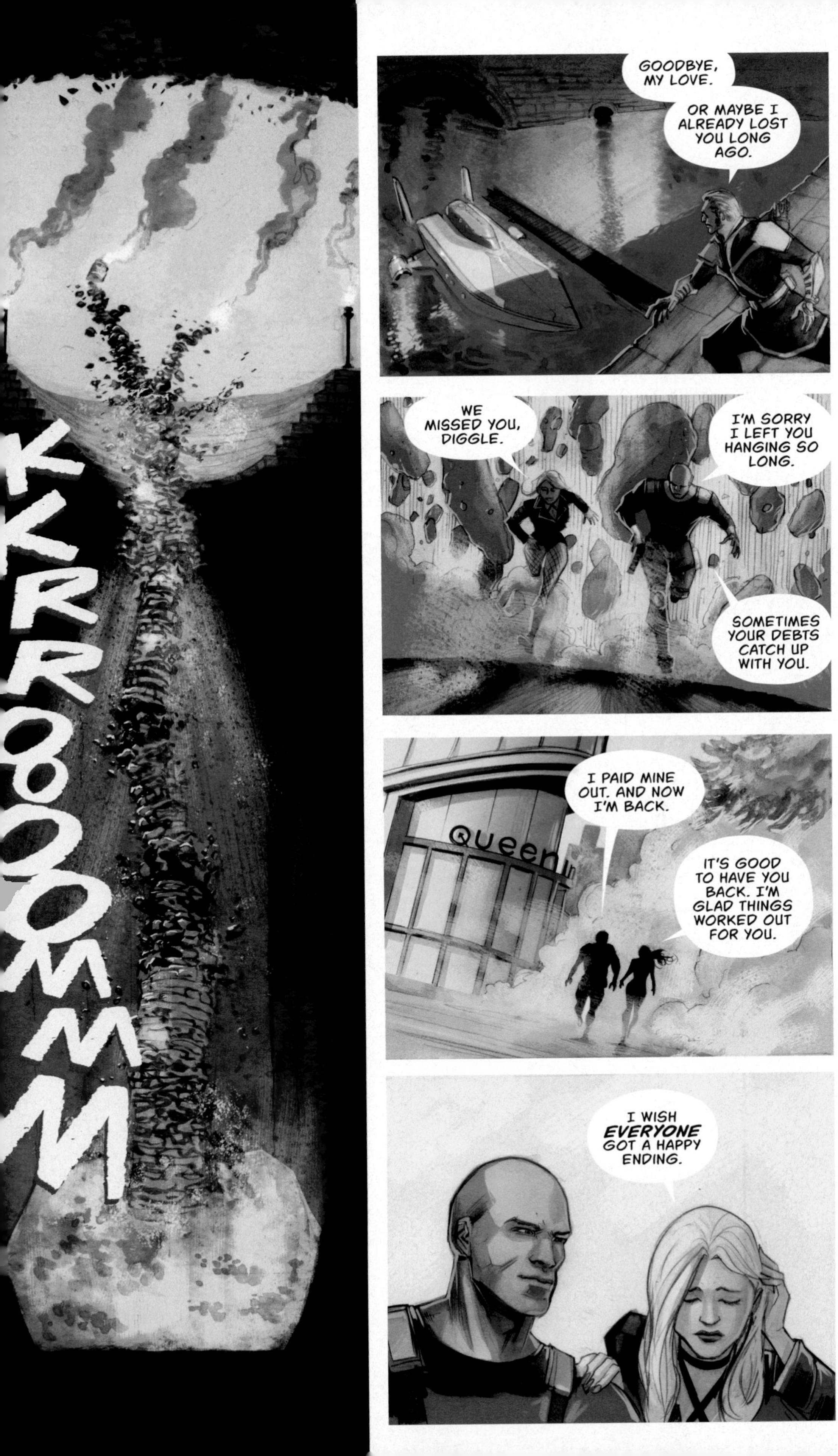
KKRROOOMMM
GOODBYE, MY LOVE.
OR MAYBE I ALREADY LOST YOU LONG AGO.
WE MISSED YOU, DIGGLE.
I'M SORRY I LEFT YOU HANGING SO LONG.
SOMETIMES YOUR DEBTS CATCH UP WITH YOU.
I PAID MINE OUT. AND NOW I'M BACK.
Queen
IT'S GOOD TO HAVE YOU BACK. I'M GLAD THINGS WORKED OUT FOR YOU.
I WISH *EVERYONE* GOT A HAPPY ENDING.

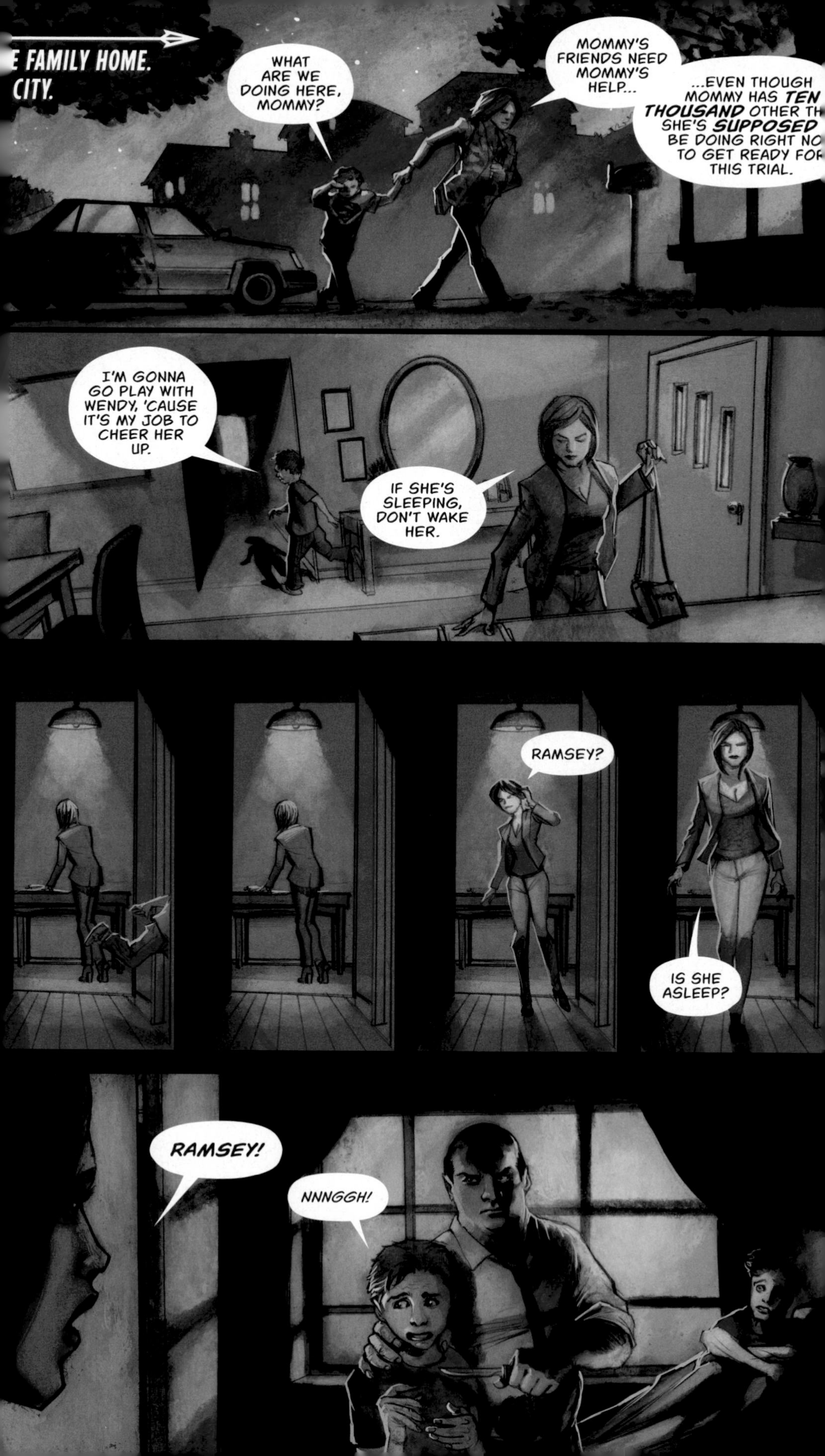
E FAMILY HOME.
CITY.
WHAT ARE WE DOING HERE, MOMMY?
MOMMY'S FRIENDS NEED MOMMY'S HELP...
...EVEN THOUGH MOMMY HAS TEN THOUSAND OTHER TH SHE'S SUPPOSED BE DOING RIGHT NO TO GET READY FOR THIS TRIAL.
I'M GONNA GO PLAY WITH WENDY, 'CAUSE IT'S MY JOB TO CHEER HER UP.
IF SHE'S SLEEPING, DON'T WAKE HER.
RAMSEY?
IS SHE ASLEEP?
RAMSEY!
NNNGGH!

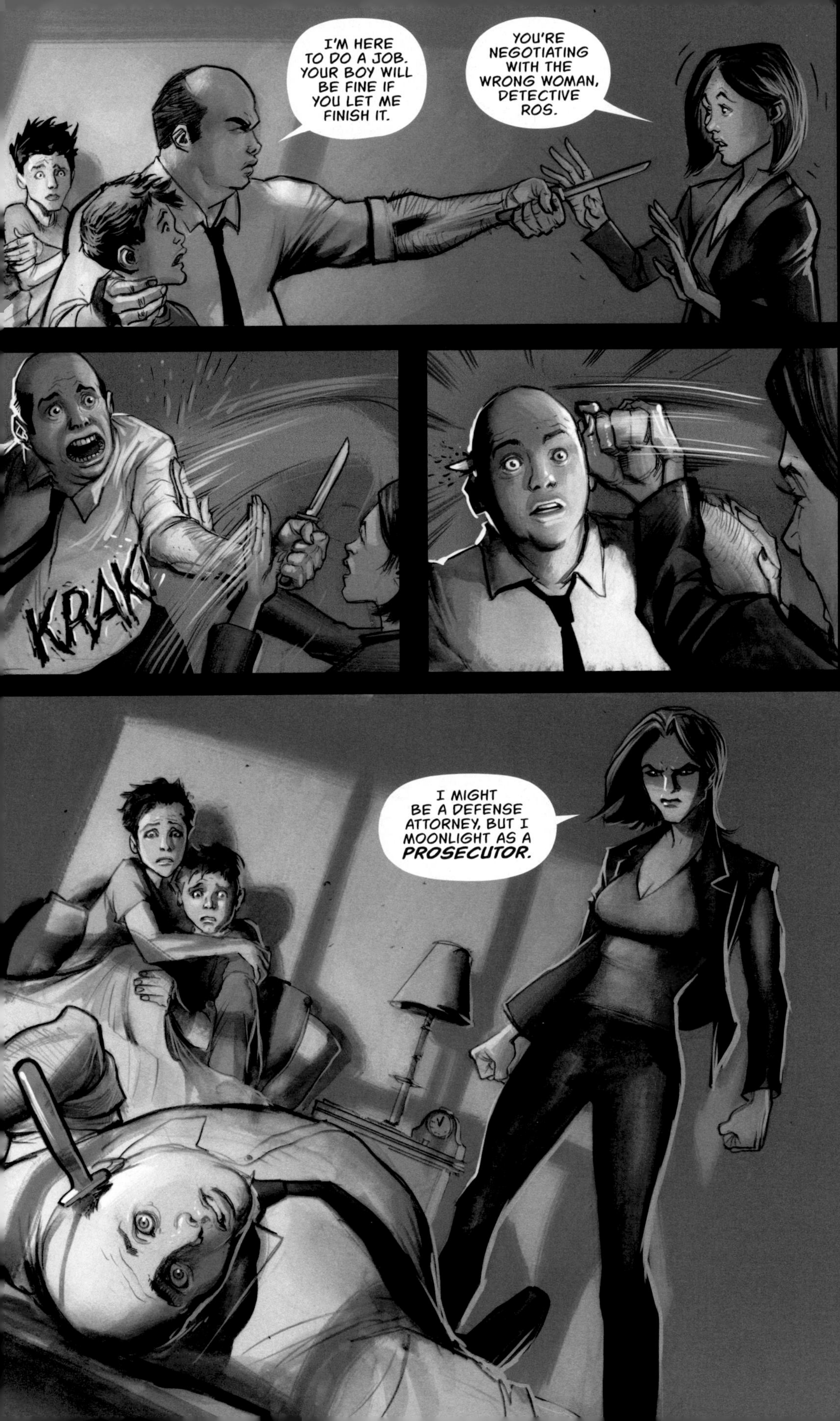
I'M HERE TO DO A JOB. YOUR BOY WILL BE FINE IF YOU LET ME FINISH IT.
YOU'RE NEGOTIATING WITH THE WRONG WOMAN, DETECTIVE ROS.
KRAK!
I MIGHT BE A DEFENSE ATTORNEY, BUT I MOONLIGHT AS A *PROSECUTOR.*

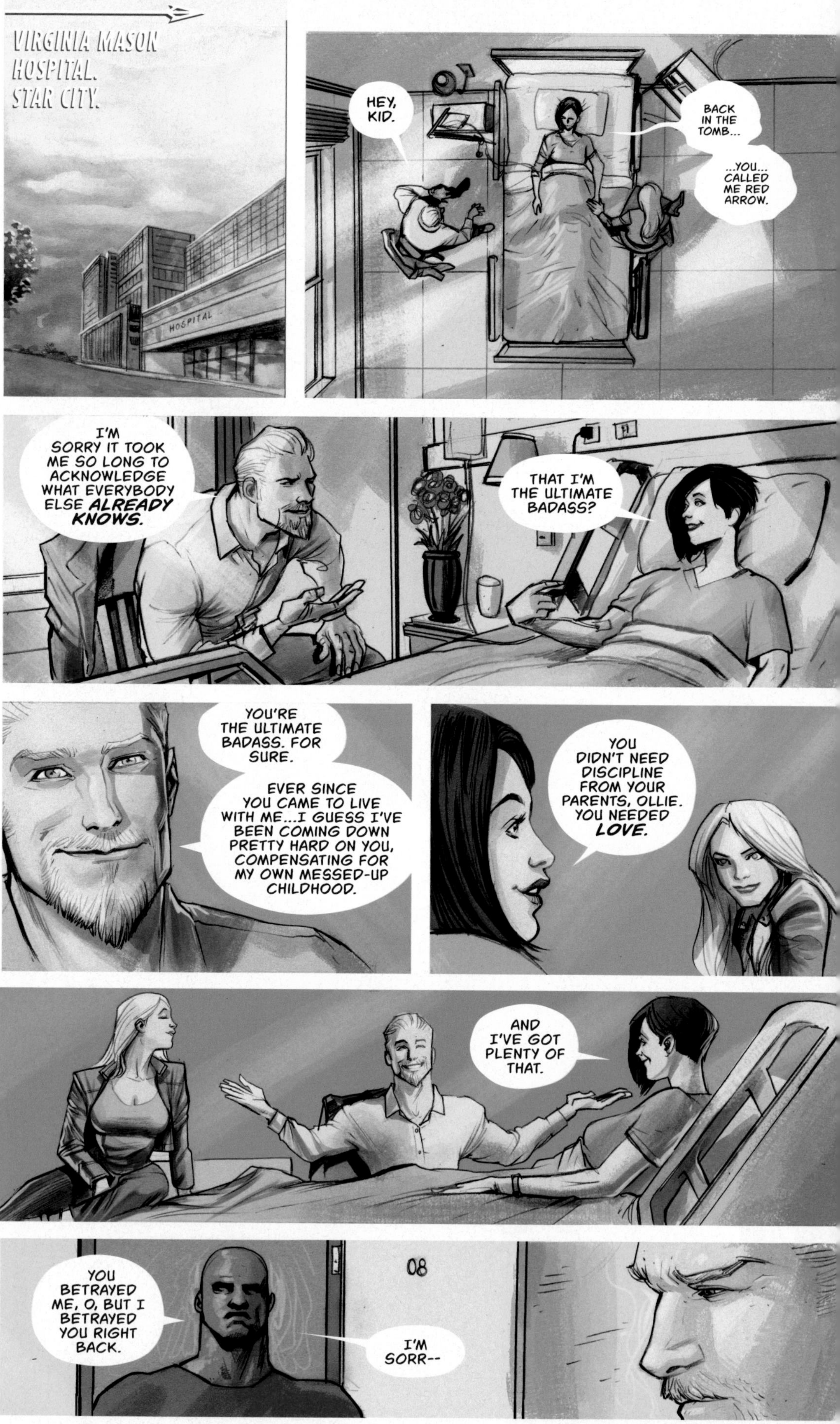
VIRGINIA MASON HOSPITAL. STAR CITY.
HOSPITAL
HEY, KID.
BACK IN THE TOMB...
...YOU... CALLED ME RED ARROW.
I'M SORRY IT TOOK ME SO LONG TO ACKNOWLEDGE WHAT EVERYBODY ELSE ALREADY KNOWS.
THAT I'M THE ULTIMATE BADASS?
YOU'RE THE ULTIMATE BADASS. FOR SURE.
EVER SINCE YOU CAME TO LIVE WITH ME...I GUESS I'VE BEEN COMING DOWN PRETTY HARD ON YOU, COMPENSATING FOR MY OWN MESSED-UP CHILDHOOD.
YOU DIDN'T NEED DISCIPLINE FROM YOUR PARENTS, OLLIE. YOU NEEDED LOVE.
AND I'VE GOT PLENTY OF THAT.
YOU BETRAYED ME, O, BUT I BETRAYED YOU RIGHT BACK.
08
I'M SORR--

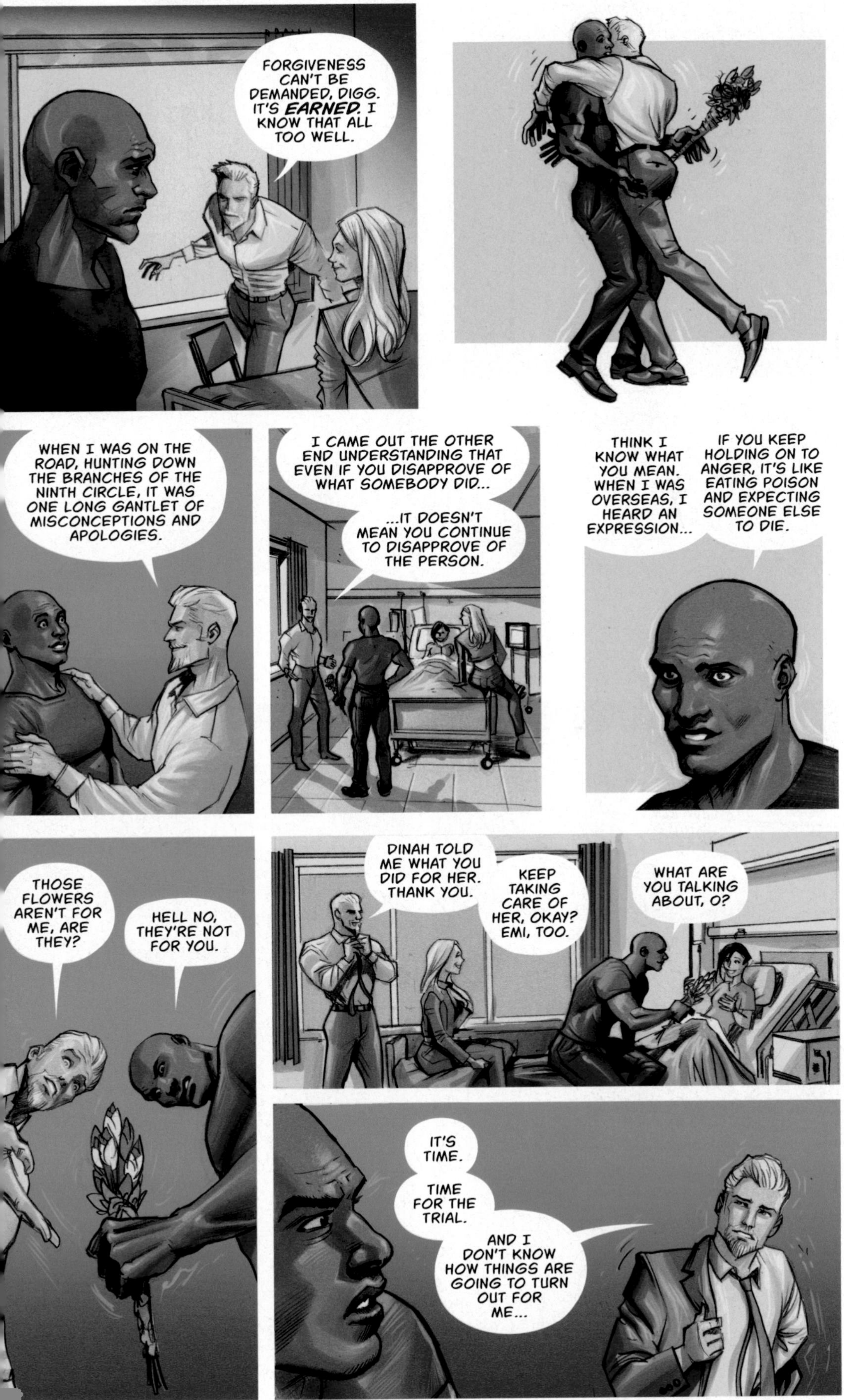
FORGIVENESS CAN'T BE DEMANDED, DIGG. IT'S **EARNED.** I KNOW THAT ALL TOO WELL.
WHEN I WAS ON THE ROAD, HUNTING DOWN THE BRANCHES OF THE NINTH CIRCLE, IT WAS ONE LONG GANTLET OF MISCONCEPTIONS AND APOLOGIES.
I CAME OUT THE OTHER END UNDERSTANDING THAT EVEN IF YOU DISAPPROVE OF WHAT SOMEBODY DID...
...IT DOESN'T MEAN YOU CONTINUE TO DISAPPROVE OF THE PERSON.
THINK I KNOW WHAT YOU MEAN. WHEN I WAS OVERSEAS, I HEARD AN EXPRESSION...
IF YOU KEEP HOLDING ON TO ANGER, IT'S LIKE EATING POISON AND EXPECTING SOMEONE ELSE TO DIE.
THOSE FLOWERS AREN'T FOR ME, ARE THEY?
HELL NO, THEY'RE NOT FOR YOU.
DINAH TOLD ME WHAT YOU DID FOR HER. THANK YOU.
KEEP TAKING CARE OF HER, OKAY? EMI, TOO.
WHAT ARE YOU TALKING ABOUT, O?
IT'S TIME.
TIME FOR THE TRIAL.
AND I DON'T KNOW HOW THINGS ARE GOING TO TURN OUT FOR ME...

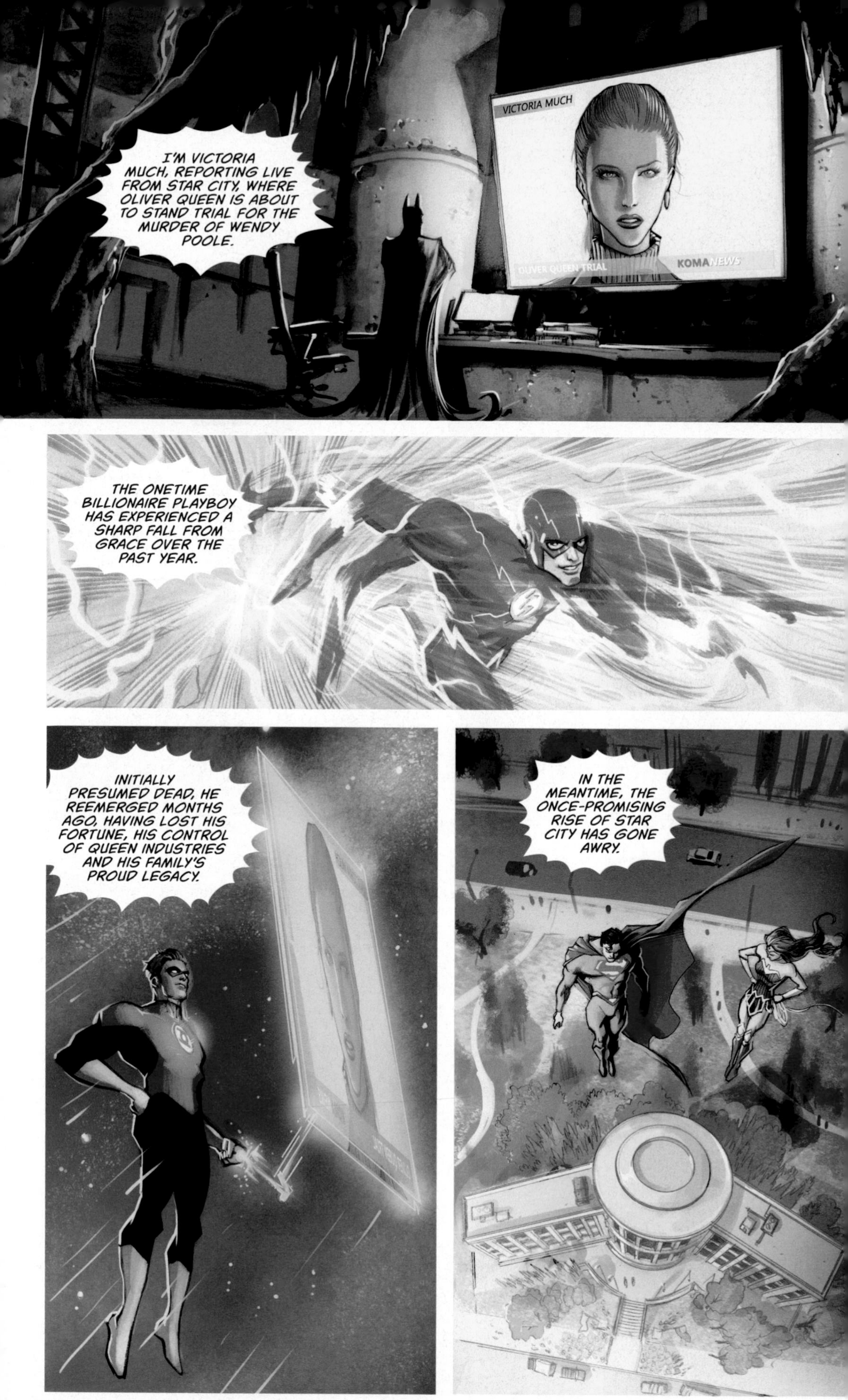

I'M VICTORIA MUCH, REPORTING LIVE FROM STAR CITY, WHERE OLIVER QUEEN IS ABOUT TO STAND TRIAL FOR THE MURDER OF WENDY POOLE.
VICTORIA MUCH
OLIVER QUEEN TRIAL
KOMA NEWS
THE ONETIME BILLIONAIRE PLAYBOY HAS EXPERIENCED A SHARP FALL FROM GRACE OVER THE PAST YEAR.
INITIALLY PRESUMED DEAD, HE REEMERGED MONTHS AGO, HAVING LOST HIS FORTUNE, HIS CONTROL OF QUEEN INDUSTRIES AND HIS FAMILY'S PROUD LEGACY.
IN THE MEANTIME, THE ONCE-PROMISING RISE OF STAR CITY HAS GONE AWRY.

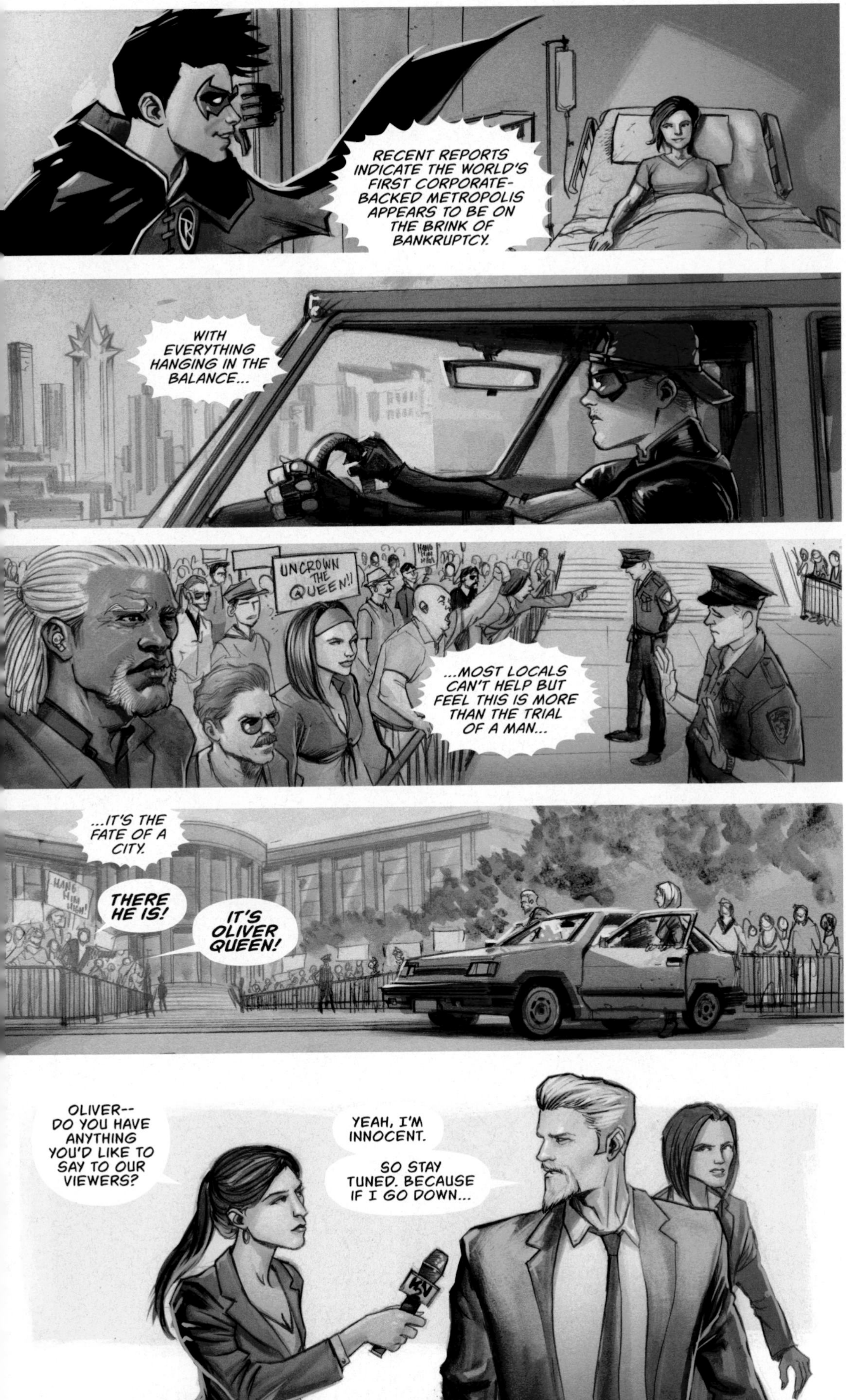
RECENT REPORTS INDICATE THE WORLD'S FIRST CORPORATE-BACKED METROPOLIS APPEARS TO BE ON THE BRINK OF BANKRUPTCY.
WITH EVERYTHING HANGING IN THE BALANCE...
UNCROWN THE QUEEN!!
HANG HIM HIGH
...MOST LOCALS CAN'T HELP BUT FEEL THIS IS MORE THAN THE TRIAL OF A MAN...
...IT'S THE FATE OF A CITY.
HANG HIM HIGH!
THERE HE IS!
IT'S OLIVER QUEEN!
OLIVER-- DO YOU HAVE ANYTHING YOU'D LIKE TO SAY TO OUR VIEWERS?
YEAH, I'M INNOCENT.
SO STAY TUNED. BECAUSE IF I GO DOWN...

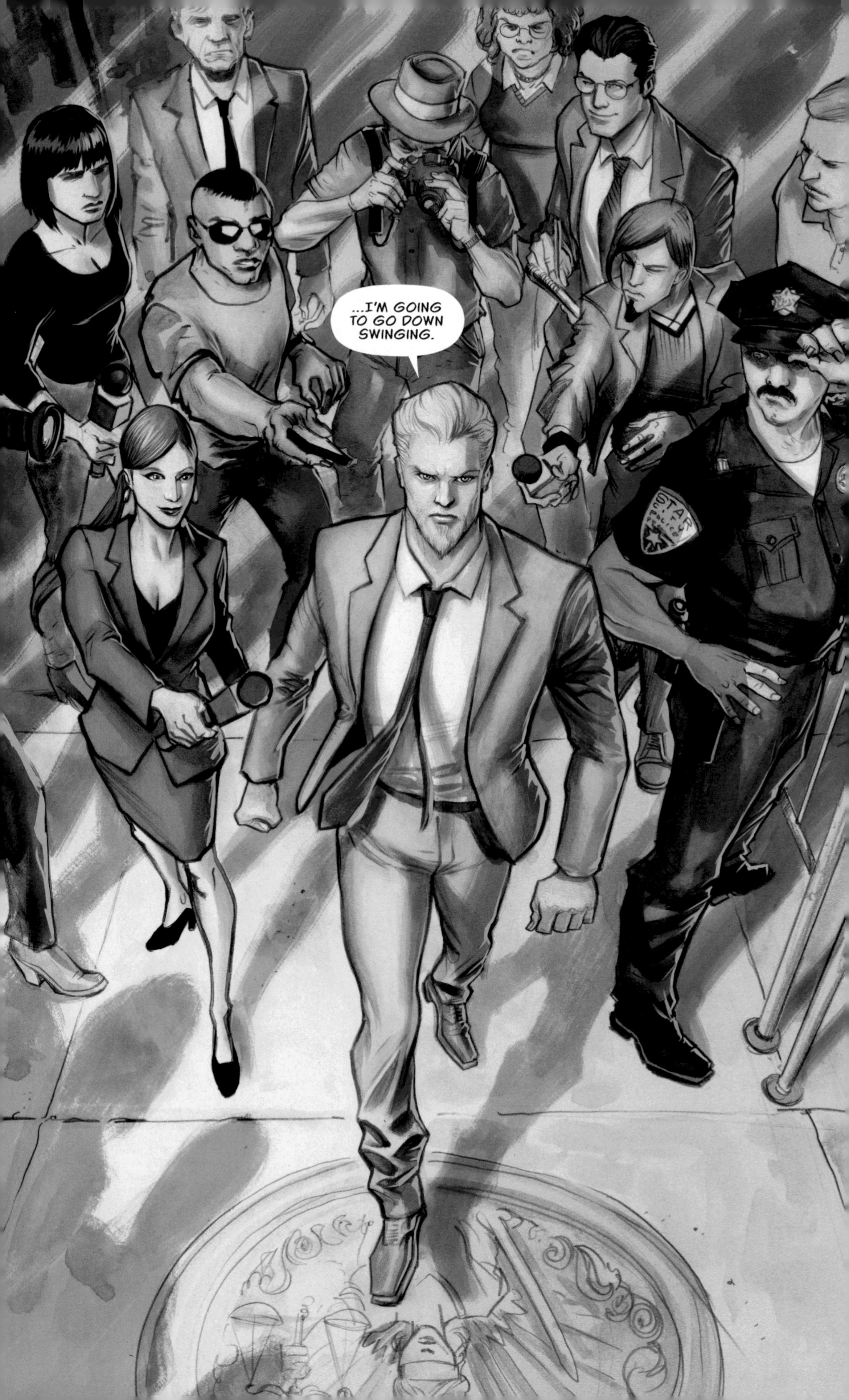
...I'M GOING TO GO DOWN SWINGING.

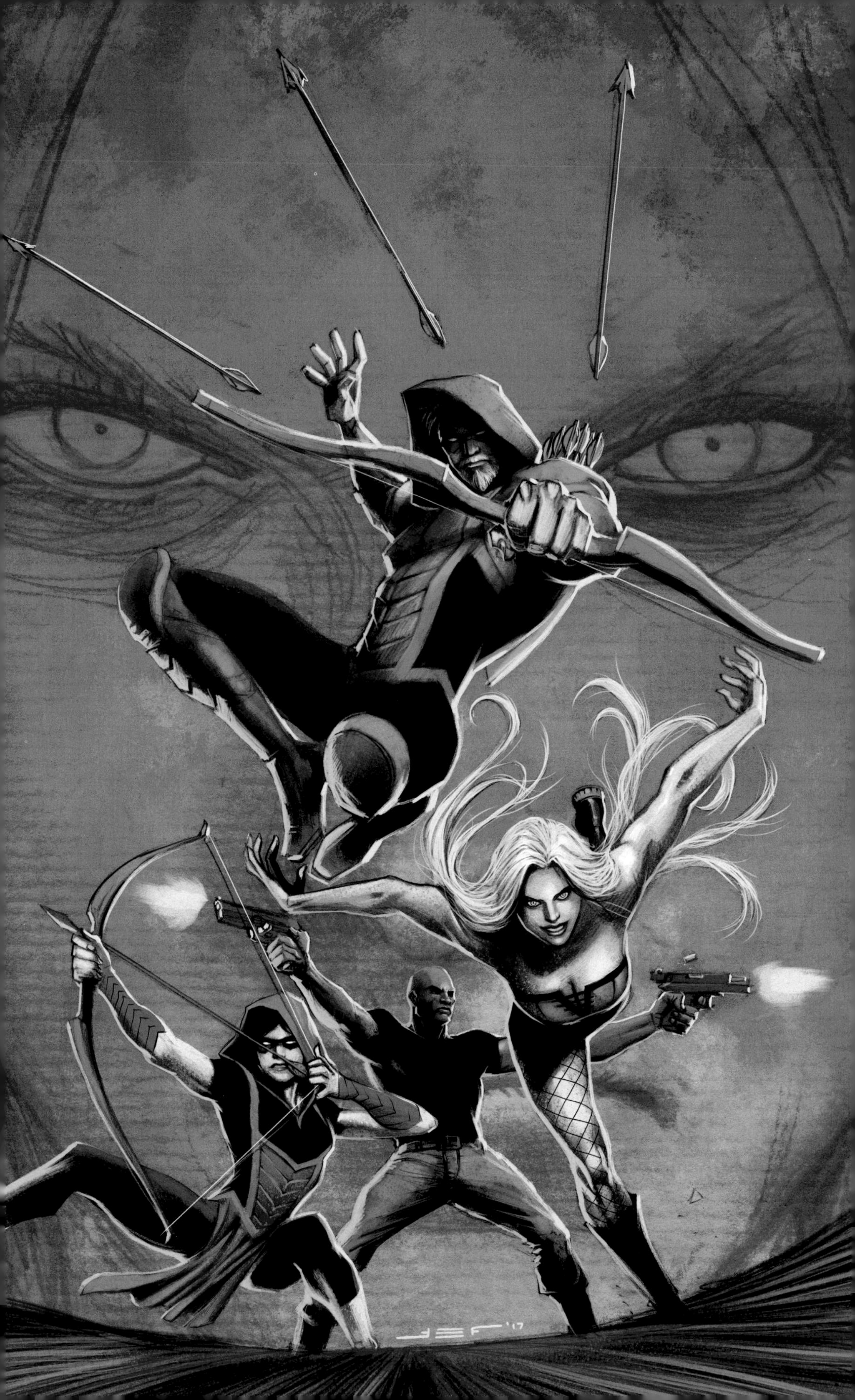

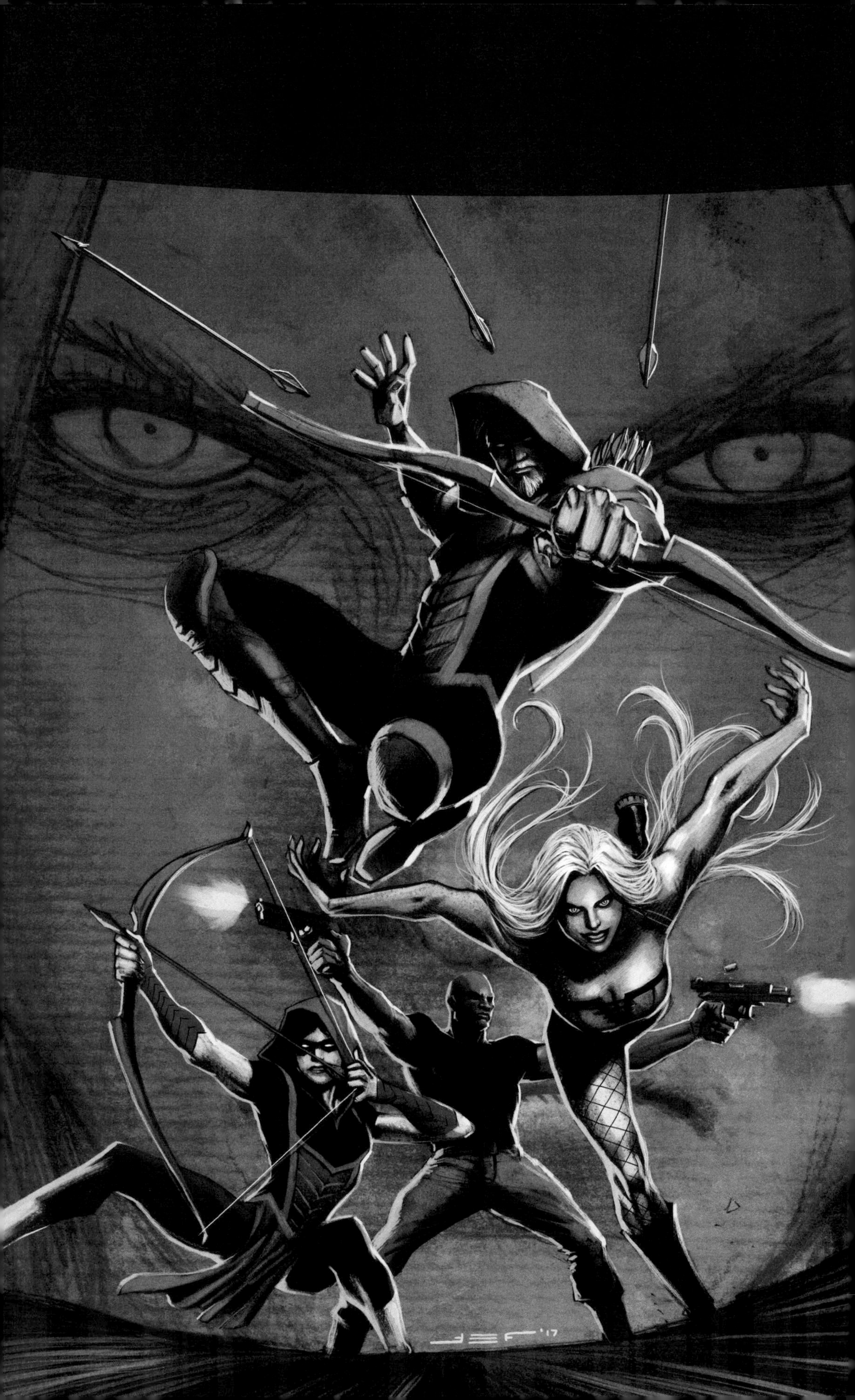

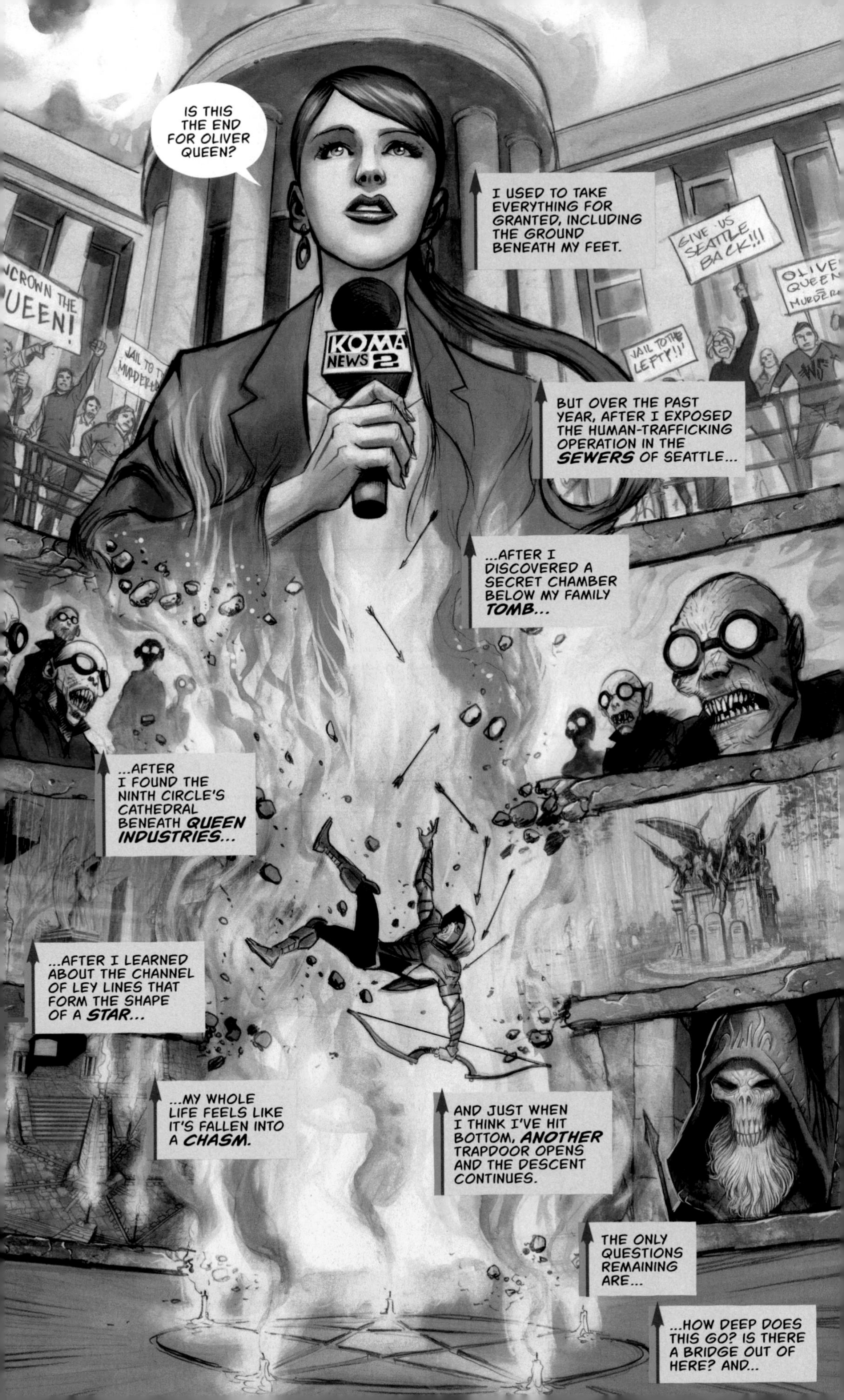
IS THIS THE END FOR OLIVER QUEEN?
KOMA NEWS 2
I USED TO TAKE EVERYTHING FOR GRANTED, INCLUDING THE GROUND BENEATH MY FEET.
GIVE US SEATTLE BACK!!!
OLIVER QUEEN = MURDERER
JAIL TO THE LEFTY!!!
BUT OVER THE PAST YEAR, AFTER I EXPOSED THE HUMAN-TRAFFICKING OPERATION IN THE SEWERS OF SEATTLE...
...AFTER I DISCOVERED A SECRET CHAMBER BELOW MY FAMILY TOMB...
...AFTER I FOUND THE NINTH CIRCLE'S CATHEDRAL BENEATH QUEEN INDUSTRIES...
...AFTER I LEARNED ABOUT THE CHANNEL OF LEY LINES THAT FORM THE SHAPE OF A STAR...
...MY WHOLE LIFE FEELS LIKE IT'S FALLEN INTO A CHASM.
AND JUST WHEN I THINK I'VE HIT BOTTOM, ANOTHER TRAPDOOR OPENS AND THE DESCENT CONTINUES.
THE ONLY QUESTIONS REMAINING ARE...
...HOW DEEP DOES THIS GO? IS THERE A BRIDGE OUT OF HERE? AND...

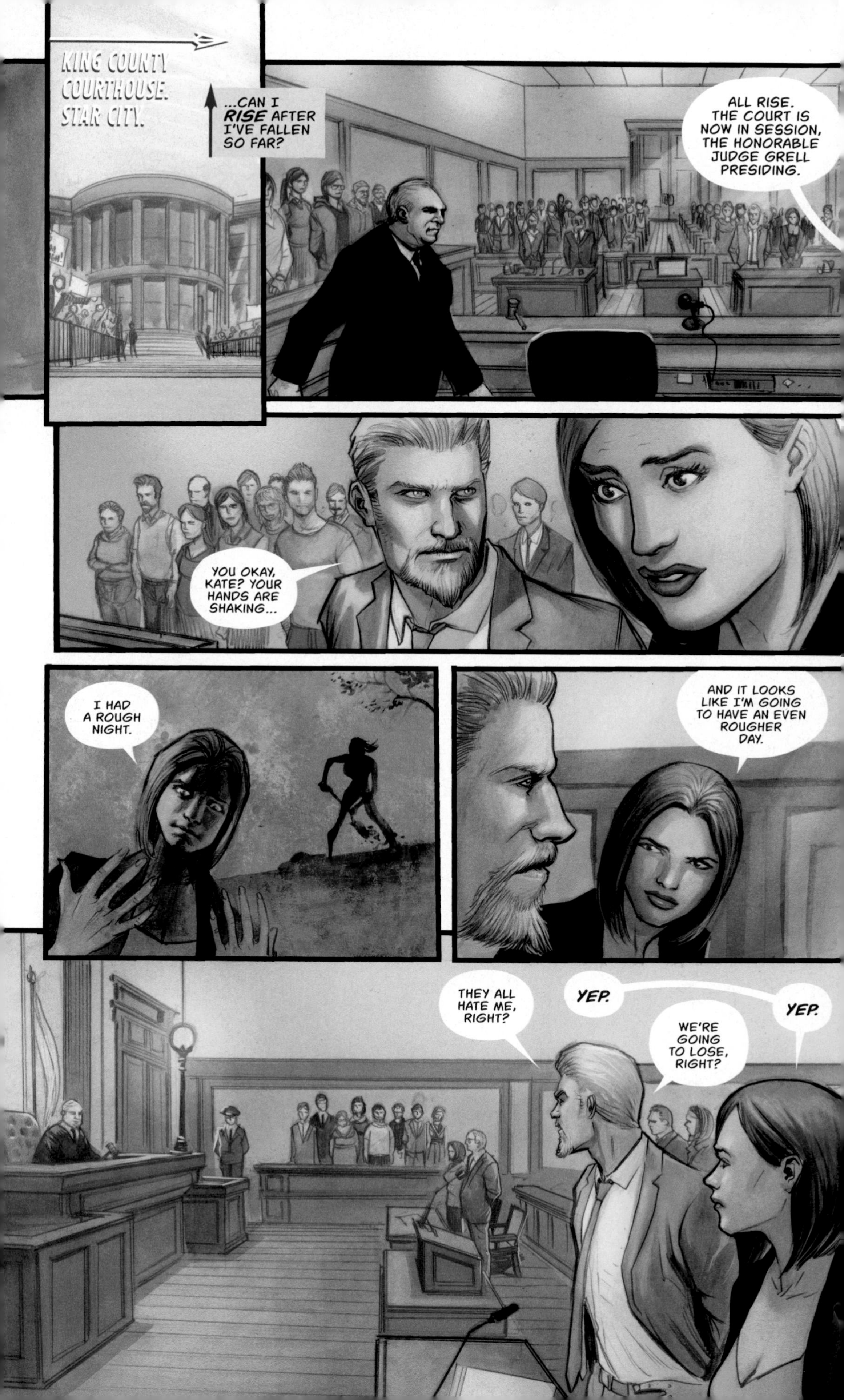
KING COUNTY COURTHOUSE. STAR CITY.
...CAN I RISE AFTER I'VE FALLEN SO FAR?
ALL RISE. THE COURT IS NOW IN SESSION, THE HONORABLE JUDGE GRELL PRESIDING.
YOU OKAY, KATE? YOUR HANDS ARE SHAKING...
I HAD A ROUGH NIGHT.
AND IT LOOKS LIKE I'M GOING TO HAVE AN EVEN ROUGHER DAY.
THEY ALL HATE ME, RIGHT?
YEP.
WE'RE GOING TO LOSE, RIGHT?
YEP.

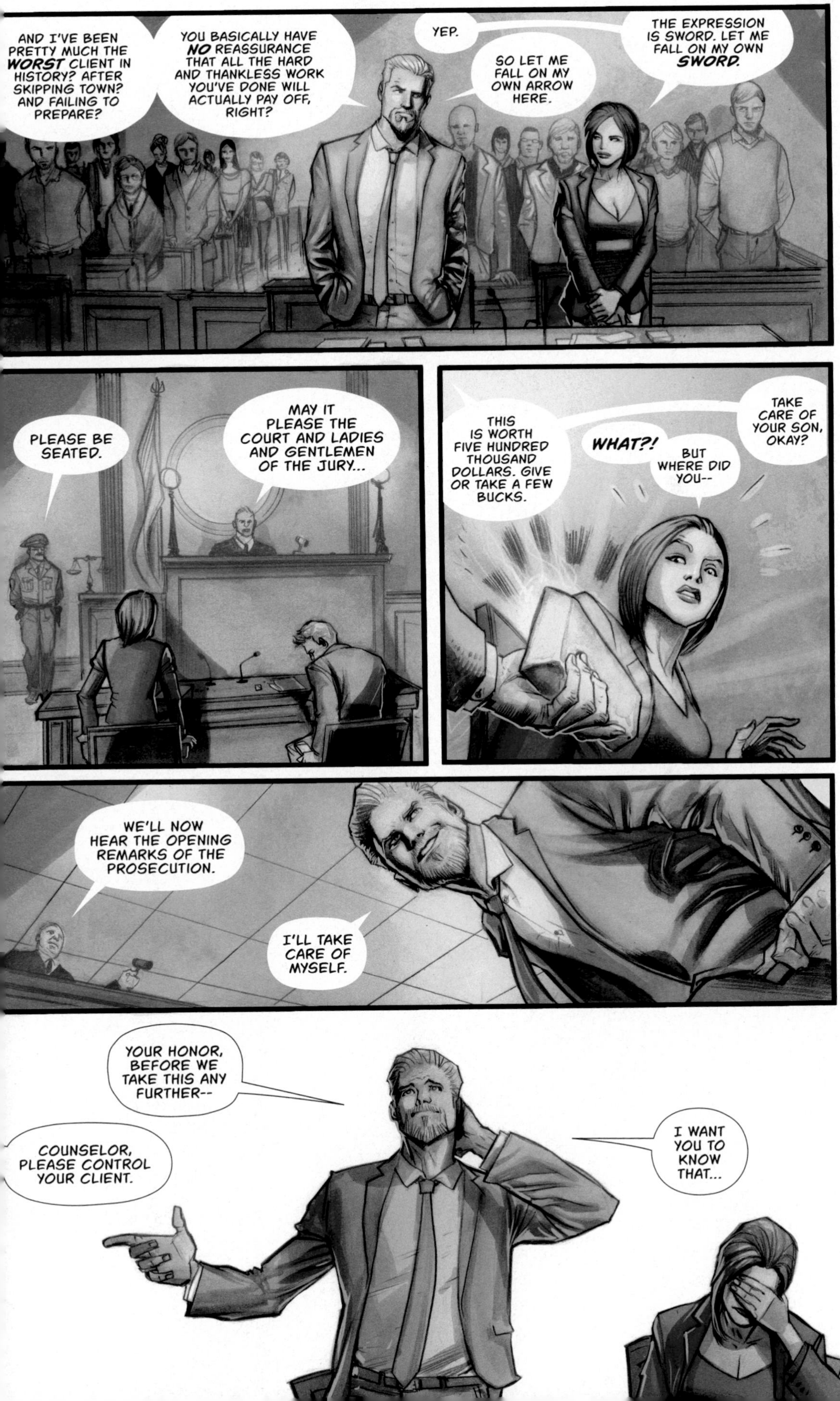
AND I'VE BEEN PRETTY MUCH THE WORST CLIENT IN HISTORY? AFTER SKIPPING TOWN? AND FAILING TO PREPARE?
YOU BASICALLY HAVE NO REASSURANCE THAT ALL THE HARD AND THANKLESS WORK YOU'VE DONE WILL ACTUALLY PAY OFF, RIGHT?
YEP.
SO LET ME FALL ON MY OWN ARROW HERE.
THE EXPRESSION IS SWORD. LET ME FALL ON MY OWN SWORD.
PLEASE BE SEATED.
MAY IT PLEASE THE COURT AND LADIES AND GENTLEMEN OF THE JURY...
THIS IS WORTH FIVE HUNDRED THOUSAND DOLLARS. GIVE OR TAKE A FEW BUCKS.
TAKE CARE OF YOUR SON, OKAY?
WHAT?!
BUT WHERE DID YOU--
WE'LL NOW HEAR THE OPENING REMARKS OF THE PROSECUTION.
I'LL TAKE CARE OF MYSELF.
YOUR HONOR, BEFORE WE TAKE THIS ANY FURTHER--
COUNSELOR, PLEASE CONTROL YOUR CLIENT.
I WANT YOU TO KNOW THAT...

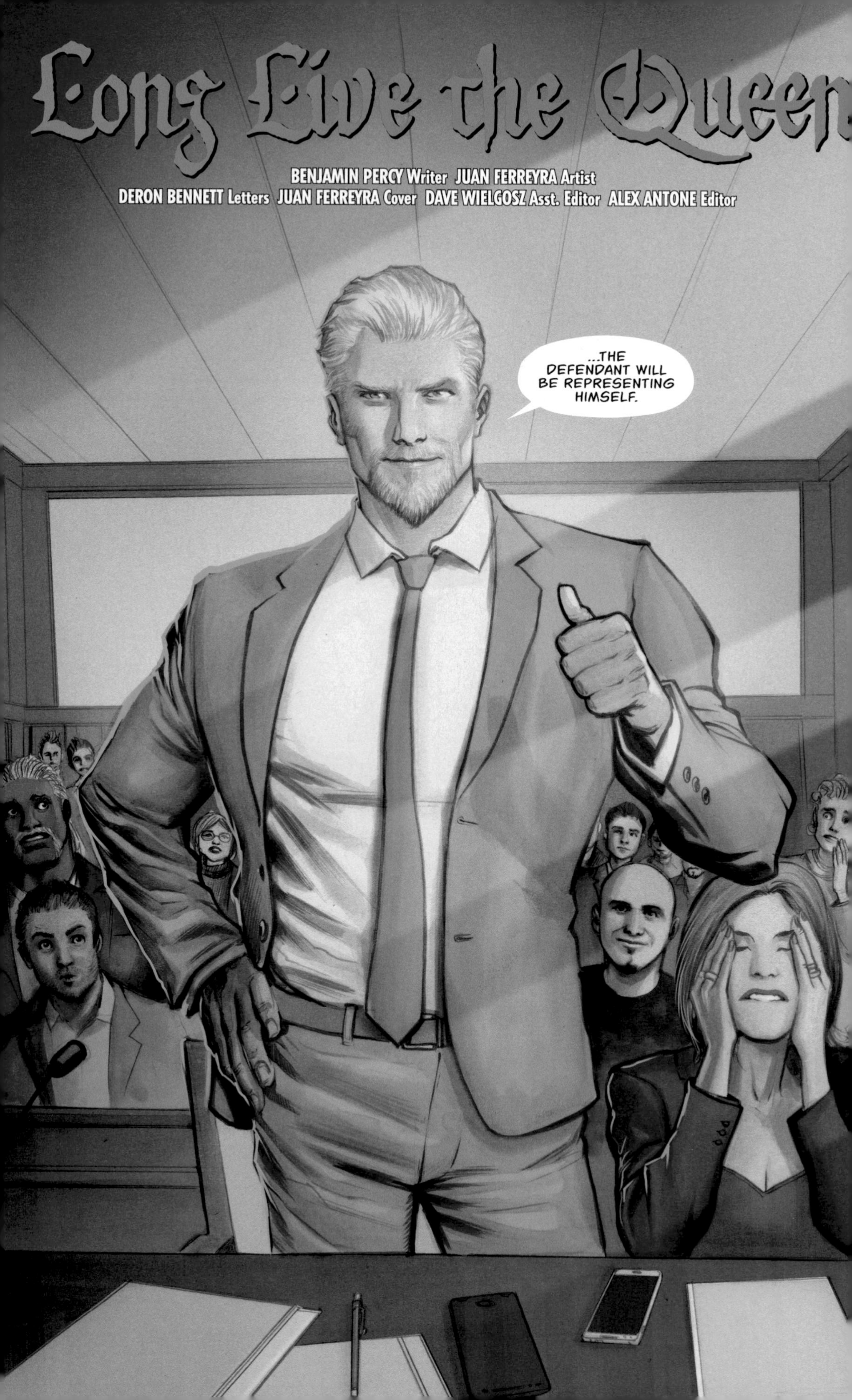
Long Live the Queen
BENJAMIN PERCY Writer JUAN FERREYRA Artist
DERON BENNETT Letters JUAN FERREYRA Cover DAVE WIELGOSZ Asst. Editor ALEX ANTONE Editor
...THE DEFENDANT WILL BE REPRESENTING HIMSELF.

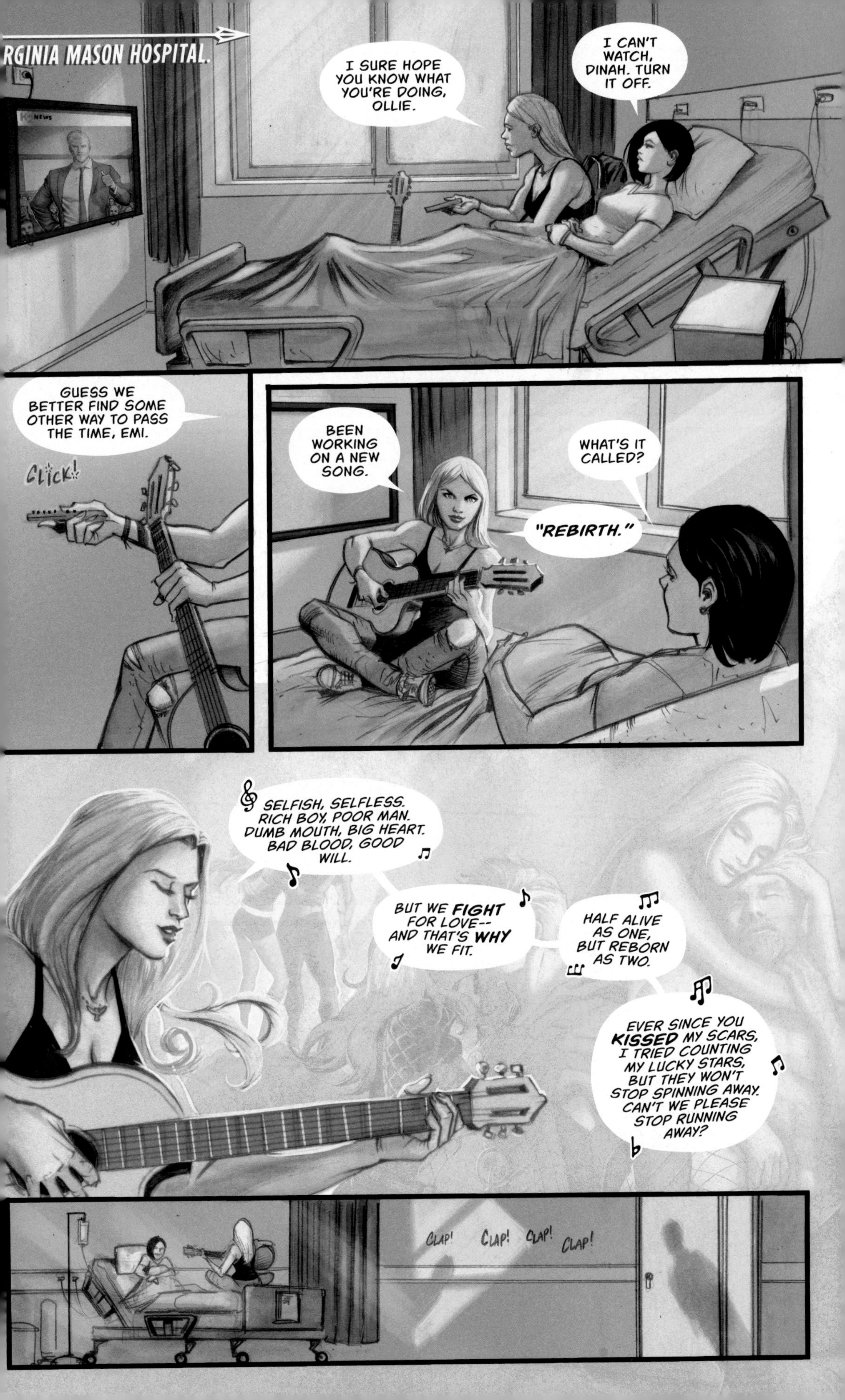
RGINIA MASON HOSPITAL.
NEWS
I SURE HOPE YOU KNOW WHAT YOU'RE DOING, OLLIE.
I CAN'T WATCH, DINAH. TURN IT OFF.
GUESS WE BETTER FIND SOME OTHER WAY TO PASS THE TIME, EMI.
CLICK!
BEEN WORKING ON A NEW SONG.
WHAT'S IT CALLED?
"REBIRTH."
SELFISH, SELFLESS. RICH BOY, POOR MAN. DUMB MOUTH, BIG HEART. BAD BLOOD, GOOD WILL.
BUT WE FIGHT FOR LOVE-- AND THAT'S WHY WE FIT.
HALF ALIVE AS ONE, BUT REBORN AS TWO.
EVER SINCE YOU KISSED MY SCARS, I TRIED COUNTING MY LUCKY STARS, BUT THEY WON'T STOP SPINNING AWAY. CAN'T WE PLEASE STOP RUNNING AWAY?
CLAP! CLAP! CLAP! CLAP!

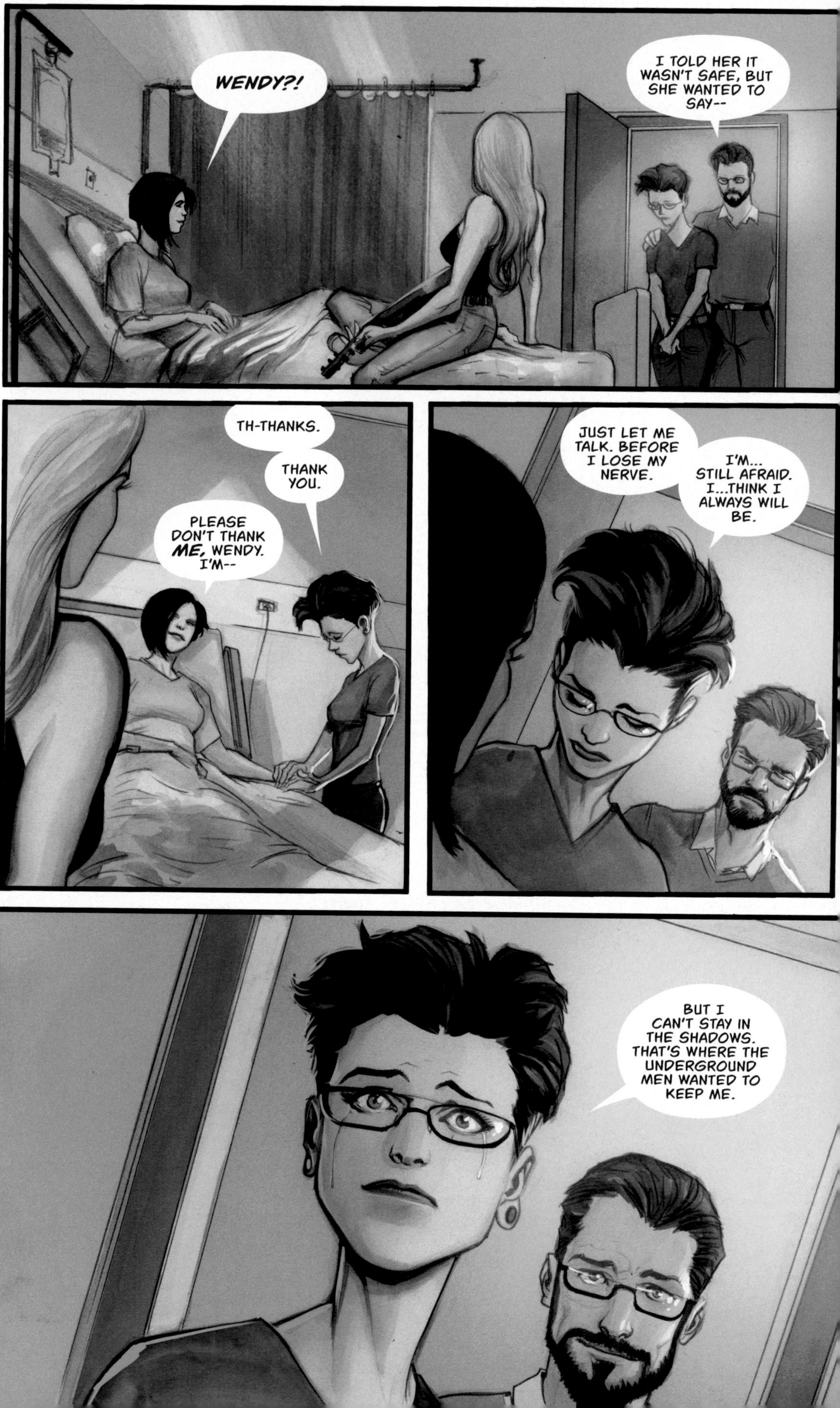
WENDY?!
I TOLD HER IT WASN'T SAFE, BUT SHE WANTED TO SAY--
TH-THANKS.
THANK YOU.
PLEASE DON'T THANK ME, WENDY. I'M--
JUST LET ME TALK. BEFORE I LOSE MY NERVE.
I'M... STILL AFRAID. I...THINK I ALWAYS WILL BE.
BUT I CAN'T STAY IN THE SHADOWS. THAT'S WHERE THE UNDERGROUND MEN WANTED TO KEEP ME.

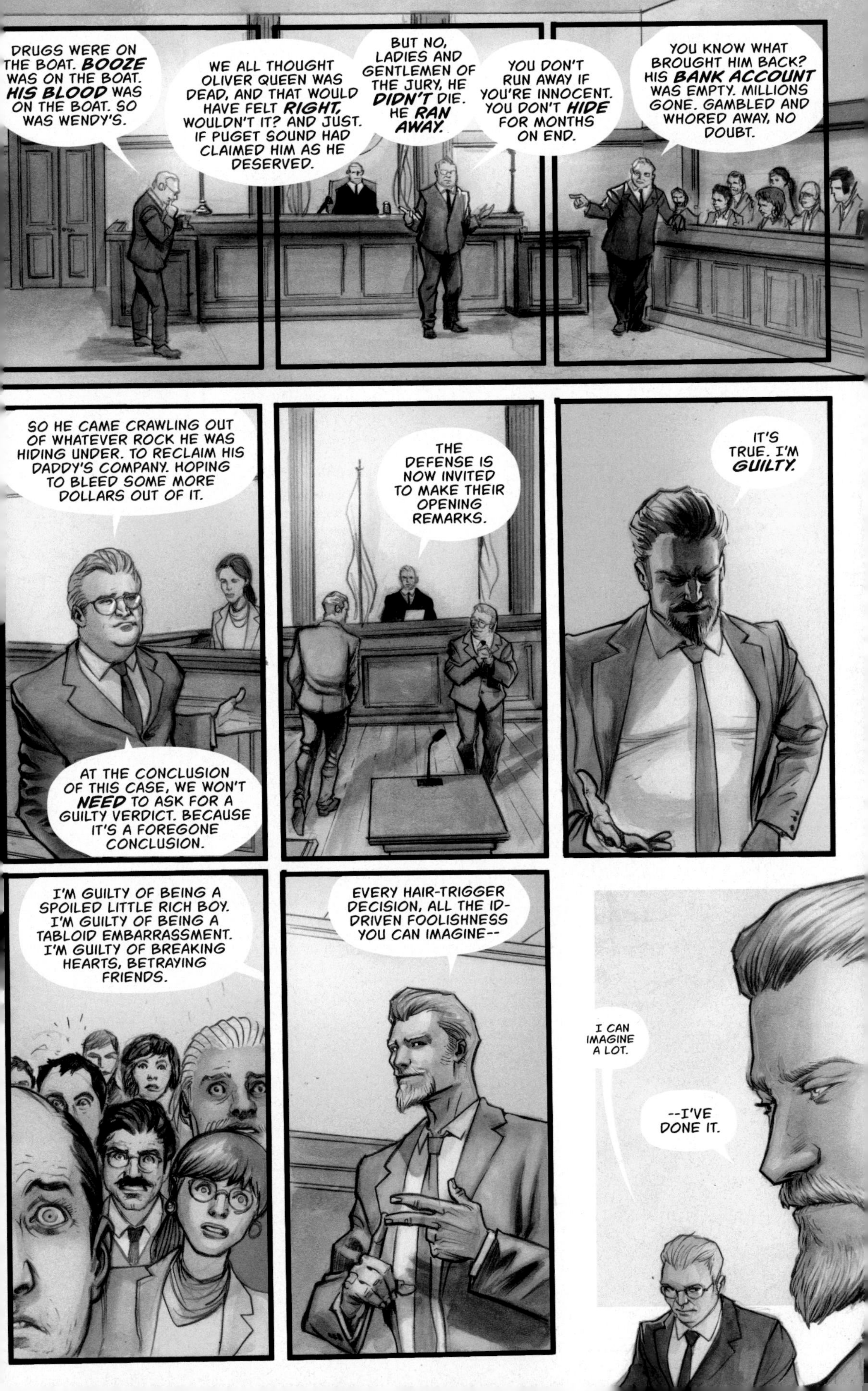
DRUGS WERE ON THE BOAT. BOOZE WAS ON THE BOAT. HIS BLOOD WAS ON THE BOAT. SO WAS WENDY'S.
WE ALL THOUGHT OLIVER QUEEN WAS DEAD, AND THAT WOULD HAVE FELT RIGHT, WOULDN'T IT? AND JUST. IF PUGET SOUND HAD CLAIMED HIM AS HE DESERVED.
BUT NO, LADIES AND GENTLEMEN OF THE JURY, HE DIDN'T DIE. HE RAN AWAY.
YOU DON'T RUN AWAY IF YOU'RE INNOCENT. YOU DON'T HIDE FOR MONTHS ON END.
YOU KNOW WHAT BROUGHT HIM BACK? HIS BANK ACCOUNT WAS EMPTY. MILLIONS GONE. GAMBLED AND WHORED AWAY, NO DOUBT.
SO HE CAME CRAWLING OUT OF WHATEVER ROCK HE WAS HIDING UNDER. TO RECLAIM HIS DADDY'S COMPANY. HOPING TO BLEED SOME MORE DOLLARS OUT OF IT.
AT THE CONCLUSION OF THIS CASE, WE WON'T NEED TO ASK FOR A GUILTY VERDICT. BECAUSE IT'S A FOREGONE CONCLUSION.
THE DEFENSE IS NOW INVITED TO MAKE THEIR OPENING REMARKS.
IT'S TRUE. I'M GUILTY.
I'M GUILTY OF BEING A SPOILED LITTLE RICH BOY. I'M GUILTY OF BEING A TABLOID EMBARRASSMENT. I'M GUILTY OF BREAKING HEARTS, BETRAYING FRIENDS.
EVERY HAIR-TRIGGER DECISION, ALL THE ID-DRIVEN FOOLISHNESS YOU CAN IMAGINE--
I CAN IMAGINE A LOT.
--I'VE DONE IT.

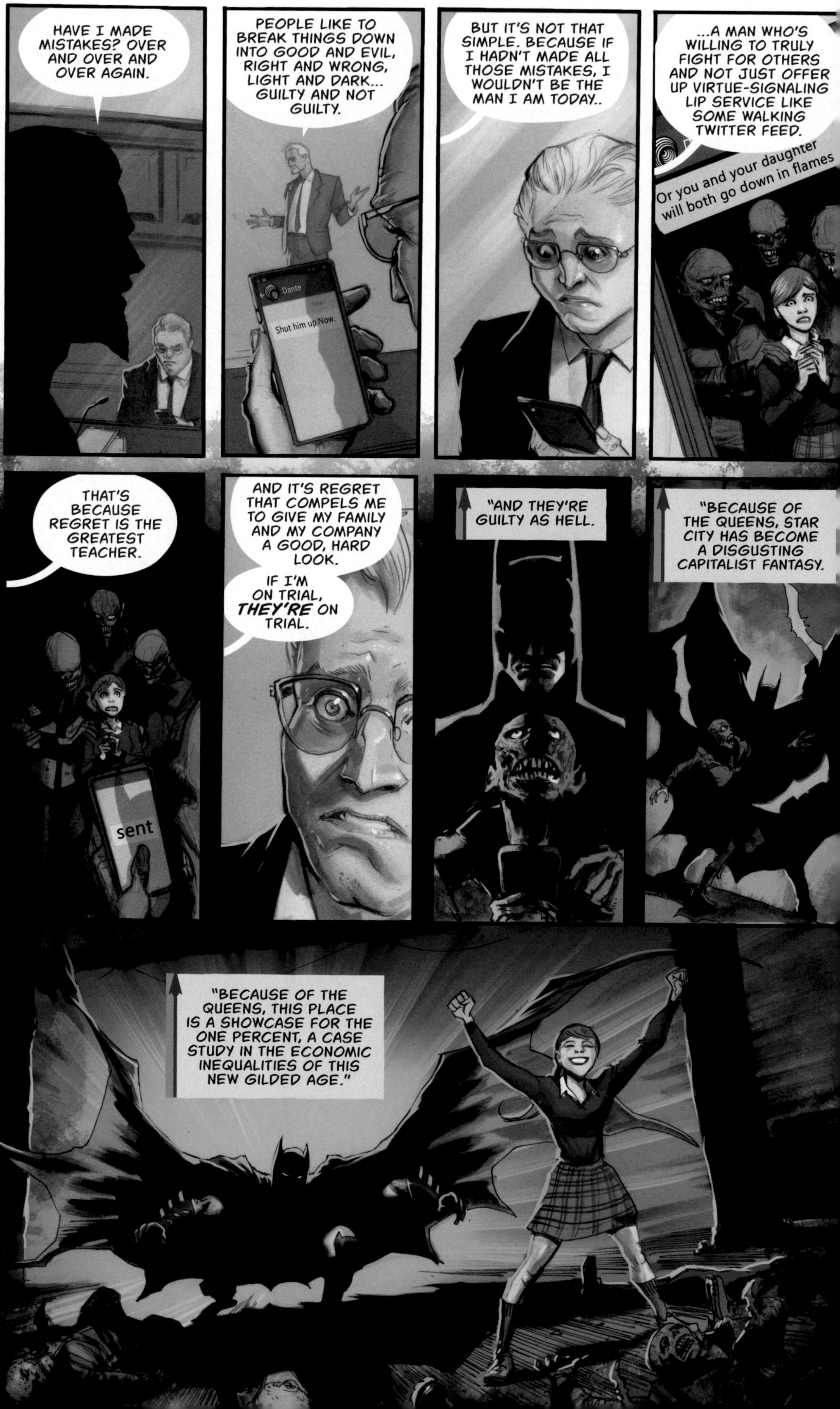

HAVE I MADE MISTAKES? OVER AND OVER AND OVER AGAIN.
PEOPLE LIKE TO BREAK THINGS DOWN INTO GOOD AND EVIL, RIGHT AND WRONG, LIGHT AND DARK... GUILTY AND NOT GUILTY.
Dante
Shut him up.Now.
BUT IT'S NOT THAT SIMPLE. BECAUSE IF I HADN'T MADE ALL THOSE MISTAKES, I WOULDN'T BE THE MAN I AM TODAY..
...A MAN WHO'S WILLING TO TRULY FIGHT FOR OTHERS AND NOT JUST OFFER UP VIRTUE-SIGNALING LIP SERVICE LIKE SOME WALKING TWITTER FEED.
Or you and your daughter will both go down in flames
THAT'S BECAUSE REGRET IS THE GREATEST TEACHER.
sent
AND IT'S REGRET THAT COMPELS ME TO GIVE MY FAMILY AND MY COMPANY A GOOD, HARD LOOK.
IF I'M ON TRIAL, *THEY'RE* ON TRIAL.
"AND THEY'RE GUILTY AS HELL.
"BECAUSE OF THE QUEENS, STAR CITY HAS BECOME A DISGUSTING CAPITALIST FANTASY.
"BECAUSE OF THE QUEENS, THIS PLACE IS A SHOWCASE FOR THE ONE PERCENT, A CASE STUDY IN THE ECONOMIC INEQUALITIES OF THIS NEW GILDED AGE."

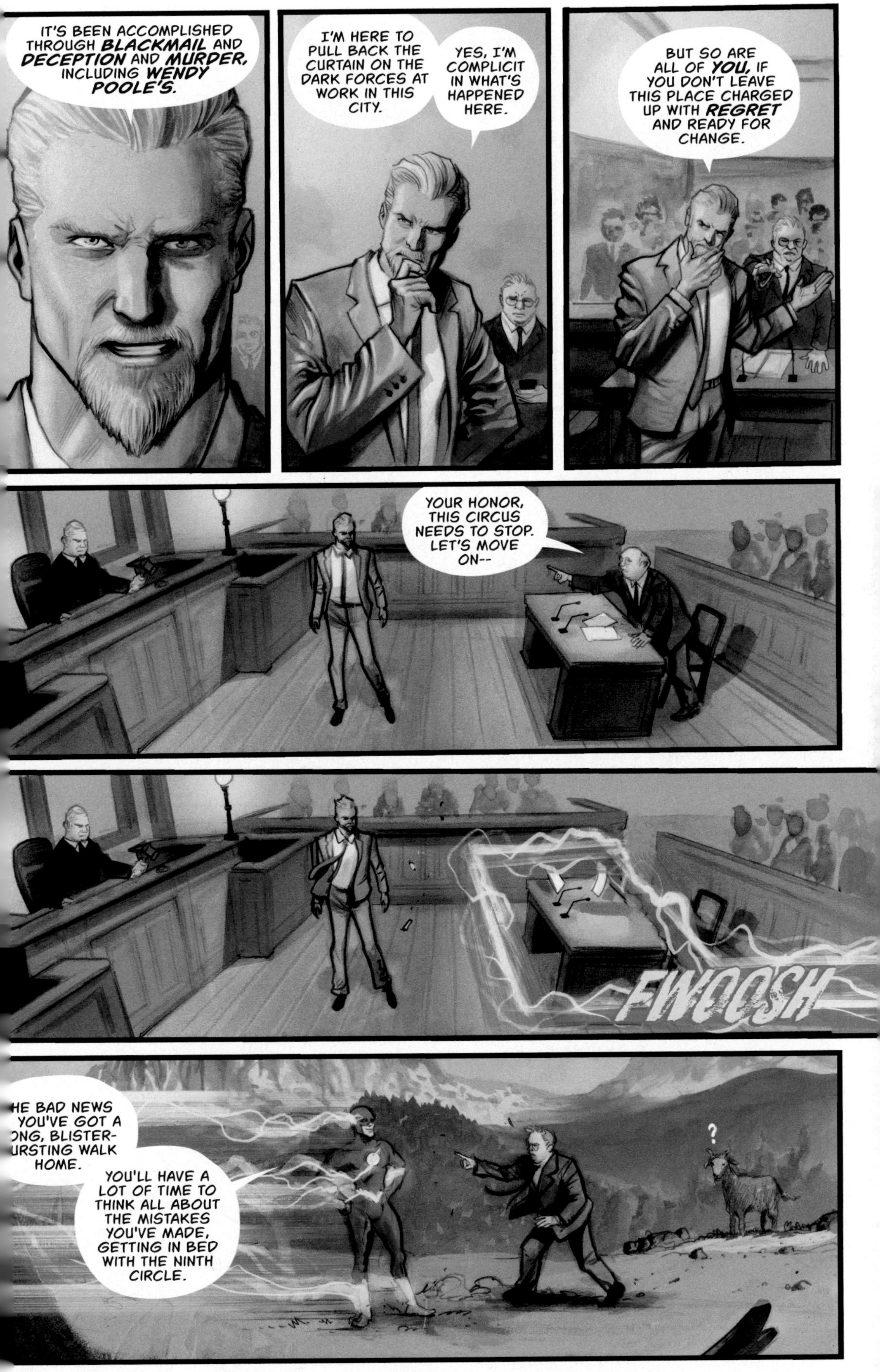
IT'S BEEN ACCOMPLISHED THROUGH BLACKMAIL AND DECEPTION AND MURDER, INCLUDING WENDY POOLE'S.
I'M HERE TO PULL BACK THE CURTAIN ON THE DARK FORCES AT WORK IN THIS CITY.
YES, I'M COMPLICIT IN WHAT'S HAPPENED HERE.
BUT SO ARE ALL OF YOU, IF YOU DON'T LEAVE THIS PLACE CHARGED UP WITH REGRET AND READY FOR CHANGE.
YOUR HONOR, THIS CIRCUS NEEDS TO STOP. LET'S MOVE ON--
FWOOSH
HE BAD NEWS YOU'VE GOT A ONG, BLISTER-URSTING WALK HOME.
YOU'LL HAVE A LOT OF TIME TO THINK ALL ABOUT THE MISTAKES YOU'VE MADE, GETTING IN BED WITH THE NINTH CIRCLE.
?

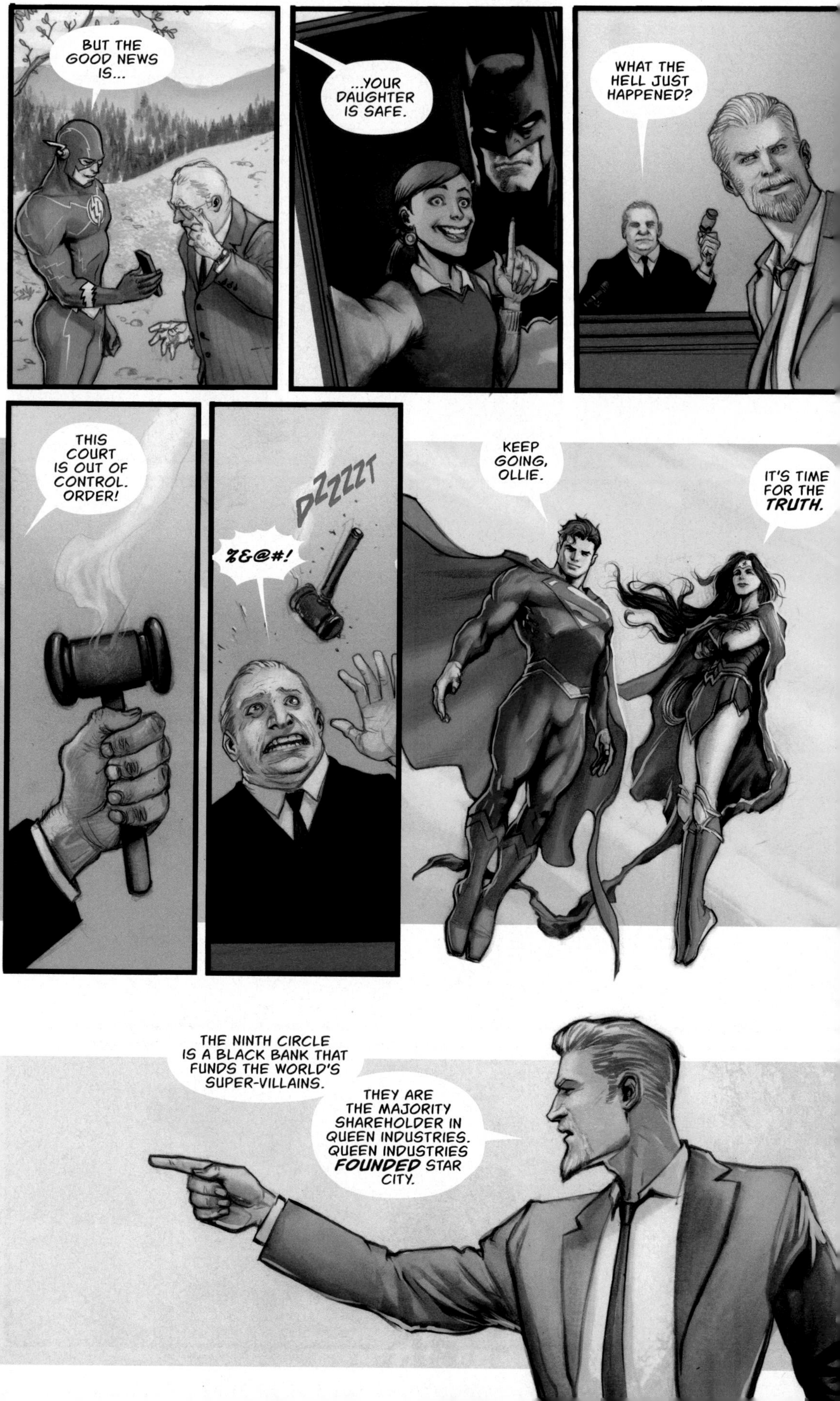
BUT THE GOOD NEWS IS...
...YOUR DAUGHTER IS SAFE.
WHAT THE HELL JUST HAPPENED?
THIS COURT IS OUT OF CONTROL. ORDER!
DZZZZT
%&@#!
KEEP GOING, OLLIE.
IT'S TIME FOR THE TRUTH.
THE NINTH CIRCLE IS A BLACK BANK THAT FUNDS THE WORLD'S SUPER-VILLAINS.
THEY ARE THE MAJORITY SHAREHOLDER IN QUEEN INDUSTRIES. QUEEN INDUSTRIES FOUNDED STAR CITY.

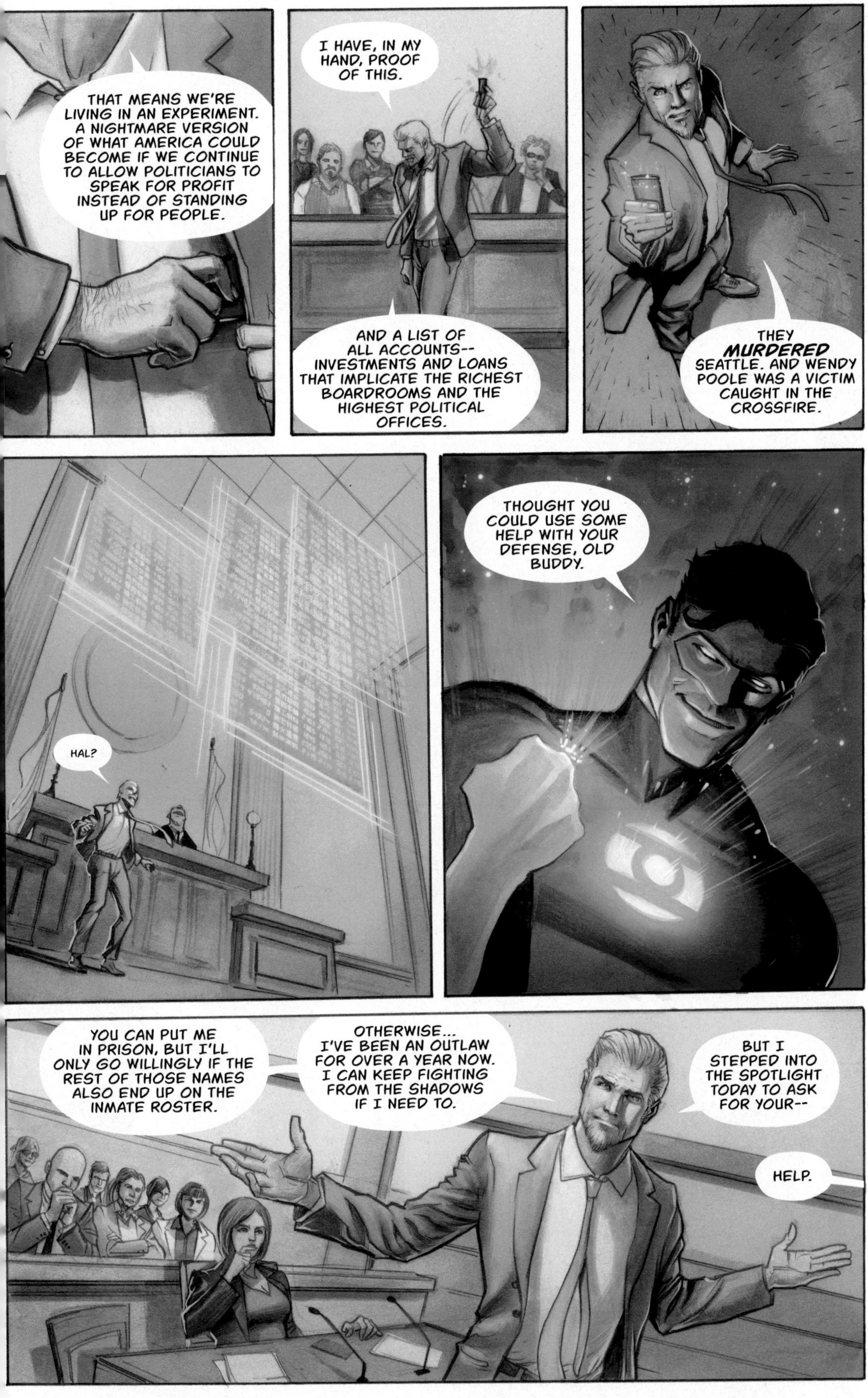
THAT MEANS WE'RE LIVING IN AN EXPERIMENT. A NIGHTMARE VERSION OF WHAT AMERICA COULD BECOME IF WE CONTINUE TO ALLOW POLITICIANS TO SPEAK FOR PROFIT INSTEAD OF STANDING UP FOR PEOPLE.
I HAVE, IN MY HAND, PROOF OF THIS.
AND A LIST OF ALL ACCOUNTS-- INVESTMENTS AND LOANS THAT IMPLICATE THE RICHEST BOARDROOMS AND THE HIGHEST POLITICAL OFFICES.
THEY ***MURDERED*** SEATTLE. AND WENDY POOLE WAS A VICTIM CAUGHT IN THE CROSSFIRE.
HAL?
THOUGHT YOU COULD USE SOME HELP WITH YOUR DEFENSE, OLD BUDDY.
YOU CAN PUT ME IN PRISON, BUT I'LL ONLY GO WILLINGLY IF THE REST OF THOSE NAMES ALSO END UP ON THE INMATE ROSTER.
OTHERWISE... I'VE BEEN AN OUTLAW FOR OVER A YEAR NOW. I CAN KEEP FIGHTING FROM THE SHADOWS IF I NEED TO.
BUT I STEPPED INTO THE SPOTLIGHT TODAY TO ASK FOR YOUR--
HELP.

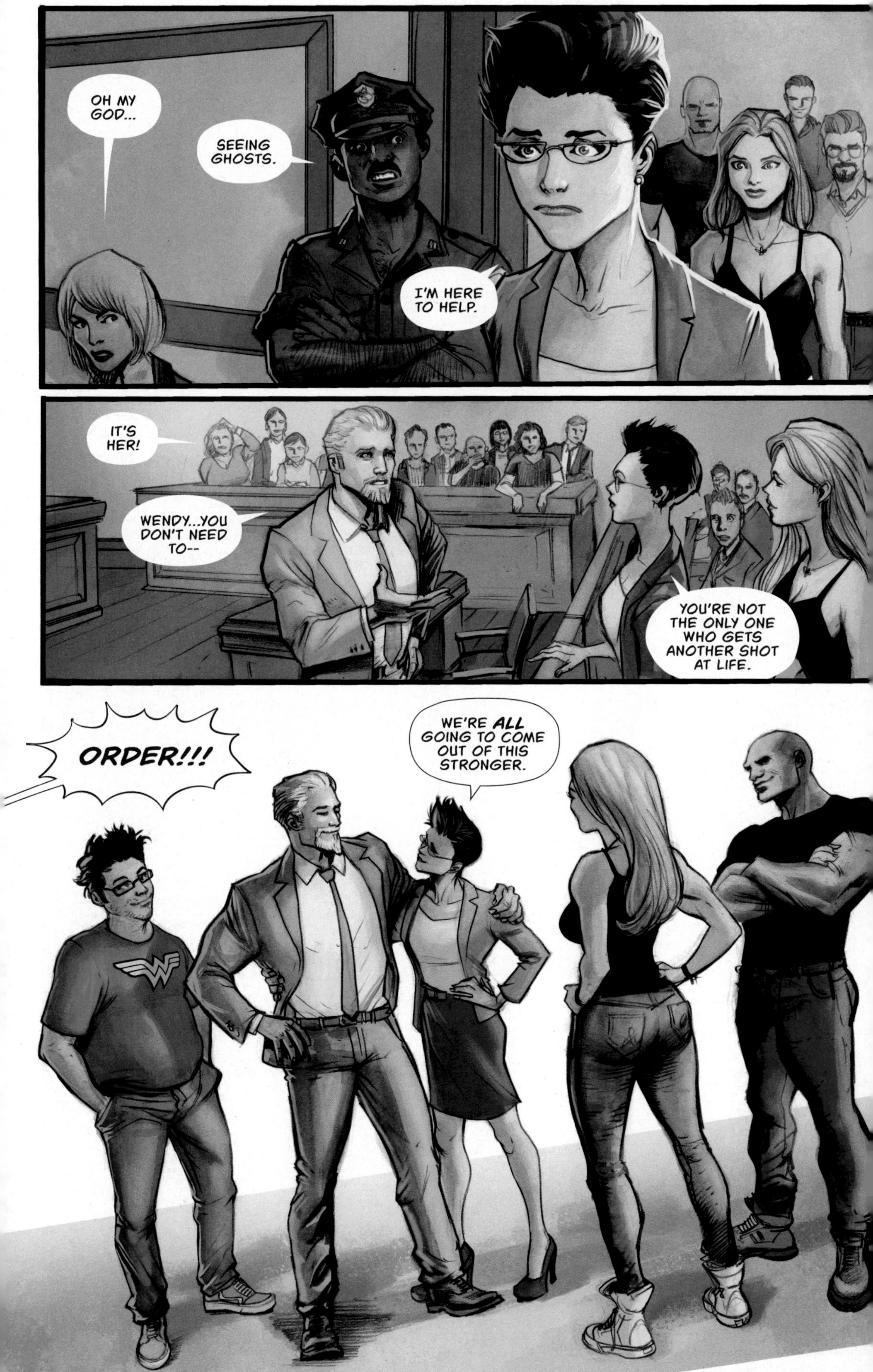
OH MY GOD...
SEEING GHOSTS.
I'M HERE TO HELP.
IT'S HER!
WENDY...YOU DON'T NEED TO--
YOU'RE NOT THE ONLY ONE WHO GETS ANOTHER SHOT AT LIFE.
ORDER!!!
WE'RE ALL GOING TO COME OUT OF THIS STRONGER.

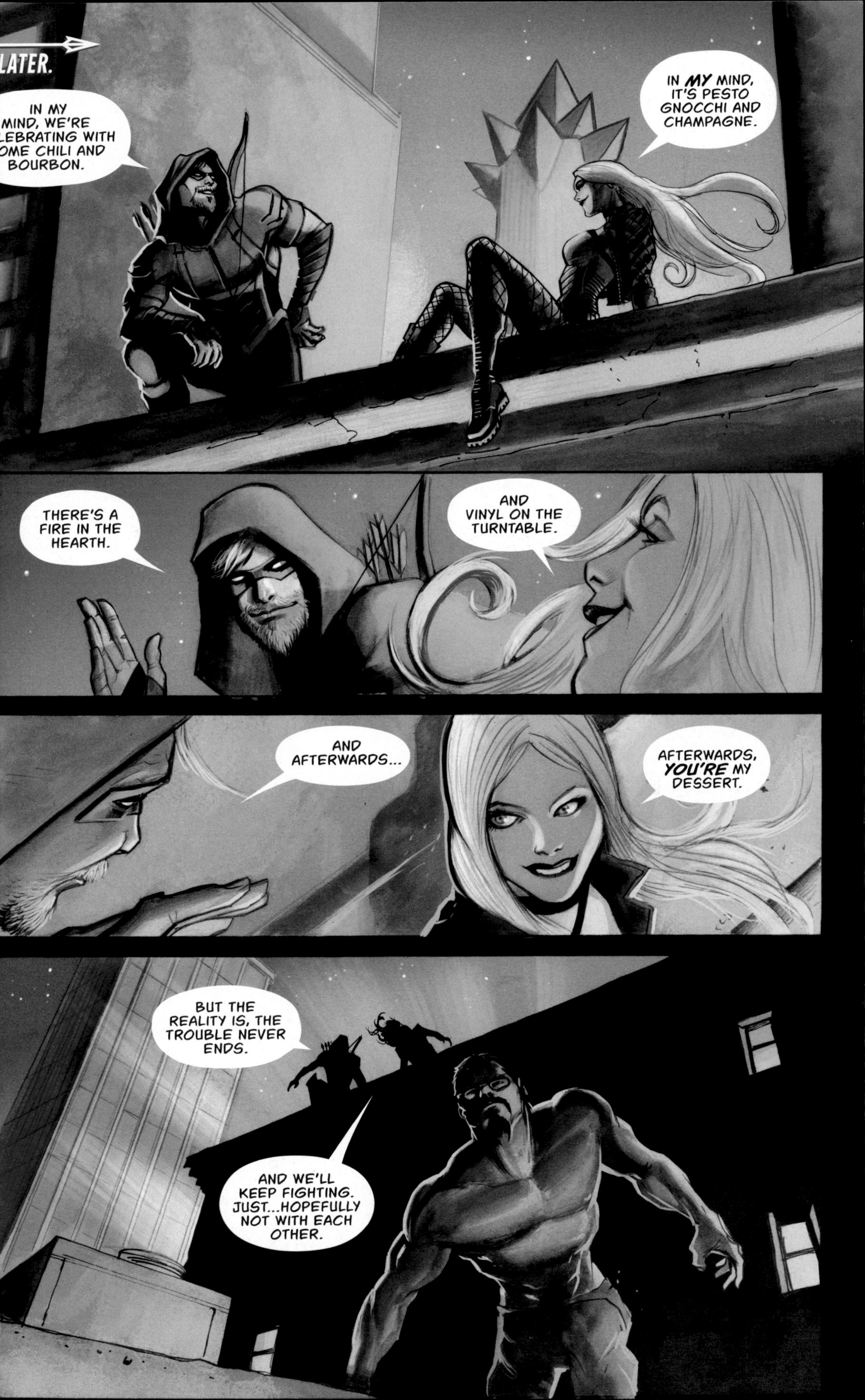

LATER.
IN MY MIND, WE'RE LEBRATING WITH OME CHILI AND BOURBON.
IN MY MIND, IT'S PESTO GNOCCHI AND CHAMPAGNE.
THERE'S A FIRE IN THE HEARTH.
AND VINYL ON THE TURNTABLE.
AND AFTERWARDS...
AFTERWARDS, YOU'RE MY DESSERT.
BUT THE REALITY IS, THE TROUBLE NEVER ENDS.
AND WE'LL KEEP FIGHTING. JUST...HOPEFULLY NOT WITH EACH OTHER.

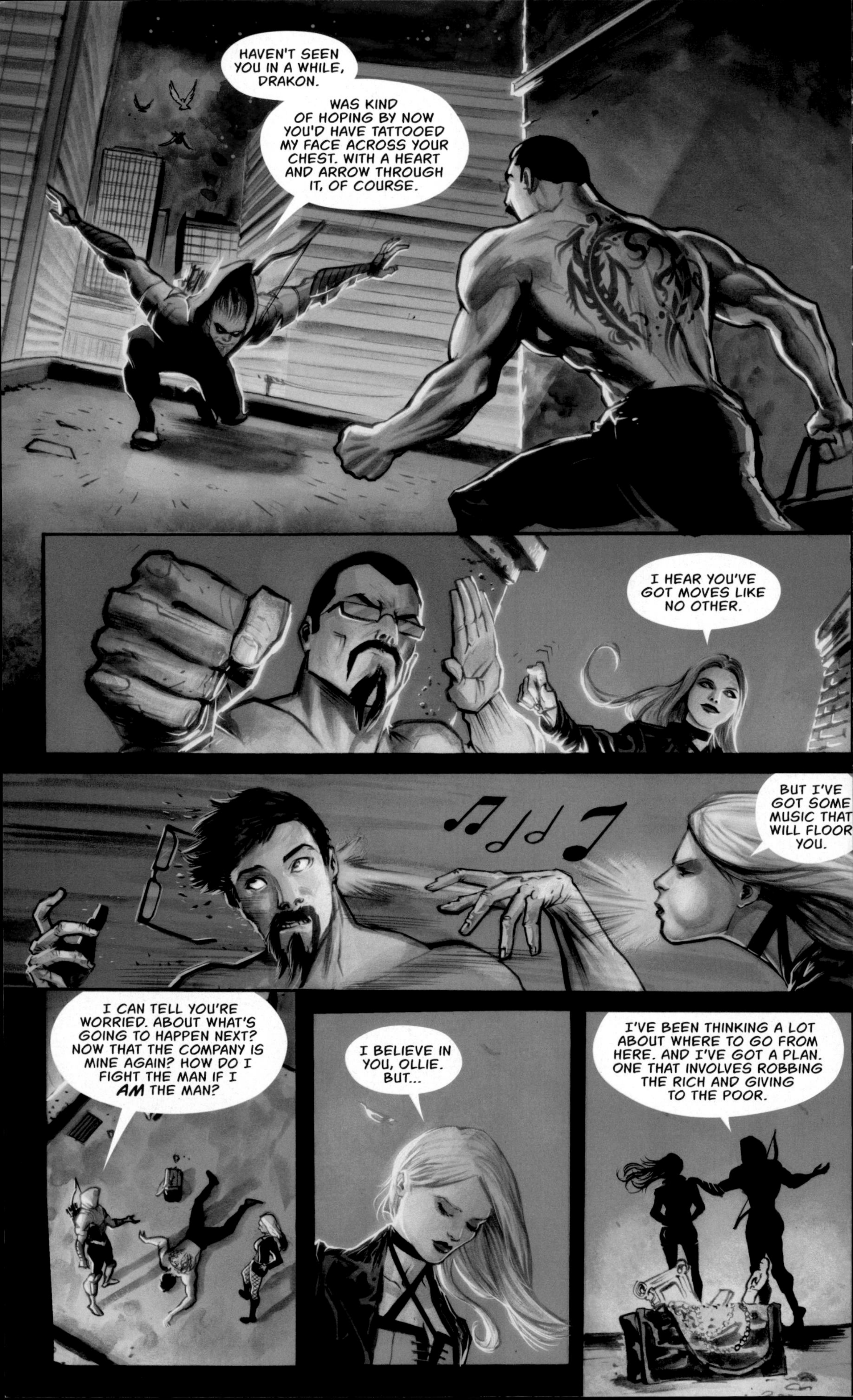
HAVEN'T SEEN YOU IN A WHILE, DRAKON.
WAS KIND OF HOPING BY NOW YOU'D HAVE TATTOOED MY FACE ACROSS YOUR CHEST. WITH A HEART AND ARROW THROUGH IT, OF COURSE.
I HEAR YOU'VE GOT MOVES LIKE NO OTHER.
BUT I'VE GOT SOME MUSIC THAT WILL FLOOR YOU.
I CAN TELL YOU'RE WORRIED. ABOUT WHAT'S GOING TO HAPPEN NEXT? NOW THAT THE COMPANY IS MINE AGAIN? HOW DO I FIGHT THE MAN IF I AM THE MAN?
I BELIEVE IN YOU, OLLIE. BUT...
I'VE BEEN THINKING A LOT ABOUT WHERE TO GO FROM HERE. AND I'VE GOT A PLAN. ONE THAT INVOLVES ROBBING THE RICH AND GIVING TO THE POOR.

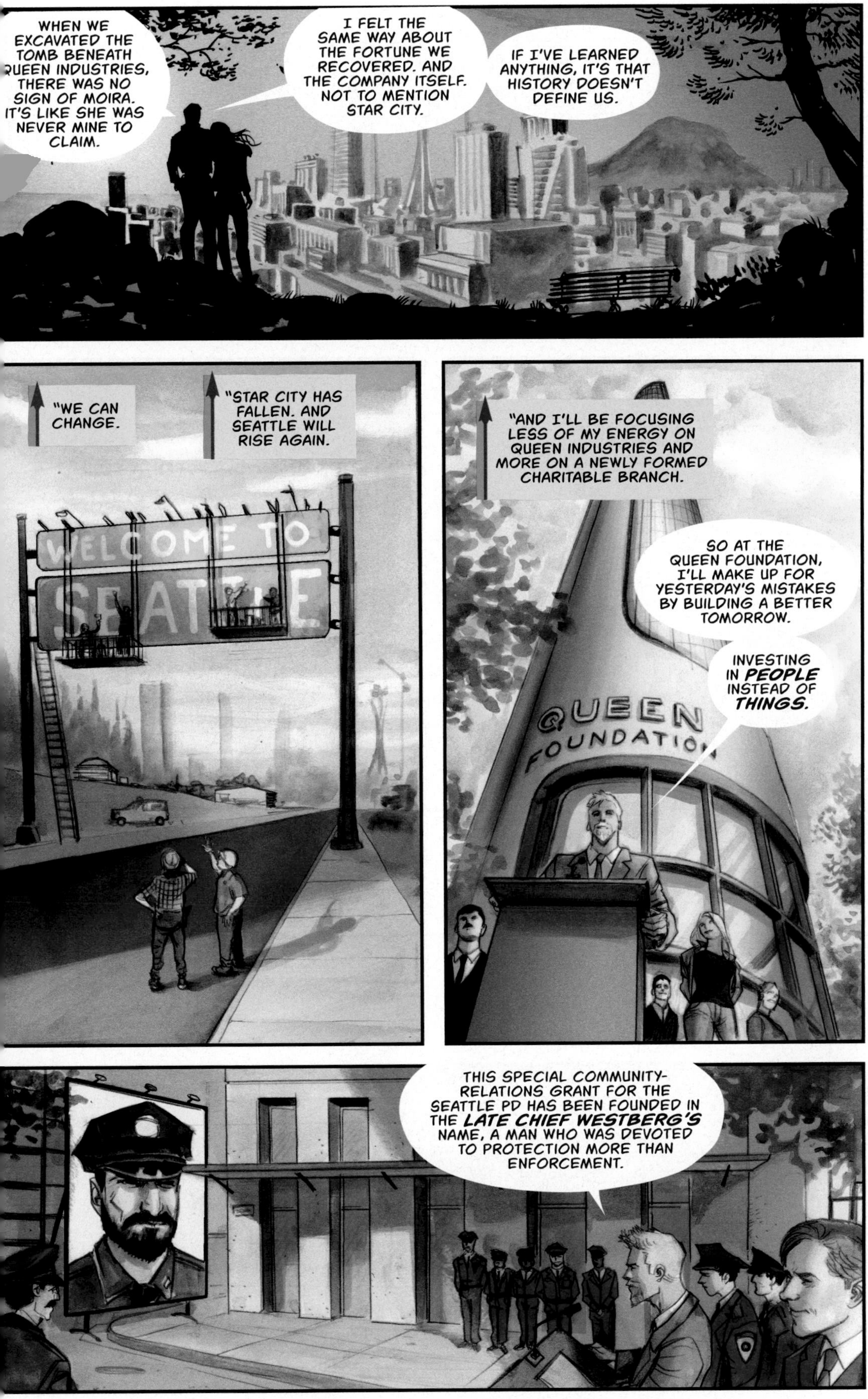
WHEN WE EXCAVATED THE TOMB BENEATH QUEEN INDUSTRIES, THERE WAS NO SIGN OF MOIRA. IT'S LIKE SHE WAS NEVER MINE TO CLAIM.
I FELT THE SAME WAY ABOUT THE FORTUNE WE RECOVERED. AND THE COMPANY ITSELF. NOT TO MENTION STAR CITY.
IF I'VE LEARNED ANYTHING, IT'S THAT HISTORY DOESN'T DEFINE US.
"WE CAN CHANGE.
"STAR CITY HAS FALLEN. AND SEATTLE WILL RISE AGAIN.
WELCOME TO SEATTLE
"AND I'LL BE FOCUSING LESS OF MY ENERGY ON QUEEN INDUSTRIES AND MORE ON A NEWLY FORMED CHARITABLE BRANCH.
SO AT THE QUEEN FOUNDATION, I'LL MAKE UP FOR YESTERDAY'S MISTAKES BY BUILDING A BETTER TOMORROW.
INVESTING IN *PEOPLE* INSTEAD OF *THINGS.*
QUEEN FOUNDATION
THIS SPECIAL COMMUNITY-RELATIONS GRANT FOR THE SEATTLE PD HAS BEEN FOUNDED IN THE *LATE CHIEF WESTBERG'S* NAME, A MAN WHO WAS DEVOTED TO PROTECTION MORE THAN ENFORCEMENT.

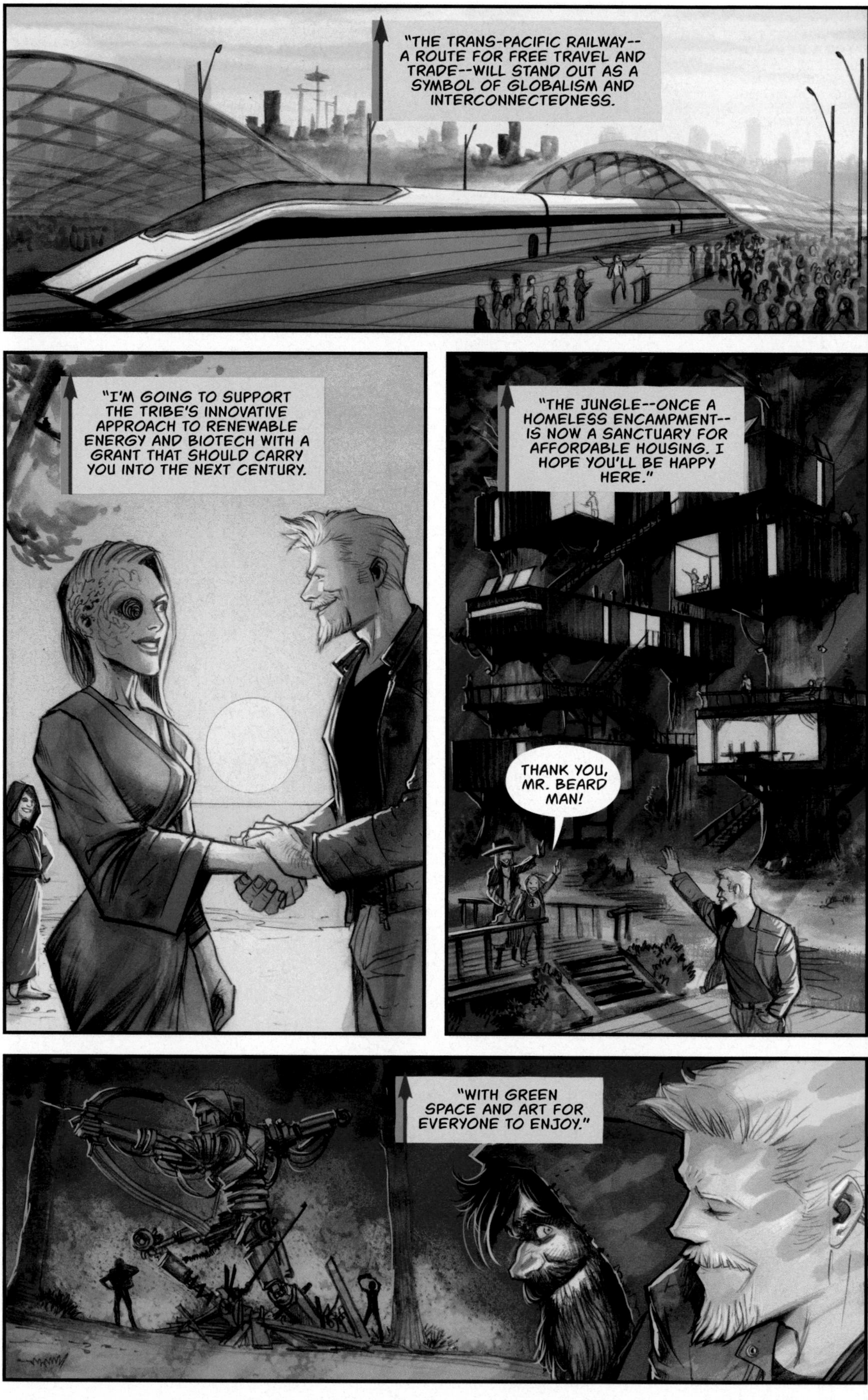
"THE TRANS-PACIFIC RAILWAY--A ROUTE FOR FREE TRAVEL AND TRADE--WILL STAND OUT AS A SYMBOL OF GLOBALISM AND INTERCONNECTEDNESS.
"I'M GOING TO SUPPORT THE TRIBE'S INNOVATIVE APPROACH TO RENEWABLE ENERGY AND BIOTECH WITH A GRANT THAT SHOULD CARRY YOU INTO THE NEXT CENTURY.
"THE JUNGLE--ONCE A HOMELESS ENCAMPMENT--IS NOW A SANCTUARY FOR AFFORDABLE HOUSING. I HOPE YOU'LL BE HAPPY HERE."
THANK YOU, MR. BEARD MAN!
"WITH GREEN SPACE AND ART FOR EVERYONE TO ENJOY."

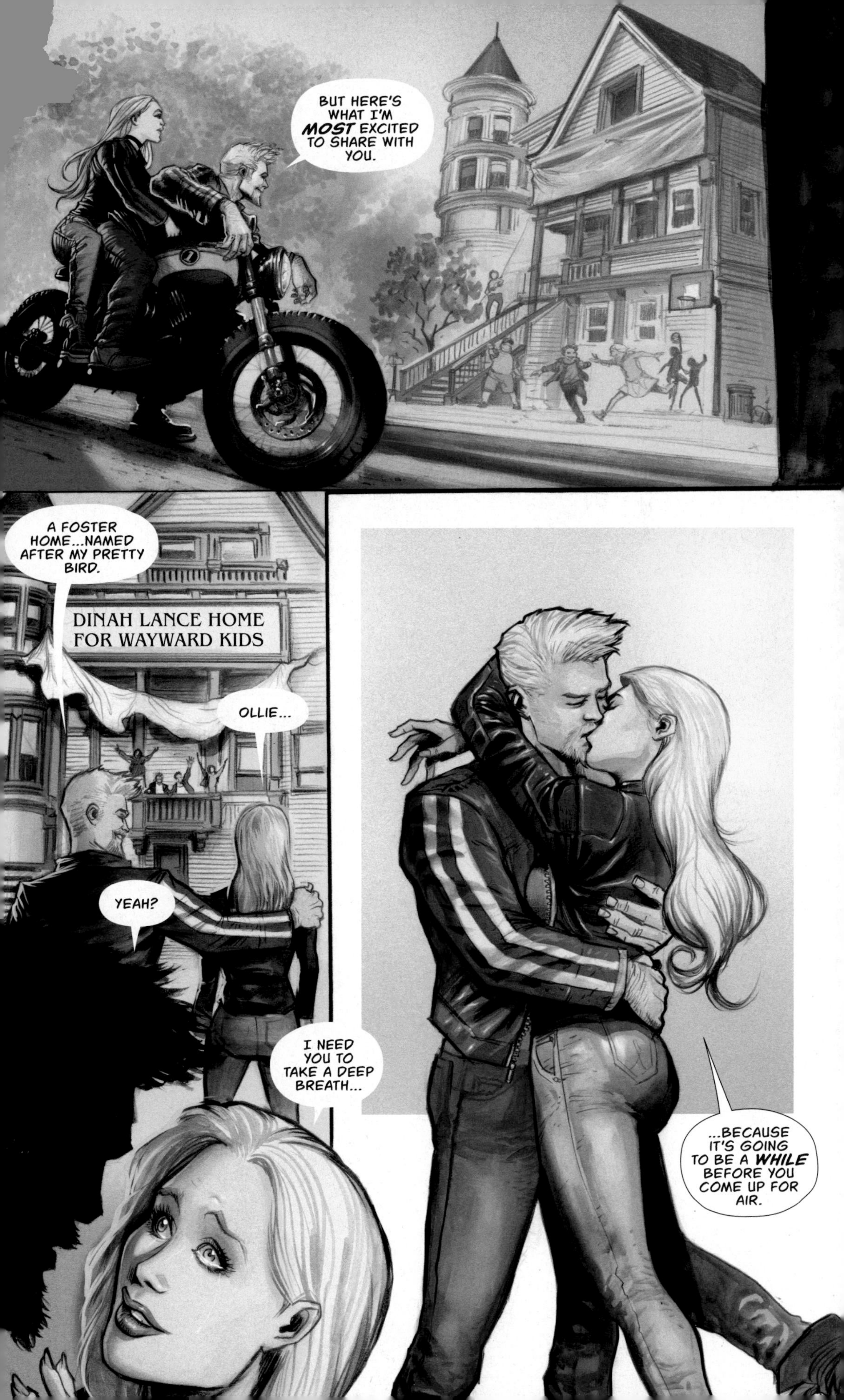
BUT HERE'S WHAT I'M MOST EXCITED TO SHARE WITH YOU.
A FOSTER HOME...NAMED AFTER MY PRETTY BIRD.
DINAH LANCE HOME FOR WAYWARD KIDS
OLLIE...
YEAH?
I NEED YOU TO TAKE A DEEP BREATH...
...BECAUSE IT'S GOING TO BE A WHILE BEFORE YOU COME UP FOR AIR.

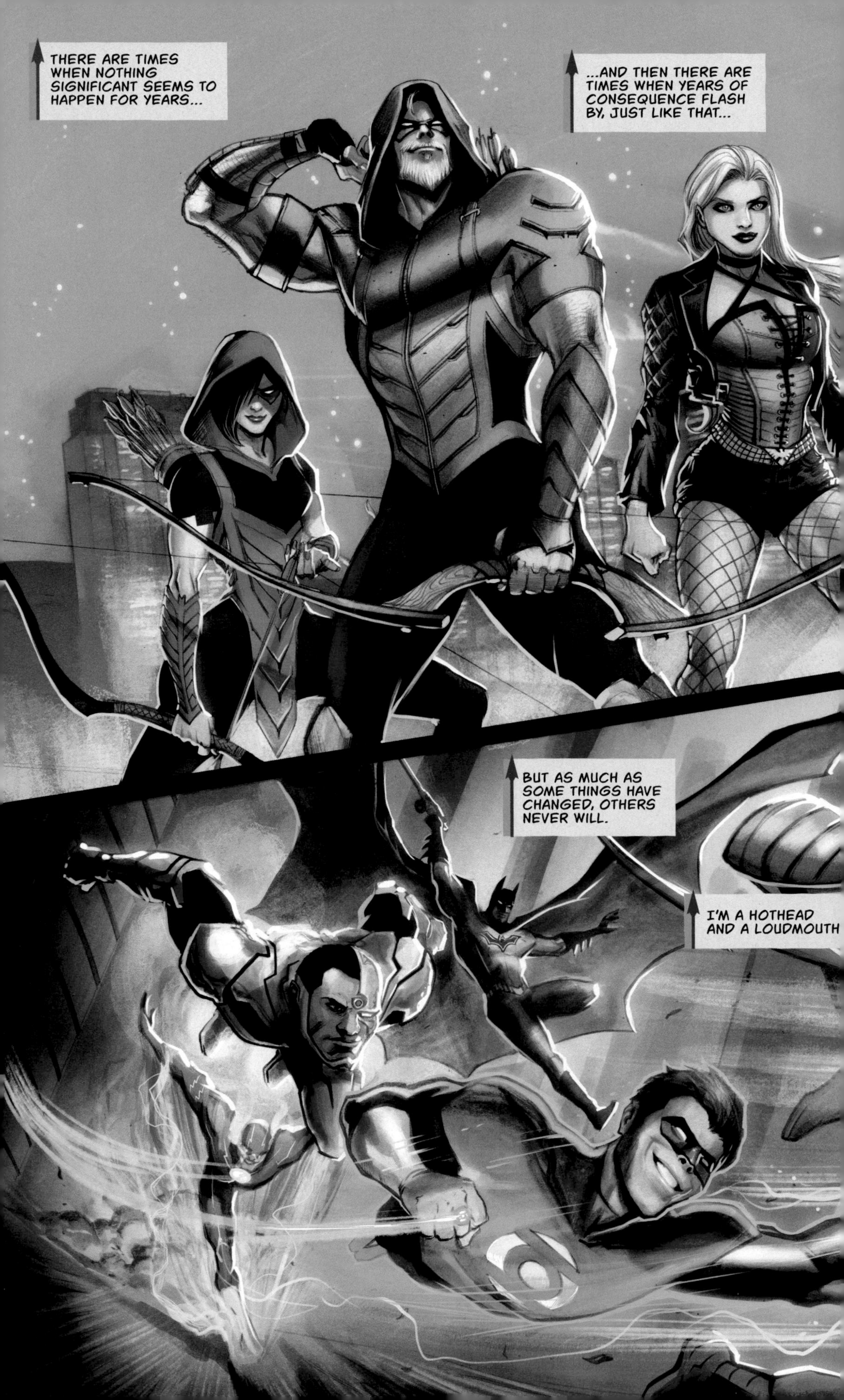
THERE ARE TIMES WHEN NOTHING SIGNIFICANT SEEMS TO HAPPEN FOR YEARS...
...AND THEN THERE ARE TIMES WHEN YEARS OF CONSEQUENCE FLASH BY, JUST LIKE THAT...
BUT AS MUCH AS SOME THINGS HAVE CHANGED, OTHERS NEVER WILL.
I'M A HOTHEAD AND A LOUDMOUTH

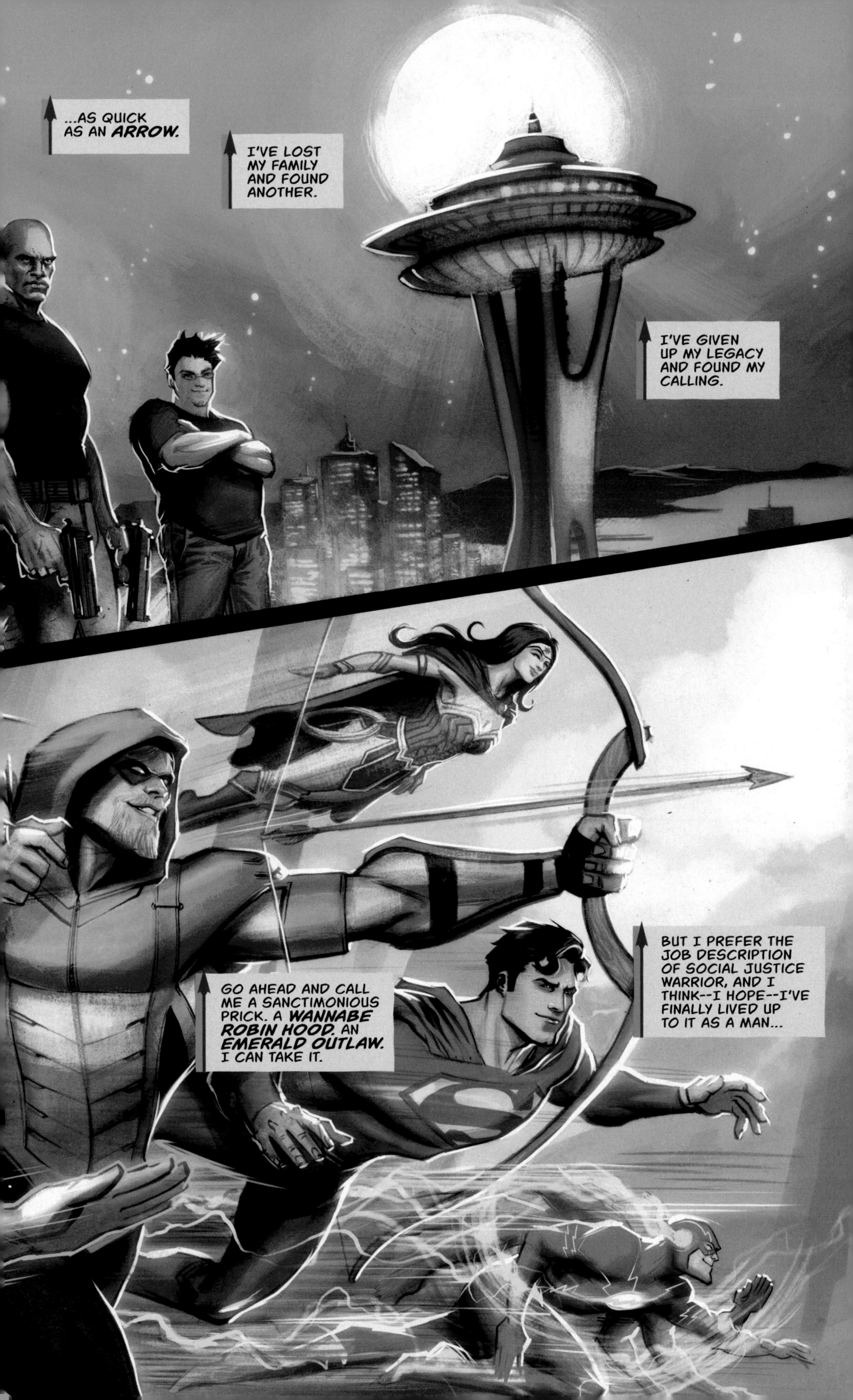
...AS QUICK AS AN ARROW.
I'VE LOST MY FAMILY AND FOUND ANOTHER.
I'VE GIVEN UP MY LEGACY AND FOUND MY CALLING.
GO AHEAD AND CALL ME A SANCTIMONIOUS PRICK. A WANNABE ROBIN HOOD. AN EMERALD OUTLAW. I CAN TAKE IT.
BUT I PREFER THE JOB DESCRIPTION OF SOCIAL JUSTICE WARRIOR, AND I THINK--I HOPE--I'VE FINALLY LIVED UP TO IT AS A MAN...

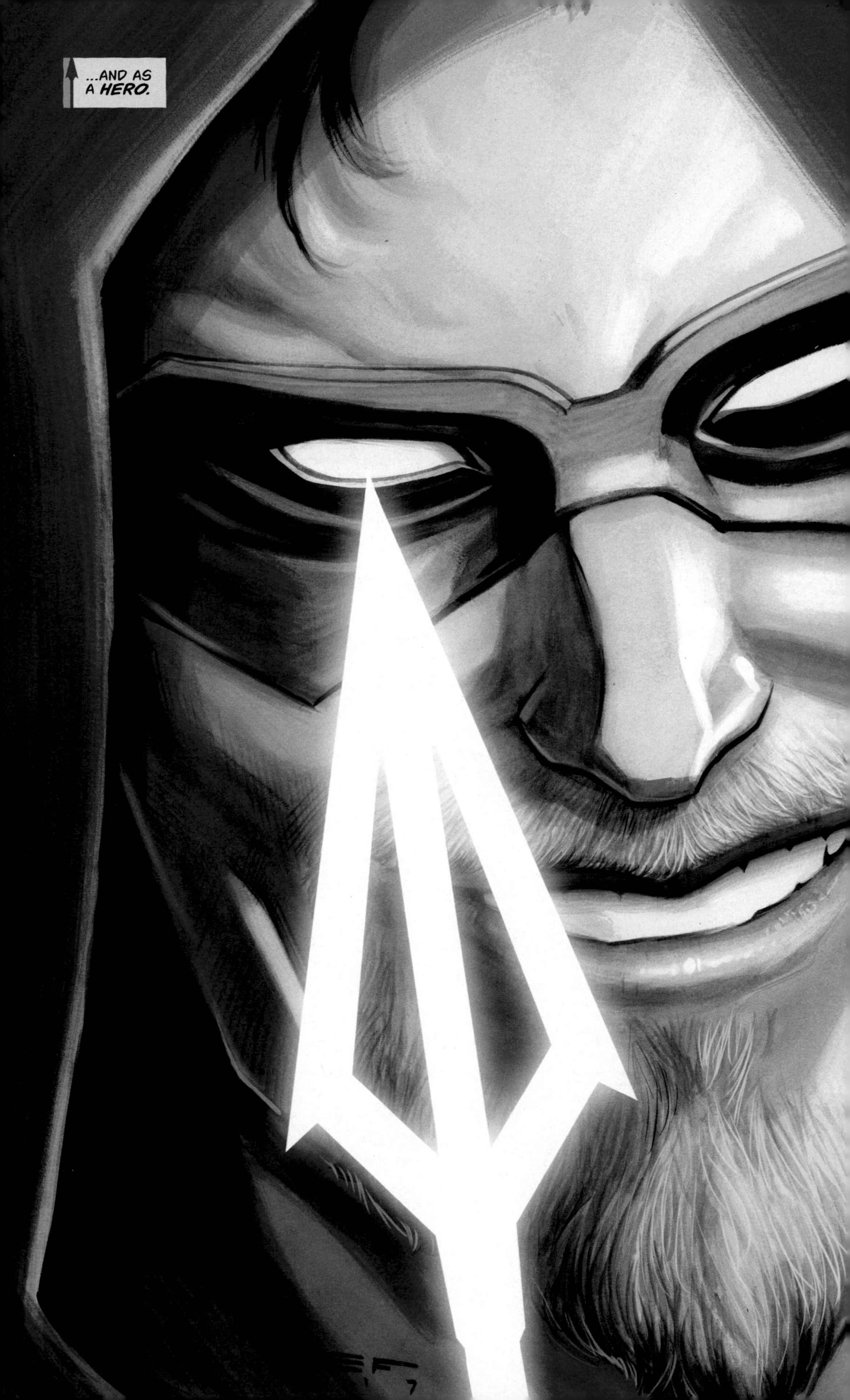
...AND AS A HERO.

GREEN ARROW

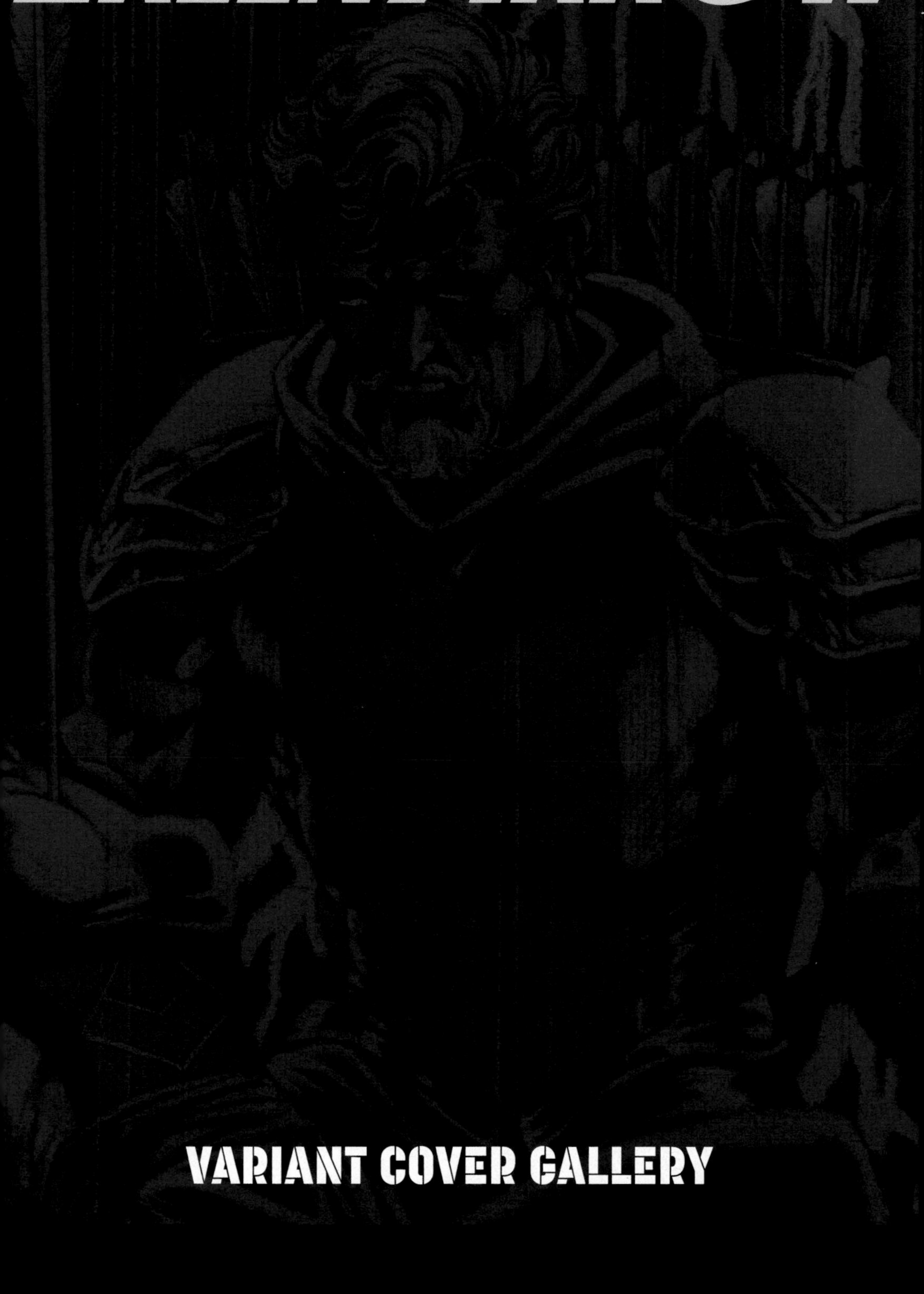

VARIANT COVER GALLERY

GREEN ARROW #33 variant cover
by MIKE GRELL and LOVERN KINDZIERSKI

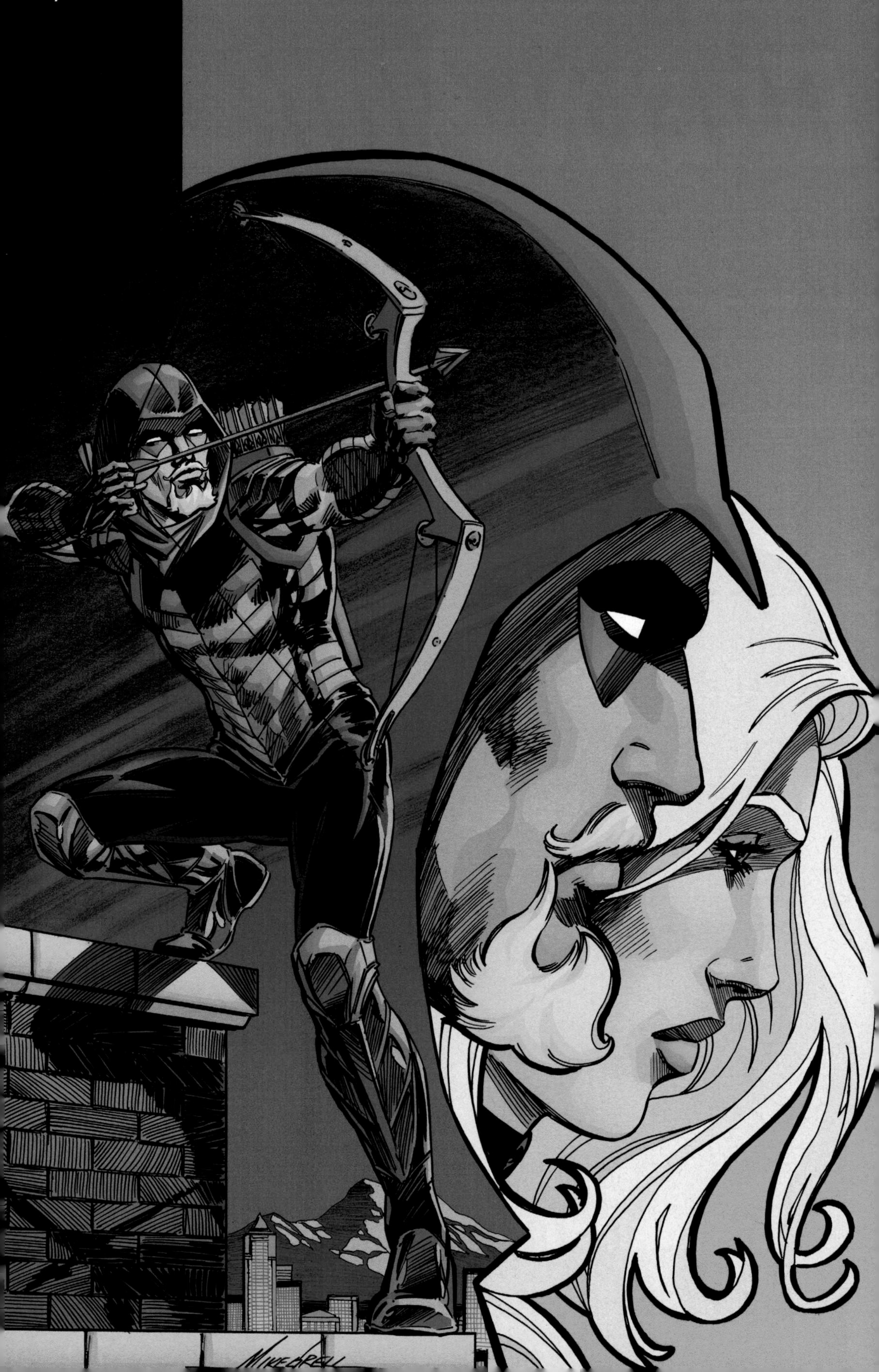

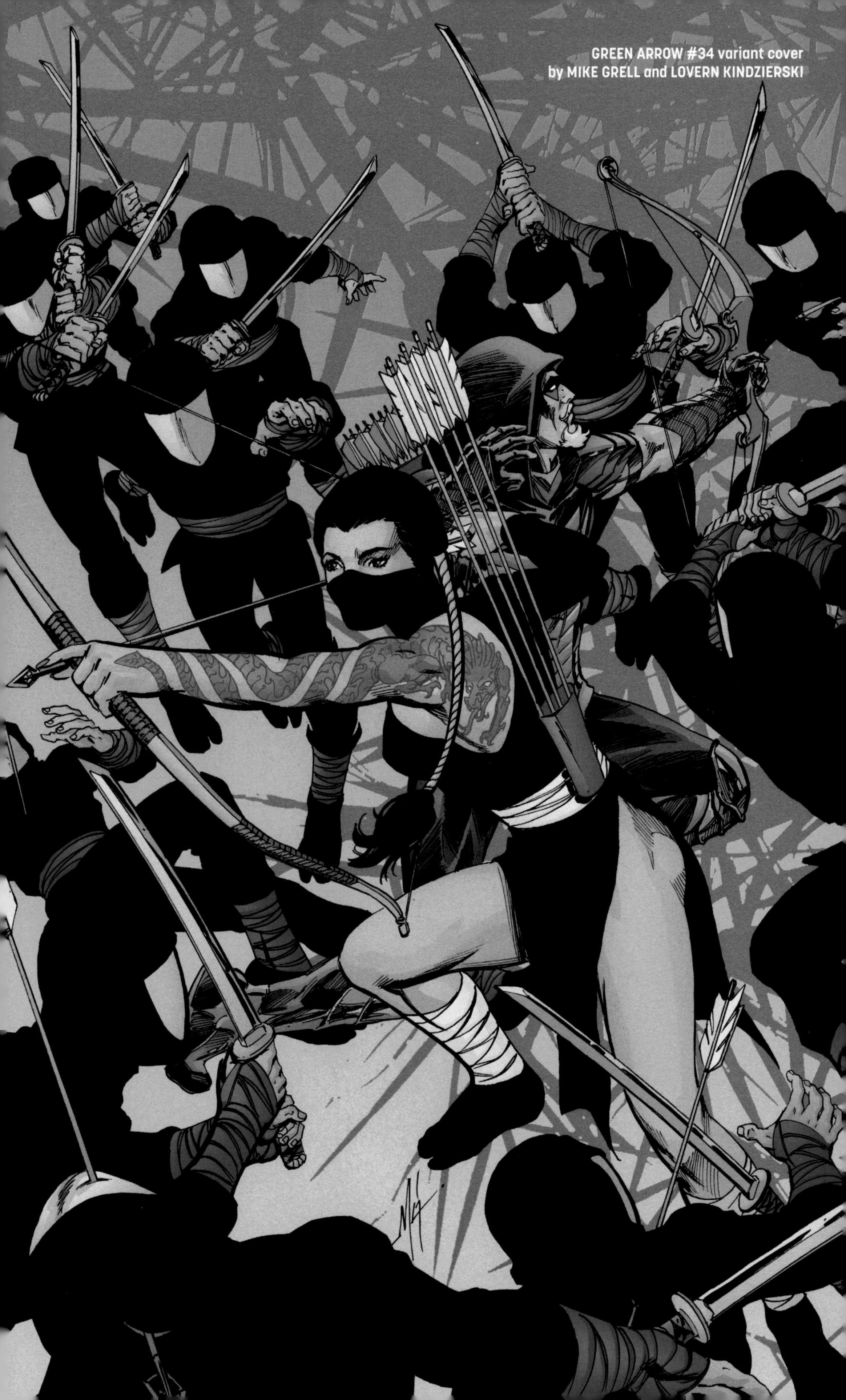

GREEN ARROW #34 variant cover
by MIKE GRELL and LOVERN KINDZIERSKI

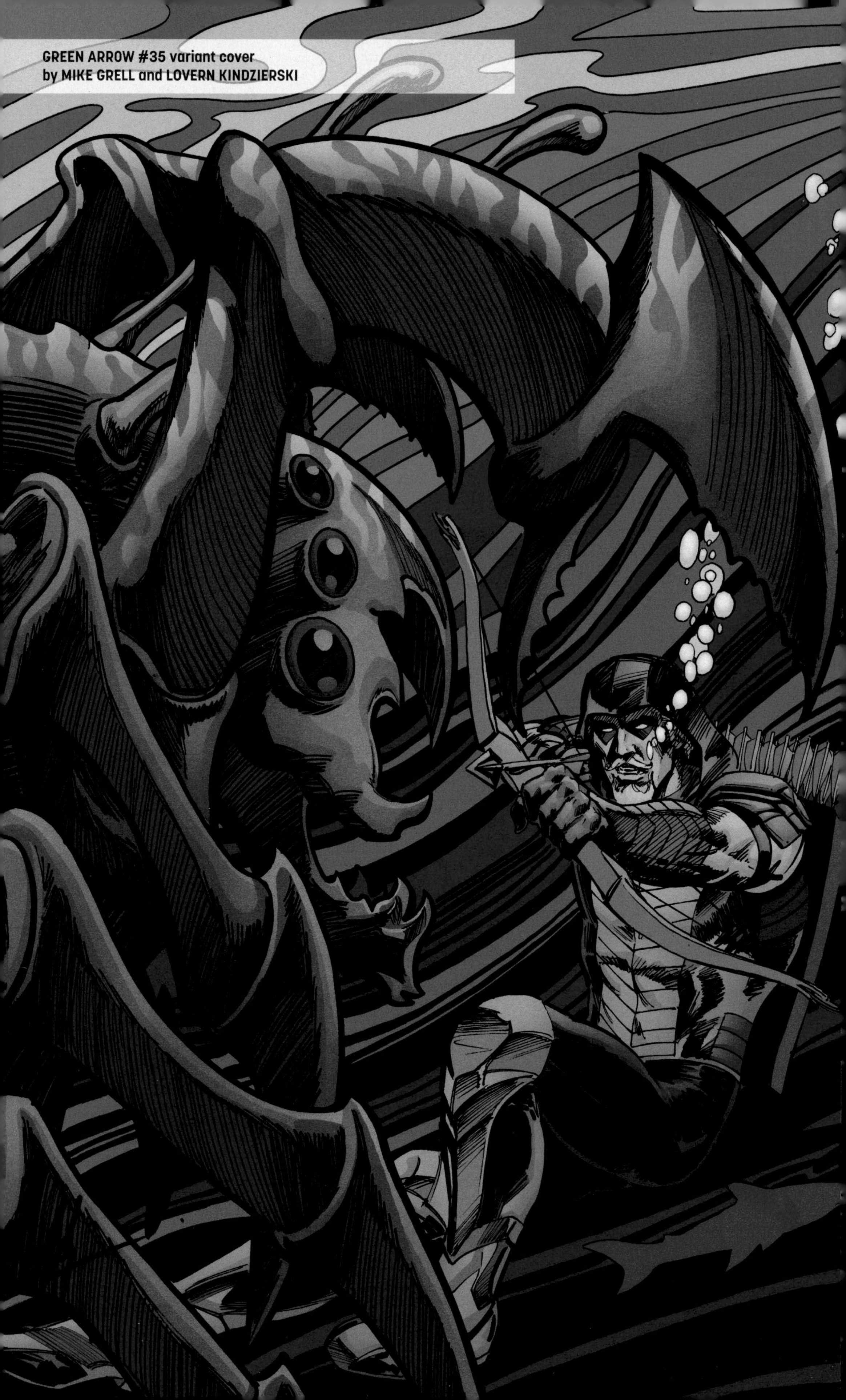

GREEN ARROW #35 variant cover
by MIKE GRELL and LOVERN KINDZIERSKI

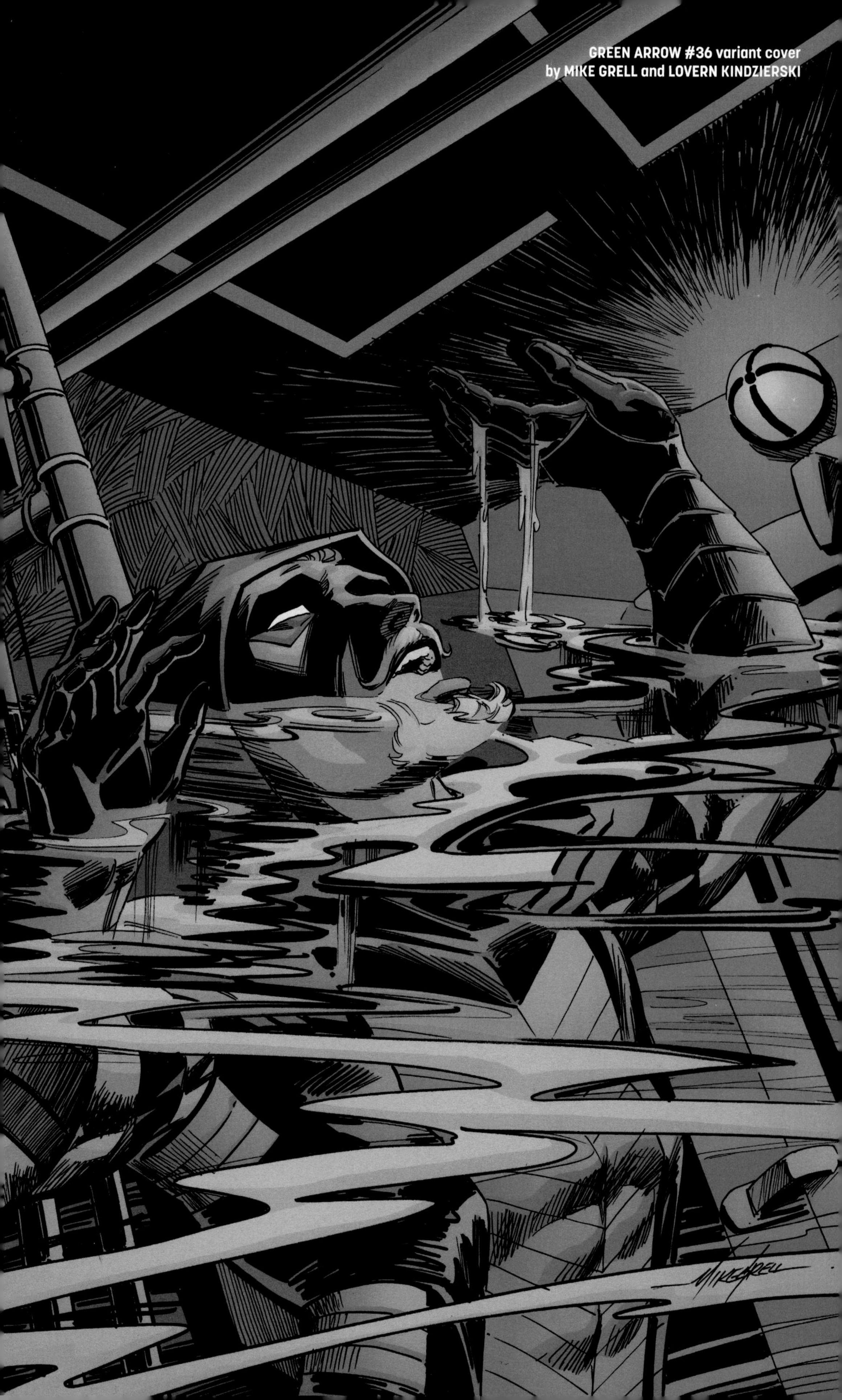

GREEN ARROW #36 variant cover
by MIKE GRELL and LOVERN KINDZIERSKI

GREEN ARROW #37 variant cover by MIKE GRELL

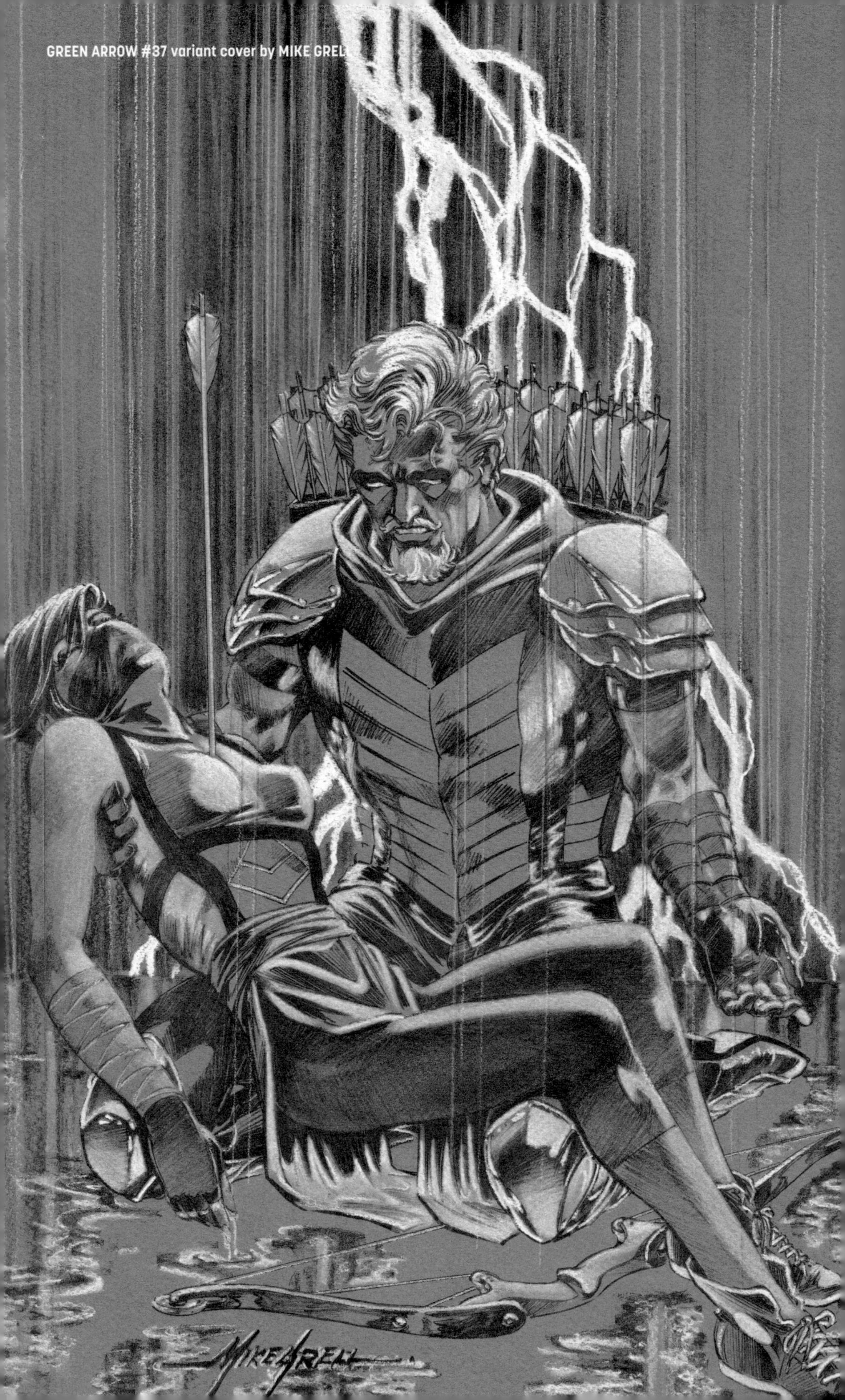

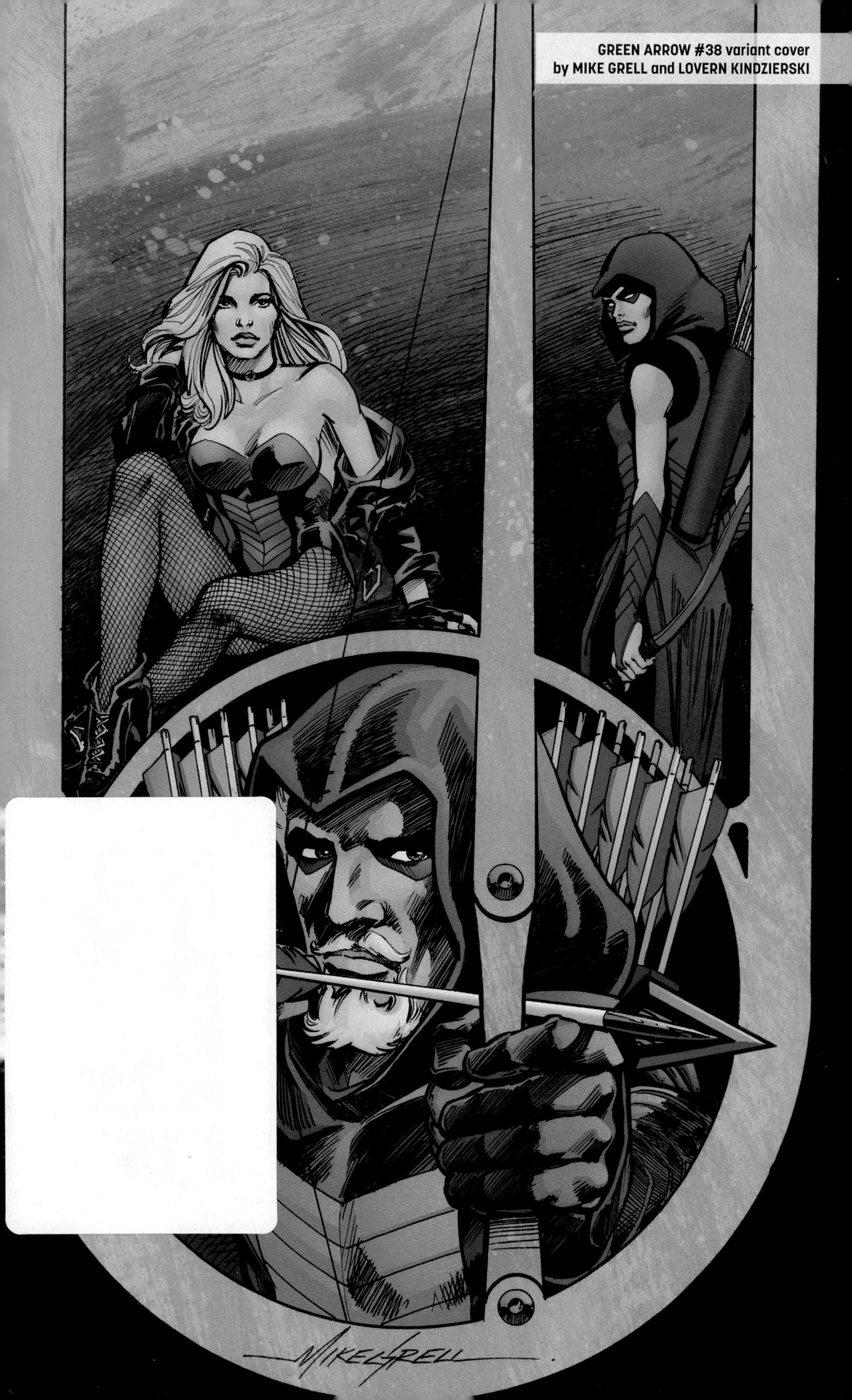

GREEN ARROW #38 variant cover
by MIKE GRELL and LOVERN KINDZIERSKI

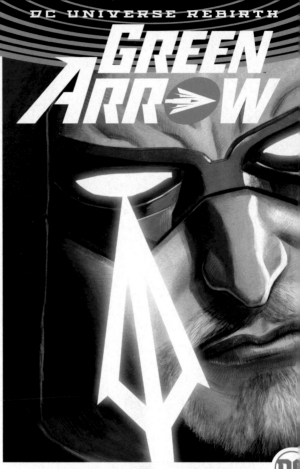

"The world that Schmidt creates feels real and lived in." **– NEWSARAMA**

"The artwork from Otto Schmidt is delightful and quirky." **– NERDIST**

DC UNIVERSE REBIRTH

GREEN ARROW

VOL. 1: THE DEATH & LIFE OF OLIVER QUEEN

BENJAMIN PERCY

with OTTO SCHMIDT & JUAN FERREYRA

BATGIRL AND THE BIRDS OF PREY VOL. 1: WHO IS ORACLE?

TITANS VOL. 1: THE RETURN OF WALLY WEST

DEATHSTROKE VOL. 1: THE PROFESSIONAL